SLAVES FROM THE TAMIL COAST AND EUROPEAN TRADE AROUND THE WORLD, 1547-1792

Slaves from the Tamil Coast and European Trade around the World, 1547-1792

S. JEYASEELA STEPHEN

MANOHAR
2025

First published 2025
First eBook edition 2025

ISBN 978-93-6080-075-8 (hardbound)
ISBN 978-93-6080-148-9 (eBook)

Published by

Ajay Kumar Jain *for*
Manohar Publishers & Distributors
4753/23 Ansari Road, Daryaganj
New Delhi 110 002

Cover design by Kamal Purna Jammual

Typeset by Kohli Print, Delhi 110 051

Printed and bound in India

Contents

Tables

Acknowledgements

The completion of this book is like a long sea journey. Although at times, I felt all by myself, steering my tiny nutshell through storm and bad weather, I was really surrounded by ever so many good forces working towards a safe passage. In the course of my research on textile trade of the Tamil coast with the Portuguese, Dutch, French and English, I came across some documents on slave trade. I continued to look for more and accumulated substantial material during my visits to many archives. I heard the voices of the slaves through the data when I wrote, but it took a long time to complete since I continued to unearth as many documents as possible. The historical records do not remain flat or lack nuance, but give individual expression and emotion, making it easy to understand the journey made by slaves through several agents, brokers, private merchants and East India Companies. This work illustrates the inspiring and interesting study on European slave trading in the Tamil Coast with the markets around the globe and reconstructs the world of human beings who were held captive for an indefinite period of time, coerced into extremely dependent and exploitative power relationships, denied rights (including rights over their labour, lives and bodies) and often vulnerable to forced relocation by various means and forced to labour against their will. The selection of the chapters explains to a large extent, the transcultural, transcontinental and transnational interactions in broad global historical perspective.

I have incurred enormous debts to the generosity, interest, guidance and friendship of a significant number of organizations. As with any project on transoceanic networks, mine was reliant on a global community of support, encouragement and expertise. My greatest debt is to the authorities and staff of Archivo General de Indias, Seville; Rigsarkivet, København; Archiv der Franckesche Stiftungen, Halle; Unitats Archive, Herrnhut; Nationaal Archief, Den Haag; British Library, London; Archives Nationales, Paris; Bibliothèque Nationale, Paris; Centre des Archives d'Outre-Mer, Aix-en-Provence; Archivo General de la Nación, México City; Archivo Histórico del Municipio de Colima, Colima; Family History Library Genealogical Society of Utah, Salt Lake City; Moravian Archives, Bethlehem, Pennsylvania; National Archives of Mauritius, Archives Departmentales de La Reunion, Saint-Denis; Western Cape Archives, Cape Town; Arsip Nasional Republik Indonesia, Jakarta; National Archives of the Philippines, Manila; Sri Lanka National Archives, Colombo; Tamil Nadu State Archives, Chennai; National Archives of India, Puducherry and Historical Archives of Goa, Panaji. As the Corona Virus pandemic devastated the world, my travel came to a halt in January 2020 and I could not collect documents anymore. I had never imagined beforehand such effects of which I had no clue. I am delighted that the book could be completed despite these challenges.

I am grateful to Manohar Publishers for undertaking this publication. It is hoped that the book would advance our understanding of the history of slavery from the Tamil coast connecting various geographical regions with an interest in global history or transnational history including global migrations, interactions and trade routes.

Puducherry S. JEYASEELA STEPHEN
8 December 2024

Abbreviations

ADR	Archives Departmentales de la Reunion, Saint-Denis
AFSt	Archiv der Franckesche Stiftungen, Halle
AGI	Archivo General de Indias, Seville
AGN	Archivo General de la Nación, México City
AHMC	Archivo Histórico del Municipio de Colima, Colima, México
AN	Archives Nationales, Paris
ANRI	Arsip Nasional Republik Indonesia, Jakarta
ARE	*Annual Report on Epigraphy*
BL	British Library, London
BNP	Bibliothèque Nationale de Paris
CAOM	Centre des Archives d'Outre-Mer, Aix-en-Provence
CJ	Council of Justice
DCB	*Diary and Consultation Book*
DI	*Documenta Indica*
DK	*Danske Kancelli*
DR	*Dagregister*
EFI	*English Factories in India*
FHLGSU	Family History Library Genealogical Society of Utah, Salt Lake City
FMC	*Fort Marlborough Consultation*
GM	*Generale Missiven*
HAG	Historical Archives of Goa, Panaji
HB	Hallesche Berichte
IOR	India Office Records
KK	Kommerce Kollegiet
MAB	Moravian Archives, Bethlehem, Pennsylvania
MDR	Monçoes do Reino
NA	Nationaal Archief, Den Haag

NAFR	*Nouvelles Acquisitions Françaises*
NAIP	National Archives of India, Puducherry
NAM	National Archives of Mauritius
NAP	National Archives of the Philippines, Manila
NHB	Neue Hallesche Berichte
OBP	Overgekomen Brieven en Papieren
OIOC	*Oriental and India Office Collection*
RA	Rigsarkivet, København
SII	*South Indian Inscriptions*
SLNA	Sri Lanka National Archives, Colombo
TNSA	Tamil Nadu State Archives, Chennai
UA	Unitats Archive, Herrnhut
VOC	Verenigde Oost-Indische Compagnie
WCA	Western Cape Archives, Cape Town
YFC	*York Fort Consultation*

CHAPTER 1

Introduction

Maritime historians of the early modern age have produced works that deal with European presence, commercial expansion, goods and commodities traded, interaction with people, migration and scientific encounters around the world. Tapan Raychaudhuri, R.N. Banerjee and S. Arasaratnam were the pioneers to focus on the Coromandel Coast and they dealt chiefly with merchants, trading practices, organizational and institutional aspects of the Dutch and the English East India Companies and the overall structure of overseas commerce.[1] Following them a group of historians culled statistical data from European records to know the concrete realities on economic and social history of the Coromandel (including Tamil and Telugu country) and their seminal studies, linked the local developments with commercial exchange that took place at the global level.[2] Yet there are many new and unexplored avenues on the European impact of maritime trade and so this book aims to explore the slave trade and human migration from the Tamil coast to ports around the world.

S. Arasaratnam and Markus Vink outlined the subject of slave trade that was carried out in the Bay of Bengal and Indian Ocean.[3] Sanjay Subrahmanyam, while covering the region of South India never touched on the slave trade of the Europeans.[4] In fact no reliable study that dwells upon Tamil society and the impact of slave trading developed through various new trading routes connecting the new slave markets that emerged in the age of colonial slavery is available. There is a pressing need to have this regional study in order to examine and compare the slave trade of the Europeans in the

Atlantic which affected largely the African and American society in the early modern period at the global level. Colonialism was a global phenomenon that not only defined the territories subjected to its rationale and destructive rule, but also shaped European history in profound yet still reluctantly recognized ways. A majority of the works deal emphatically with British colonialism. They do not discuss aspects of other European overseas empires. A more pluralistic approach to the question of colonialism and postcolonial legacy must begin with identifying the parameters of the various participating empires.

The book seeks to explain how Europeans sought to understand slavery prevalent in Tamil country. Thereafter they developed trading strategies and operations in slave trade. Each of the East India Companies dealt with slaves and slave trade separately but their volume and value of business had differed owing to various reasons. The sprawling slave trade networks through intercontinental trade led to personal interest and corporate policy enabling the circulation of slaves around the world. The East India trading companies fashioned their own system and practices, with a conscious blend of collaboration with local agents, brokers and merchants in slave trade.

Slavery in Medieval Tamil country was a mode of labour. It is to be mentioned that overseas transportation of slaves never happened prior to the coming of the Europeans. How slaves were exported overseas and this change occurred needs to be examined. One could ask broader questions, such as whether there are any shadow sides and links between slave trade of the East India Companies and colonialism. Did large scale exploitation develop through the slave trade and had slavery and labour been linked and combined together? How did slavery and slave trade cause further damage towards descendants of slaves and their next generation? What types of crimes were committed against humanity by the European trading companies? Thus, the stories of slavery and slave trade remain untold till date and should be traced.

SOURCES AND METHODS

Transnational methods are most suitable for writing maritime history to understand the process of globalization that dates back to the sixteenth century. European empires began to expand overseas and the inter-imperial connections and cross-cultural interactions are important for the progression of colonial expansion. By studying the flows of people, commodities and ideas which crossed national boundaries in this period, historians could offer new insights in the operation of colonialism.

The study culls information from Portuguese and Spanish records on the slave trade. It also uses Dutch, Danish, French and English East India Company documents and German missionary reports. The work focuses on the basic questions of how and why the slave trade was generated and sustained by these European companies from the Tamil coast. It evaluates explicitly and makes it known whether the slave traffic arose from the demand side or the supply side. It argues that the European capitalism developed since the mid-sixteenth century, had created necessary conditions that turned a human being into a commodity for sale. It led to produce a colonial proletariat in the form of manual labour undertaken both by the European privateers and the East India Companies. As a result slaves came to be widely transported and transplanted from many European trading enclaves on the Tamil coast to various destinations in Asia, Africa and America.

THE BOOK'S STRUCTURE

Chapter 1 introduces the theme, maritime history of the Tamil Coast from a historiographical perspective. Chapter 2 traces the presence of slaves in Tamil society and situates the sale of slaves engraved on stones and employed by medieval temples and madams. Slavery had continued as one notices the slave sale deeds on palm leaves. The chapter thus deals with the theme particularly of Tamil society and slaves in transition from medieval to pre-colonial rule.

Chapter 3 outlines the Portuguese slave trade developed from the Tamil Coast to Goa and Cochin in India, with ports of Melaka and Aceh in South East Asia during 1547 and 1625. It discusses how the Kings of Portugal in Lisbon and the Viceroys in Goa issued regulations on slavery and slave trade from time to time. Portuguese private merchants purchased slaves from Tamil Coast. The study traces the accounts of a Tamil slave in Goa in 1548 and escape of a Tamil slave in Cochin from his master in 1558. The Jesuit missionaries on the Tamil Coast wrote at length on slavery and slave trade in their letters sent to Europe during 1545-1552. The discussion on slavery and slaves took place at the Provincial Council held in Goa in 1567 and it framed rules from the ecclesiastical point of view. However, private Portuguese slave trade thrived from Nagapattinam to Melaka from 1616 to 1625. Portuguese slave trade had also extended from Nagapattinam to Aceh in Sumatra in 1621.

Chapter 4 evaluates the slave exports from the Tamil Coast to the foreign long-distance markets through the Portuguese slave trade conducted with Spanish Manila and further growth of Spanish slave trade with Mexico during 1616 and 1704. Private Portuguese trade in slaves flourished from Nagapattinam to Manila between 1616 and 1689. One finds numerous sale and resale of Tamil slaves in Manila of various castes including paraiyars, vellalars, valaiyars, reddis and Tamil Muslims. These slaves in Manila were largely employed in the coconut palm cultivation works in 1646. The Spaniards transported the Tamil slaves purchased again in Manila and exported them to colonial Mexico. These slaves who crossed the Pacific were employed in the coconut palm tree plantations in Mexico in 1619. Some Tamil slaves in Mexico were also employed in textile workshops. One finds a slave of the udaiyar caste in Manila sold and transported and again resold in Mexico in 1643.

Chapter 5 enumerates the export of slaves from Pazhaverkadu to Jakarta by the Dutch Company during 1621-65. An exercise is made to cull statistics from the Dutch records.

2,911 slaves were purchased in 1621-4 in Pazhaverkadu and exported to Jakarta. 880 slaves were transported in 1625 in ships to Jakarta. 1,082 slaves were transported during 1627-31. Slave purchases dwindled when slaves were not available. Therefore one finds 87 slaves exported during 1634-7 and 265 slaves were purchased during 1640-5 and exported to Jakarta. However, later the Dutch purchases swelled and increased and the company purchased 2,117 slaves in 1646 and 1,915 slaves in 1647. The export and supply decreased to 56 between 1648 and 1651 because slaves were not available. 1,059 slaves were exported to Jakarta during 1660-5. One also finds the export of 98 persons captured during naval sieges against Portuguese being declared as slaves from Pazhaverkadu to Jakarta between 1630 and 1643. The death of 1,086 slaves occurred during the slave voyages from Pazhaverkadu to Jakarta during 1622-48.

Chapter 6 examines the Dutch slave trade and shipping slaves from Pazhaverkadu to Syriam in Myanmar between 1638 and 1679. The study also traces the rules framed for slave trade by the Dutch East India Company. The chapter also analyses slave exports from Devanampattinam and Porto Novo to Jakarta, Aceh and Banten under the Dutch Company during 1624-88. According to statistics culled from records, 1,683 slaves were exported during 1624-30 in Dutch ships from Devanampattinam to Jakarta. 461 slaves purchased in Kunimedu during 1624-7 were exported from Devanampattinam to Jakarta. 197 slaves were sent in 1635-6 from Devanampattinam to Jakarta. 27 slaves were exported in 1651. 166 slaves were transported in 1660-2 from Devanampattinam to Jakarta. 133 slaves were exported in 1644 in Dutch ships from Tirumullaivasal to Jakarta. 729 slaves were again purchased and exported in 1646 from Tirumullaivasal. 1,976 slaves were purchased and exported from Karaikal to Jakarta during 1646-7. 31 slaves were again purchased and exported from Karaikal in 1651. The voluminous slave trade led to the resistance of the local ruler banning slave trade of the Dutch Company in 1688.

Chapter 7 discusses Dutch slave trade operated from Nagapattinam to Colombo, Banten, Jakarta, Melaka and the social realities of the enslaved between 1655 and 1704. It is found that 4,195 slaves were purchased and exported during 1655 and 1656 in Dutch ships from Nagapattinam to Colombo. 6,793 Tamil slaves were purchased and exported between 1659 and 1661 in ships from Nagapattinam to Colombo. 46 slaves were purchased in 1660 and exported to Banten. 1,202 slaves were purchased in 1660 and exported to Jakarta. 213 slaves were purchased in 1660 and exported to Melaka. 5 slaves were purchased in 1663 and sent in Dutch ships from Sadurangapattinam to Melaka. The Dutch company transported 703 Portuguese soldiers and residents as war prisoners declared as slaves from Nagapattinam to Jakarta in 1658. One finds re-distribution of Nagapattinam slaves by the Dutch Company from Colombo to Jakarta during 1678-83. The study also dwells on the continued slave purchases and trade at Nagapattinam under the Dutch during 1694 and 1704.

The chapter also explores the Dutch slave trade conducted from Nagapattinam to Cape Town and Colombo during 1705 and 1791. Slave purchases and exports continued from Nagapattinam to Africa in 1705-39 and also in 1763-75. One finds purchase and sale of many slaves on the Coromandel Coast by the naval officers of the Dutch Company during 1737 and 1743. The study dwells on the growth of slave exports from Nagapattinam to Sri Lanka during 1766-91.

Chapter 8 elaborates slave trade and traffic in Tuticorin developed under the Dutch company from 1660 to 1791. Transportation of slaves began from Tuticorin to Cape Town in South Africa and to the Netherlands on a large scale during 1694-1734. The slave trade of the Dutch Company continued to South Africa and Sri Lanka during 1730-80. One finds manumission of Tuticorin slaves in Colombo between 1739 and 1791. According to statistics 1710 slaves were transported from the port of Tuticorin to Sri Lanka between 1755 and 1791. The study covers domestic slavery prevalent in

Tuticorin and the pathetic lives of the slaves too. The chapter also outlines an interesting case study of a slave from Tuticorin and the circuits of his journey to the Netherlands, Germany and British North America during 1739-63. Madhan, a Tamil slave abducted from his father was sold to an employee of the Dutch Company in Tuticorin in 1739. He travelled along with his master to the Netherlands in 1741. His master took him to Germany where he was converted and received baptism with the new name, Samuel Johannes in 1746. Even after becoming a Christian, he remained a slave. He was sent to the seminary at Barbay for his education and he stayed there from 1746 to 1753. He was sent to Herrnhut and he ran away in March 1754. The surrender and arrest of Samuel Johannes at Barby had been reported in May 1754. Thereafter Samuel Johannes was transported to Pennsylvania in British North America. He lived there since 1754 and got married to an African slave. Finally he died in 1763. This chapter underlines the living experience of the Tamil slave.

Chapter 9 explores the English East India Company export of slaves from Madras to St Helena colony in South Atlantic between 1654 and 1712 for development of sugar plantations. It also traces the English Company slave trade from Madras to Bengkulu on the West Coast of Sumatra between 1682 and 1748 where the transported slaves had been employed in the shipyard.

Chapter 10 focuses on slavery, slave trade and the seascapes of Tranquebar under the Danes between 1632 and 1790. It outlines the beginning of the Danish slave trade in 1632 and the subsequent growth of the private traders shipping slaves to the port of Kedah in Malaysia and Aceh in Sumatra during 1646-7. The Lutheran missionaries who noticed the system of slavery in Tranquebar communicated the details to Europe. They described the local slavery and made comparison with slavery prevalent in Germany. The Lutheran missionaries also explained the various methods of slave traps adopted by the native slave dealers in Tranquebar. Slaves were converted to Christianity in the Danish colony as found in the records of

1707-8. The internal migration facilitated increasing slave exports from Tranquebar to Aceh in Sumatra and Cape Town in South Africa between 1727 and 1749. Pratap Singh the king of Thanjavur reacted sharply to the slave purchases and growth of trade by the Danes between 1741 and 1744. This made the Danish Governor issue an order of prohibition for slave trade in Tranquebar in 1745. As a result after introduction of prohibition illegal slave trade came to be developed by the traders between 1745 and 1753. The Danish governor who sensed the threat and danger from the native ruler, came to introduce the abolition of slave trade and the order was issued in Tranquebar in 1753. Government orders were again issued for ending the slavery in Tranquebar between 1783 and 1790. The study traces Tranquebar born slaves found in Sri Lanka, Cape Town, Mauritius and Denmark between 1775 and 1794.

Chapter 11 illuminates the export of slaves from Pondicherry under the French East India Company. The role of the native brokers and merchants and the rulers is explored in this context. The Nawab of Arcot had his own policy towards French slave trade and so the Company had to adopt several methods for obtaining slaves for overseas export. Shipping and French slave trade during 1707 and 1760 had extended from Pondicherry to Mauritius and Reunion. A statistics of 588 slaves exported during 1729-32 had been furnished. The French Company developed purchase of slaves from Karaikal. One notices sale of 26 male and 23 female slaves and transportation to Mauritius and Le Reunion during 1766-76. Case studies of slaves have been presented: while the first deals with a slave of Pondicherry exported to France in 1750 and the legal battle held during 1759, the second traces how a slave exported from Mauritius to Pondicherry after his stay for many years, made his escape and returned in a ship to Pondicherry in 1785. Interesting insights emerge from the slave register maintained at Pondicherry and one finds the geographical origin of slaves with place names in the hinterland, the selling price in Pondicherry port town held in the slave auction on various dates in 1783.

Chapter 12 deals with the conclusion and reports the findings of the study. The book explains the fluidity of oceans that calls for a global perspective and the transnational perspectives to analyse oceans, seas and waterways. There has been a shift in maritime studies by looking not from hinterland to sea but from ocean to coast in the modern period. This study thus brings for a rigorous incorporation of the littoral Tamil communities into world history. It shows that oceans can change understandings of global networks of connectivity and also geographic concepts of borders and horizons, subverting notions of imperial hierarchies of power. Understanding the oceans as vibrant living spaces this volume provides a way to transcend spatial and temporal categories to dive deeper into oceanic movement of people and colonial history.

NOTES

1. Tapan Raychaudhuri, *Jan Company in Coromandel, 1603-1690: A Study in the Interrelations of European Commerce and Traditional Economies*, The Hague, 1962; R.N. Banerjee, *Economic Progress of the East India Company on the Coromandel Coast, 1702-1746*, Nagpur, 1974; Sinnapah Arasaratnam, *Merchants, Companies and Commerce on the Coromandel Coast, 1650-1740*, Delhi, 1980.
2. Bhaskarjyoti Basu, *The Central Coromandel in the Eighteenth Century*, Ph.D. Dissertation, Visva-Bharati, 1989; Bhaswathi Bhattacharaya, *The Dutch East India Company on the Coromandel Coast, 1740-1780, A Study of its Decline*, Ph.D. Dissertation, Visva-Bharati, 1992; Lalitha Iyer, *Trade and Finance on the Coromandel Coast, 1757-1853*, Ph.D. Dissertation, University of Hyderabad, 1993; S. Jeyaseela Stephen, *The Coromandel Coast and its Hinterland: Economy, Society and Political System, 1500-1600*, Manohar, Delhi, 1997; Kanakalatha Mukund, *The Trading World of the Tamil Merchant: Evolution of Merchant Capitalism in the Coromandel*, Hyderabad, 1999; Arvind Sinha, *The Politics of Trade: Anglo-French Commerce on the Coromandel Coast, 1763-1793*, Manohar, Delhi, 2002; P. Swarnalatha, *The World of the Weaver in the Northern Coromandel, 1750-1850*, Hyderabad, 2005;

S. Jeyaseela Stephen, *Expanding Portuguese Empire and the Tamil Economy, Sixteenth-Eighteenth Centuries*, Delhi, 2009; Radhika Seshan, *Trade and Politics on the Coromandel Coast, Seventeenth and Early Eighteenth Centuries*, Delhi, 2012; S. Jeyaseela Stephen, *Oceanscapes: Tamil Textiles in the Early Modern World*, Delhi, 2014.

3. S. Arasaratnam, 'Slave Trade in the Indian Ocean, in K.S., Mathew, ed., *Mariners, Merchants and Oceans*, Delhi, 1995, pp. 195-208; Markus Vink, 'The World's Oldest Trade: Dutch Slavery and Slave Trade in the Indian Ocean in the Seventeenth Century', *Journal of World History*, vol. 14, no. 2, June 2003, pp. 131-46.
4. Sanjay Subrahmanyam, *The Political Economy of Commerce, Southern India, 1500-1650*, London, 1990.

CHAPTER 2

The Slaves in Tamil History and Society

Puranaanuru refers to *ilipirappalan* (man of low birth) the lower classes and servants in Tamil country, in the ancient period.[1] Adimai employed by Tiruvalluvar refers only to a servant of low rank.[2] The couplet says that if the citizenry turns indolent, it would enslave them to an enemy king. Hence the view of K.K. Pillay who cites this as the existence of slavery is called into question.[3] Many Tamil literary texts such as *Pattinapaalai*, *Maduraikanchi*, *Pathittrupaththu* and *Manimekhalai* refer to women captured after successful battles.[4] Tholkappiyam refers to slavery but it was not widespread.[5] Slavery had developed gradually as an institution in the early medieval period. Hence the view of V. Kankasabhai that slavery was unknown to the Tamils may also be questioned.[6] Slavery existed in the post-sangam period in some form. Men and women offered themselves as slaves to individuals and families. Since the slaves were apparently the people of the lowest status possible in Tamil society; inscriptions mention their sale or transfer deed to identify them precisely as property. The identity of the slave had been defined and specified just as the exact limits of a piece of land donated to the temple.

Numerous inscriptions mention the terms *adiyaar* and *adiyaazhl* (serving) referring to the fact of subordination. It signifies exclusively 'slave' rather than indicate another meaning of the term that is 'devotee'. A record from Tiruchirappalli area mentioned a Chandrasekhara arasa mayinthan of Nandivarman mangalam, the village headman who purchased Ooransolai and her daughter and granddaughter Velanpratti and Amainthankandi by name as *kuli azhl* (wage labourer) in AD 942. They were employed for six years. He decided to sell them in AD 948 and sold all the three of them to the temple of Vayalur to sing hymns in the temple and be *kavarippina varkal* (flywhisk women) for the deity.[7] Again one finds an inscription of South Arcot area in the early eleventh century which states that the mother of a *vellalar* was given to be an *adiyaazhl* for the temple deity and that her son was to be responsible for the cultivation of the temple garden that had been donated.[8] Thus *vellalars* were also donated as slaves to temples and they worked there.

The term *adimai* had also been used exclusively in inscriptions referring to slave. One inscription mentioned and used the term uvachcha *adimai* (a male drummer).[9] Thus *adiyaar*, *adiyaazhl* and *adimai* had been used interchangeably, referring to slaves. These men and women slaves were unfree, employed in the beginning on a large scale in agriculture and also in the houses. They were given shelter to live in the backyards of the houses, fed and given clothes for maintenance. As these slaves could not be liberated at all they were given or resold and came to be attached to the temples.

Slaves were grouped along with the land and cattle as property and this is revealed from an inscription of AD 1150.[10] Another inscription mentions the inheritance right of a slave who was a married woman and had no issue.[11] A Brahmin of Nangur possessed 15 men and 7 women slaves and he decided to sell all of them as he could not afford to maintain them anymore. The cultivating tenants of the place in AD 1219 purchased 5 men and 5 women, and paid 1,000 *kasus* as the price. The buyers were allowed to retain the ownership of slaves on a hereditary basis.[12]

THE SALE OF SLAVES ENGRAVED ON STONES AND EMPLOYED BY TEMPLES

The temples in Tamil country became owners of slaves mainly in three ways. At first one finds receipt of slaves whom people had gifted to the temples.[13] It is mentioned in a record that a

Brahmin who owned slaves had sold 2 women and 5 men for 30 *kasus*, again 15 persons for 2 *kasus*, and yet again 6 persons for 13 *kasus* to the temple. The Brahmin also remitted the entire amount to the temple treasury. The sale of slaves was generally conducted through the registration of a deed on a palm leaf in Tamil prepared at the time to avoid problems and complications in future. In an instance, it is reported that the seal of the *aranmani* (royal palace) was affixed on a palm leaf record by mistake when slaves were sold. A rectification to this effect was later made by stamping the seal of the temple since the sale of the slaves was done to the temple.[14]

Secondly, in many cases people voluntarily sold themselves as slaves to the temples. It is reported that eight persons sold themselves in Thanjavur area to a temple but the prices are not stated.[15] Two women, their dependents and relatives sold themselves to the same temple; while seven of them were sold for 30 *kasus*, 15 of them were sold for 30 *kasus*.[16] It is found again that six persons were sold to the same temple for 13 *kasus*.[17] Thus the minimum sale price of a slave was around 2 *kasus* and the maximum was 4 *kasus* excluding registration charges of the sale deed. The price of slaves had increased in AD 1175. One finds four *devaradiyars* who were employed were sold to Tiruvalangadu temple for 700 *kasus*.[18] During the famine of AD 1201, many people had voluntarily become slaves and a *vellalan* (cultivator) sold himself along with his wife and two daughters to escape starvation after borrowing 110 *kasus* from temple. It is said that 3 *nalis* paddy was sold for one *kasu* which was very expensive at that time and so they had sold themselves.[19] Marutha Rajayakondan sold his daughter Ramadevi in AD 1425 to the temple of Ariyamangalam near Tiruchendur.[20] Five girls of Rajarajapuram enslaved themselves in AD 1448 to god in Appan temple and settled as *irandam kudi* (second settlers) of Sermaadevi village.[21]

Third, it is noticed that temples had come to purchase slaves as they needed them for work.[22] An inscription in AD 1196-7 gives a list of 100 slaves purchased by the temple of Viratanesvara both males and females, from several places by an order of the king.[23] The slaves sold to temples were marked with *sulam* (trident).[24] They were differentiated from the slaves who belonged to the king marked with ilaicinai.[25]

The slaves in temples were assigned several duties. Some female slaves dehusked paddy.[26] Some washed the clothes.[27] Some looked after filling the lamps with oil.[28] Thus they did divine services in temples. They were given accommodation, food and clothes for maintenance but not given any wages.

SLAVES SOLD AND EMPLOYED IN MADAMS

Women attached to a madam in the twelfth century were part of a list of people who were bound themselves in service to the temple in perpetuity.[29] A record mentions women given as hereditary servants to a madam at Tiruvaikkali in Thanjavur area in the thirteenth century.[30] One finds that a *kal thachar* (stone mason), his wife and their four sons were sold as *adimai* (slaves) to the madam at Achutha mangalam in Thanjavur area.[31] It is reported in an inscription that Vaiyiradha Rayar had a number of slaves who formed part of the dowry of his wife. He sold them with the consent of his wives to a madam.[32] Thus it is seen that men and women who were sold or given to madams in perpetual servitude.

SLAVE SALE DEEDS ON PALM LEAVES: SLAVERY AND THE SOCIAL HISTORICAL PROCESS

Three palm leaf manuscripts describe in detail the condition of slaves during the period 1509-29. They record that one Thiyagraja Mudaliar sold a slave named Rayaan son of Santhosi, of the parayiar caste in the presence of an arbitrator for 10 pons. Ramachandra Nayinar, a resident of Reddi Kadalangudi village sold four of his slaves called Muthan, Vellichan, his wife Parvathy and a male slave to Subramanya Mudaliar of Manganallur for fourteen pons. Subba Padaychi sold his slaves called Raman, his wife Mukkatai and their children to Appachi Mudaliar of Ganja village for 80 pons.

These evidences show that the family as a whole entered into slavery in the Thanjavur region where rice cultivation was intensive.[33]

These deeds recording the sale of slaves were called *aazhl-vilai-piramana-isavu-thittu*. The sale was done through an auction and the prices were recorded in the presence of an arbitrator. These manuscripts display the signature of slaves, witnesses and that of the writer of the document.[34] A standard clause in the sale deeds was that the slaves were to be property of the purchaser as long as the mountain, river Cauvery, the earth and the grass lasted. The sale of paraiyar had increased in this period. In one instance a family of seven paraiyars was sold for eight and a half pagoda in 1593.[35] Most of the slaves in the rural areas were owned by the local elite and wealthier members of the Tamil society. However, it is unclear from records whether owning a slave in that period was perceived as a symbol of social status.

Slavery developed because of socio-economic distress, poverty, famines, drought and debt. According to records, the owners of the slaves found in the medieval sale transactions, were mainly landlords. Thus, the most odious form of private property existed in the form of the sale of human beings. A slave was said to be a saleable person who was then regarded as the property of the buyer. The Tamil society had an open system of slavery with an established hierarchy which placed slaves at the bottom of the social order. Thus there is no lacking of indigenous Tamil primary sources to understand the society than to depend on the accounts of foreigners. Untouchability and slavery came in the way of the material well being of the people and also deprived them of civil rights.

NOTES

1. *Puranaanuru*, ed. U.V. Swaminatha Aiyar, Madras, 1971, 9: 1-5.
2. *Thirukural*, ed. M. Virasamy Pillai, Madras, 1849, 608.
3. K.K. Pillay, *A Social History of the Tamils*, Madras, 1969, rpt. 1975, p. 199.

4. *Pattinappaalai*, ed. U.V. Swaminatha Aiyar, in *Pathupattu*, Madras, 1974, line 246; *Pathitrupaththu*, ed. Avvai Duraisamy Pillai, 2nd edn., South India Saiva Siddhanta Pathippu Kazhagam, Tirunelveli, 1955, song 3, line 9; *Manimekhalai*, ed. Venkatsamy Nattar, South India Saiva Siddhanta Pathippu Kazhagam, Tirunelveli, 1992, chapter 18, line 119; *Maduraikanchi*, ed. U.V. Swaminatha Aiyar, in *Pathupattu*, Madras, 1974, line 583; C. Balasubramanian, *The Status of Women in Tamilnadu during the Sangam Age*, Madras, University of Madras, 1976.
5. *Tholkappiyam*, Porul Athikaaram, ed. V.U. Chidambaram Pillai, Madras, 1941, 74.
6. V. Kanakasabhai Pillai, *The Tamils Eighteen Hundred Years Ago*, Madras, 1966, p. 114. S. Manickam opines that Tamil literary sources on slavery are scanty and they are not corroborated by other evidences. This view is also called into question. S. Manickam, *Slavery in Tamil Country—A Historical Overview*, CLS, Madras, 1982, p. 25.
7. *Annual Report on Epigraphy* (including Indian and South Indian Epigraphy from 1881 to 1922, 1923-45, 1950 to 2005), New Delhi/ Madras, 1887-2005 (hereafter *ARE*), 149 of 1936.
8. *South Indian Inscriptions*, Publications of the Archaeological Survey of India, vols. I to XXXIV, New Delhi, 1890-1990 (hereafter *SII*), vol. XXII, no. 141.
9. *ARE*, 280 of 1927.
10. *ARE*, 429 of 1918.
11. *ARE*, 538 of 1918.
12. *ARE*, 499 of 1904.
13. *ARE*, 289 of 1910.
14. *ARE*, 499 of 1904.
15. *ARE*, 149 of 1937.
16. *ARE*, 218 of 1925, 219 of 1925.
17. *ARE*, 217 of 1925.
18. *ARE*, 80 of 1913.
19. *ARE*, 86 of 1911.
20. *ARE*, 365 of 1949.
21. *ARE*, 638 of 1916.
22. *ARE*, 223 of 1917.
23. *ARE*, 230 of 1917.
24. *ARE*, 230 of 1921.
25. *ARE*, 141 of 1922.

26. *ARE*, 122 of 1912
27. *ARE*, 578 of 1916.
28. *ARE*, 248 of 1916.
29. *ARE*, 76 of 1925, 84 of 1925.
30. *ARE*, 276 of 1925.
31. *ARE*, 409 of 1925.
32. *ARE*, 94 of 1926.
33. *Kalvettu*, vol. 17, pp. 1-6; S. Jeyaseela Stephen, *The Coromandel Coast and its Hinterland: Economy, Society and Political System 1500-1600*, Delhi, 1997, pp. 180-1.
34. S. Jeyaseela Stephen, *The Coromandel Coast*, p. 181.
35. *ARE*, 296 of 1911.

CHAPTER 3

Portuguese Slave Trade from the Tamil Coast to Goa and Cochin in India and to Melaka and Aceh in South East Asia, 1547-1625

According to available Tamil sources, Slaves were never exported overseas according to available ancient and medieval sources though humans were purchased and sold like goods in the inland of Tamil country. There was non-governmental trade of export of slaves and also by private individuals. Marco Polo the medieval traveller noted that slaves were exported from the ports of Bengal.[1] This fact had been also affirmed by the Duarte Barbosa the Portuguese traveller in the early sixteenth century.[2]

THE KINGS OF PORTUGAL IN LISBON, THE VICEROYS IN GOA AND THE REGULATIONS ISSUED ON SLAVERY AND SLAVE TRADE

Vasco da Gama arrived at Calicut on the western coast of India in 1498 and later the Portuguese began to expand their commercial operations on the Tamil coast. Enslavement and slave trade commenced when the Portuguese settled in the coastal fringes. Lourenço Moreno and Diogo Pereira wrote in 1510 to the king of Portugal in Lisbon concerning the slavery that was getting in the way of larger services to God and king. They mentioned that the ship captains in India were unwilling to carry sick and crippled men while in the service of the king, they would rather bring their ships full of slaves, which was an act of great inhumanity; and, if they brought some sick men it was because they were bribed. Hence they requested the king to offer a solution to this situation.[3] Thus it is learnt that slaves from India were shipped to Portugal.

Slaves and slave trade were among the issues targeted by a set of Portuguese laws enacted in 1520 known as Ordenações da Índia. A royal provision enacted in November 1521 confirmed that, despite not being included in the Ordenações Manuelinas, this code was to be enforced in Portuguese trading settlements. It gave official recognition to the enslavement of Muslims in the Indian Ocean. This was the law that confirmed the project of Portuguese royal monopoly on spices in the Indian Ocean. In this provision, any person, including officials of the Portuguese colonial administration, Christians, Muslims, and people from any other nation were forbidden to trade pepper, clover, ginger, cinnamon, mace, nutmeg, lacquer, silk and the mineral tincal.

A letter was therefore sent to Diogo Lopes de Sequeira, the governor in Goa in March 1520, where the king explained in detail the reasons for this move. According to the letter, the presence of slaves on ships coming from India was a waste of supplies, among other inconveniences. For that reason, the king restricted the presence of slaves on board of the said vessels, although he admitted that private merchants in the service of the king were not to follow the said restriction, in respect to contracts they had with other merchants. However, in the letter, the king provided that, if it was necessary for the safety of the ship, the king would allow up to 20 slaves or even more if necessary, to come on board, as long as they were men. The reason for this no-female restriction had nothing to do with social norms. The letter explained, men were allowed as long as they were able and knowledgeable enough to help in sailing the ship.[4]

The pepper and spice trade had restrictions in regard to trading officials and the commerce between Portuguese ports, but the slave trade was simply unregulated in India. Human trafficking became one choice for the small traders who were in search of profit but lacked enough capital to take part in the spice trade. The result was an active slave trade. The Portuguese legislation in this period was directed at regulating and curtailing slave trading practices, not defining legitimacy or restricting ownership of slaves. Slave trade was free, unless it represented any danger to the spice trade.

The king of Portugal received complaints regarding the Portuguese who were not freeing their baptized slaves as they should. Hence the king wrote a letter to Dom Henrique de Menezes, the Governor of Goa (1524-6) and instructed him on how to proceed in such cases, confirming that slaves were to be freed upon baptism. The same matter had been repeated again in 1533, when the king wrote to Governor D. Nuno da Cunha.[5] In 1556 before passing away, Dom João III, the king of Portugal reversed his decision and ruled that baptized slaves owned by Muslims or Hindus should be sold to Christians, but not be freed. These slaves were to be kept as slaves by their new masters.[6] The only and real obligation was that converted slaves had to be sold only to Christians.

Dom Sebastiao, the new king of Portugal (1557-78) wrote to Francisco Barreto, the Governor in Goa, that slaves owned by Muslims were to be sold to Christians upon baptism, but not regain their freedom.[7] The King of Portugal also gave instructions to the departing new Viceroy Dom Luís de Ataíde in 1568, in which he declared that Muslims illegally transporting pepper outside of the Malabar Coast could be captured and enslaved. He indicated specifically that they were to be considered as slaves being captives of just war.[8]

Dom Constantino de Bragança, the Portuguese viceroy of India (1558-61) ruled that slaves owned by Hindus should be freed upon baptism. The converted slaves brought by Hindus to be sold should then be auctioned, and after being purchased by Christians, the amount had to be delivered to its former owner. At the same time, the viceroy forbade Hindus to buy Christian slaves in the Portuguese trading settlements.[9] Mathias de Albuquerque the viceroy in Goa in 1590s ruled that baptized slaves should not be owned by Hindus.[10] Thus various regulations were enforced on slaves and slavery in India because of the tension that had developed between baptism of slaves and manumission of slaves.

THE PURCHASE SLAVES FROM THE TAMIL COAST BY THE PORTUGUESE TRADERS

Portuguese traders had settled on the Tamil coast since 1507. They purchased slaves and employed them in domestic work in their trading settlements. Thus, over a period of time a large population of slaves lived in the Portuguese settlements.[11] Slaves were not allowed to be transported overseas in ships owing to a ban issued on the export of slaves by the local nayaka rulers of Vijayanagar empire. Portuguese traders later purchased slaves from the Tamil Coast and sold them to fellow settlers in Goa and Cochin. These purchased the slaves were employed by the masters for various purposes.

A TAMIL SLAVE IN GOA, 1548

In a testament dated 2 June 1548 by Antonio de Faria e Sousa, a rich merchant at the time of his death in Goa confided that he owned 30 slaves. One finds one Tamil male slave besides 12 Chinese slaves, two from the island of Java, two from Pegu, one from Japan, one from Gujarat, one from Makassar and one from Sri Lanka. It is found that 64 per cent of these slaves of Faria were males and 36 per cent were females, while 77 per cent were adults and 23 per cent were children.[12] This record suggests that Portuguese merchants had extensive slave trading networks in Asia.

THE ESCAPE OF A TAMIL SLAVE IN COCHIN, 1558

Another Portuguese trader called Luis Rodrigues lived at Cochin. He had also built an extensive commercial network from Cochin to Bengal and Kedah. He also owned several ships that sailed from Melaka to China during the period of 1545 and 1558 and he invested funds in the purchase of Chinese commodities. He had residences in the city of Cochin and Melaka too. Luis Rodrigues owned a Tamil male slave by name Duarte and he ran away because the master had ill-treated him. It is known that Rodrigues had many slaves called Antonio, Joana and Isabel who were employed. Peter the slave was mainly employed to seal the joints of sailing vessels with oakum.[13]

THE SLAVERY AND SLAVE TRADE ON THE TAMIL COAST AND THE JESUIT MISSIONARIES, 1545-1552

Miguel Vaz the Jesuit wrote to Dom João III, the king of Portugal in 1545 and he gave details regarding the deeds of Portuguese merchants who brought slaves from the Coromandel Coast to Goa. He said that after the arrival of slaves in Goa they were resold as human cargo. The Jesuit Provincial was mainly concerned with the fate of these men and women slaves. He suggested that, rather than passing on the slaves to Muslim masters, under Portuguese dominance the slaves should be converted to Christianity, without offering any resistance.[14]

Henrique Henriques the Jesuit at Vembar on the Pearl Fishery Coast recorded a case of a slave in 1548 which was narrated to him by a slave himself. The slave was raised in the Santa Fé College of Goa and he wished to accompany the missionaries on their trip to the Moluccas and he secretly boarded the ship. After he was discovered as a stowaway passenger he was taken off the sailing vessel in Cochin and left with a Portuguese man who was asked to bring the slave back to Goa. The slave thereafter ran away and ended up in the hands of Muslim traders who tried to convert him. Rescued by a Portuguese captain, the slave told not only his own tale of resistance, but also those of many other fugitive slaves under the Muslims. Henriques through this communication illustrated the need for the missionaries to work among the slaves. Henriques also mentioned at that time that many slaves had asked Francis Xavier to intervene in their favour, in order to allow them to become Christians and to be freed. Xavier had promised them that he would try his best, but no further information had been found in his letter.[15]

Nicolao Lancillotto the Jesuit had written a letter to Ignatius Loyola in 1550 wherein he elaborated the details on the legal aspects slavery in Tamil country. One finds that the missionary had denounced Portuguese soldiers who after settling in the Tamil Coast enslaved the natives. They also baptized their slaves, without any liturgical concern. These practices, Lancillotto said had paved the way to a lack of rigour towards the local Christian community that the Jesuits were planning to correct. The missionary attributed to these forceful baptisms the general situation of Tamil Christians, who received the baptism for reasons considered by the missionary to be unholy or secular.[16]

Lancillotto gave a detailed account on the ways how an individual became a slave in India. At first he referred to the political power the local rulers had over the populace, a dominion that included the capacity to sell subjects as slaves.[17] Next he said that any individual could sell a person or relative over whom he or she had any power. He added that parents sold their children, uncles and aunts sold their nephews and nieces and the older brothers sold younger siblings. He also mentioned that there was the problem of volunteer slavery, which according to Lancillotto accounted for thousands becoming new slaves every day in Tamil country.

The missionary reiterated that all these various types of slaves were traded as merchandise, like horses and cattle in Europe. His concerns were mainly two. The first was whether the Jesuits were allowed to buy these types of slaves and, second, if it was licit to speculate on their prices. He stated that one could buy three slaves when prices were low, but should the buyer repay the seller the difference when the market changed and prices went up later on.[18]

Ignatius Loyola replied to this letter including four other earlier letters sent by Lancillotto in a single short letter dated 27 January 1552. Ignatius did not offer any concrete answer to the questioning on legitimacy of slavery. Perhaps he preferred to leave the matter to be decided by those who lived on the Tamil Coast. May be he felt that the issue could be decided locally by people who had a better understanding of the situation.[19]

THE DISCUSSION OF MISSIONARIES ON SLAVERY AND SLAVES AT THE FIRST PROVINCIAL COUNCIL IN GOA, 1567

The legitimacy of enslavement and the issue that remained unanswered for long, finally came for discussion before the ecclesiastical authorities in Goa. The missionaries deliberated the matter in the Synod of 1567 and thus came the striking blow on the unruly slave market of the Portuguese in India. It triggered a series of legal acts by the crown in order to control and curtail slavery in the name of Christian conversions and the mission. The Goa decrees are divided into four parts or Acts, in the following order: Profession of faith and presentation; conversion of the infidels and new-converts; reform of the Church and Reform of the Muslims. Enslavement and related practices were spread throughout the decrees. The text refers to young children and slaves, as a single legal entity. It explained how political power and dominance was to be organized in the colonial societies. Missionaries were central for the most basic organizational unity of a society, the family. They had power over members of their group, but especially over their children. This relationship is recreated between the master and his or her slave. The master (dominus) assumes control (dominium) over his slave.[20] The most basic notion of dominance over a slave comes from the Roman law of nations, that had been used to explain that the winning party in a just war had the right to kill subjugated enemies. The winner could also choose, instead, a less drastic punishment, by enslaving the defeated.[21]

The council of 1567 vide its decree 16 mentioned that non-Christians should not possess a Christian slave. If they happened to buy or sell one, such a slave would be considered free. It stated that the same would apply to any slave of non-Christian master on becoming Christian, who would not receive any price for him or her. If the slave was brought for sale, they should not be paid more than 12 cruzados, and this would be applicable only if the slave was sold within three months after entering the Portuguese territory. Beyond this time limit the slave would be considered free. As regards slaves, who might belong to the jurisdiction of allies, to be baptized, the mutual accord had to be respected, namely, if the allies returned slaves to the Portuguese or paid for them, the Portuguese also had to respond in the same manner.[22]

JESUIT LETTERS AND REPORTS ON SLAVERY AND SLAVES, 1571-1576

A report of 1571 has mentioned that many Portuguese had 15 to 50 female slaves each. Masters and even servants and male slaves slept with them.[23] A letter was written in 1576 to Mercurian the Jesuit Superior-General in Rome, that in India even poor native Christians had their slaves and that it was very cheap to have them and maintain them, because the only costs were cheap clothes and rice. Besides, in the Jesuit residences, the titles of captivity were examined carefully by two or three Fathers deputed by the Provincial for this purpose. The menial jobs were considered as below dignity for the whites. Those with illegal or uncertain title were freed and their service was paid for. Those who had already served for some years were also granted their letter of manumission.[24]

Alessandro Valignano the visitor of the Jesuit missions noted in 1576 that many slave masters had donated slaves to the Jesuit residences. He feared that many of such slaves were illegally captured. He wished that slaves of all Jesuit residences in the Portuguese empire ought to be set free, as it had been done in the Jesuit province of Sicily. The authorities in India had replied that it was difficult to function in India without slaves and as to the title of slavery and good treatment, this had been ensured. The Jesuit lay brothers could not do in India the type of work they were doing in Europe. It was stated that in this country no one served another, except the slaves and some native boys.[25]

Valignano instructed 'The Father of Christians' (a State appointed official usually a priest to look after the protection and welfare of converts to Christianity) in September 1595 to look after the manumission of the slaves, particularly of those owned by the Portuguese, who tended to offer more resistance. In case they failed to yield to appeals to conscience, the cases were to be entrusted to the lay attorney of the Christians.[26] It is mentioned that even the Fathers of Christians were accomplices in accepting declarations during baptism to cover the intentions of the slave buyers who claimed that the young slaves would be a burden to their parents who would kill them, or that they would be captured by pirates. The law mentioned that baptism had become a door to slavery, instead of being a door to freedom.[27]

THE THIRD PROVINCIAL COUNCIL OF GOA IN 1585 AND DISCUSSION ON THE FREEDOM OF SLAVES

The third provincial council was held in Goa in 1585 and discussion on slavery took place. It repeated the decree 13 of the First Council and decree 8 of the Second Council extending the freedom of slaves belonging to non-Christians including those in Melaka. It also repeated the prohibition of Muslims taking slaves through the Portuguese territories. A fine of 50 pardaus and excommunication was imposed upon the Captains and ship masters who permitted embarkation of such slaves without the knowledge of the Viceroy or the Prelate. They should force the masters to sell their slaves to

Christians, or failing Christian buyers to non-Christians of the Portuguese jurisdiction.[28]

The decree 30 of the Third Council referred to the practice of some slave owners giving Christian names to their slaves without baptizing them. The masters were obliged to baptize a slave within six months after acquisition or within a month if the slave was 10 years of age or less. There was a fine imposed upon the defaulters.[29]

The decree 2 of the Third Council in 1585 ordered the slave masters to redeem within one year any of their slaves who might have been captured in wars or any such conflicts. The Council considered it to be their duty of gratitude and also defence of faith. If they were not redeemed within this period and succeeded in escaping from captivity they should be considered free. There was an annexe to the proceedings of this Council and it quoted from the Justinian code stating that Christian captives of Jews, gentiles or heretics in India, could not be considered legitimate slaves, even if any of their masters might later accept Christianity.[30]

THE FIFTH PROVINCIAL COUNCIL OF GOA IN 1606: DISCUSSION ON THE SLAVE MARRIAGES, SLAVES WITH LEGAL CERTIFICATES AND FREEING

The Fifth Council repeated a decree of the Fourth about masters not impeding the marriage of their slaves and to sell them when married to freed slaves giving an impression that these could accompany them wherever they might have to go. Such sales should be restricted to the coast extending from the port of Diu in Gujarat to Kanyakumari region and not beyond. The council banned female slaves of less than 50 years of age from selling foodstuffs or do sewing work on the streets. The masters who permitted this should pay a fine of 20 pardaus for each breach of this order.[31]

The decree 15 of the fourth session of the fifth provincial council lamented that despite many bans and decrees of the past councils, the captivity of slaves and their abusive exploitation had been on the rise and there appeared to be no way of checking it. The council therefore authorized the Bishops in their respective jurisdictions to keep a watch on the ports where slave trafficking took place, deputing virtuous and responsible persons to examine the titles of captivity and hand these in writing to the respective slaves. They should also issue the certificates of legal possession to the respective slave masters. Any slave who was not thus examined and without such certificate should be considered freed.[32]

THE VARIOUS TYPES OF ILL-TREATMENT OF SLAVES RECORDED IN THE COUNCILS OF GOA

The Council held in Goa had noted the various types of ill-treatment meted out to slaves. A decree of the council in its fourth session referred to cruel treatment meted out to slaves by some masters to the point of killing some slaves. The council prohibited the practice of punishments with fire or cane and invited denunciation by those who might come to know of such punishments being practised. It prohibited forcing the slaves to work on Sundays and religious days of obligation or making them pay for things they lost or happened to break at home. The masters were advised to treat their sick slaves well and to advise them to frequent the sacraments.[33]

In 1606 the Council had noted the various other types of ill-treatment meted out to slaves and it included slaves punished cruelly with hot irons, leather straps, by pouring hot liquids, by pressing any part of their body with weights, by throwing pepper, oil, vinegar or salt into their eyes, by breaking their teeth or by whipping them repeatedly. The Council banned the said ill-treatments and said that any one violating this order should pay a fine of 50 pardaus. The Council decreed that sick slaves abandoned by their masters and living on streets and in hospital of the poor should be considered free if their masters did not take them back.[34]

PORTUGUESE PRIVATE TRADERS AND SLAVE TRADE FROM NAGAPATTINAM TO MELAKA, 1616-1625

Pedro Chirino, the Jesuit reported that the male and female slaves were brought by the Portuguese from Nagapattinam to Melaka. The women slaves were great seamstresses, cooks and very orderly and clean in their service.[35]

A Portuguese private merchant had declared in 1616 that he had transported four slaves namely Augustine, Adriana, Maria and Jacinto from Nagapattinam and Tuticorin (besides Catalina, Antonio and Pascual the three slaves from Sri Lanka) to Melaka.[36] Evidences make it clear that the Portuguese missionaries on the Tamil Coast were willing to provide the necessary paperwork to turn an illegal purchase of a slave into a long-term labour or permanent slave contract. A common line of reasoning that developed by 1616 in Tamil country was that a person was a slave if he or she had been labelled by the Roman church council. Francisco Macedo a Portuguese slave merchant in 1620 justified his property rights over slaves in 1620 and referred to the provisions contained in the provincial councils of Goa. He claimed that the Hindus and Muslims in India were declared slaves because they were enemies of Christians.[37]

There are numerous references to Portuguese slaves who continued to be transported overseas from Nagapattinam. In a letter of 24 October 1625 the Dutch factor of Coromandel had mentioned that he had captured two ships of the Portuguese sailing from Nagapattinam to Melaka which had 300 slaves.[38]

PORTUGUESE SLAVE TRADE FROM NAGAPATTINAM TO ACEH IN SUMATRA, 1621

Slave trade began to develop from Nagapattinam to Aceh. People were sometimes kidnapped and sold as slaves. Augustin de Beaulieu, a traveller reported that he met a few slaves of

Nagapattinam brought to Aceh. These slaves had requested him on 2 March 1621 to rescue them from their owners by paying money. He however could rescue only four Christian slaves who were former residents of Nagapattinam. The santa casa da misericordia (The Holy House of Mercy) of Nagapattinam paid him 400 reals towards the expenses met by him on this count. Augustin de Beaulieu had sought the help of Kunkazhali Marakkayar of Tamil Coast who was at Aceh on 23 March 1621 and he helped him to carry out this mission of rescue of slaves with success.[39]

To conclude it may be said that the Portuguese officials and missionaries discussed about the nature of slavery and slaves. Portuguese private traders from Goa and Cochin came to the Tamil Coast and purchased salves. Tamil slaves were also exported from Nagapattinam to Melaka and Aceh in South East Asia. The missionary accounts provide a graphic description of the Portuguese private traders and their excess, including their active involvement in slave trade.

NOTES

1. Marco Polo, *Travels of Sir Marco Polo*, 2 vols., tr., Yule, London, 1903, p. 115; S. Jeyaseela Stephen, 'Slavery and Society: Experience of the Dutch and the French Trading Companies in Coastal Andhra, AD 1600-1800', in *Social Evils in Andhra Desa, 17th & 18th Centuries*, ed. R. Soma Reddy, M. Radhakishna Sarma and A. Satyanaryana, Hyderabad, 1999, pp. 75-96, see p. 76.
2. M.L. Dames, ed., *The Book of Duarte Barbosa*, 2nd edition, Hakluyt Society, London, 1921 p. 147; S. Jeyaseela Stephen, *Portuguese in the Tamil Coast: Historical Explorations in Commerce and Culture, 1507-1749*, Pondicherry, 1998, pp. 155-8.
3. Letter of Lourenço Moreno and Diogo Pereira to the king dated 20 December 1510 in Raymundo Antonio de Bulhao Pato, ed., *Cartas de Afonso de Albuquerque*, Typographia da Academia Real das Sciencias de Lisboa, 1903, tomo III, p. 317.
4. Joaquim Heliodoro da Cunha Rivara, *Archivo Portuguez Oriental* (hereafter *APO-CR*), 6 fasc. in 10 vols., New Delhi, Asian Educational Services, 1992, Fasc. 5, p. 1, pp. 52-3.

5. *APO-CR*, Fasc. 5, pp. 153-4.
6. *APO-CR*, Fasc. 5, parte I, p. 311.
7. *APO-CR*, Fasc. 5, p. 320.
8. António da Silva Rêgo, *Documentação para a história das Missões do Padroado Português do Oriente*, Lisboa, Agência Geral das Colónias, 1947-58, vol. X, p. 443.
9. *APO-CR*, Fasc. 5, parte I, p. 374.
10. Jose Wicki, ed., *O Livro do Pai dos Cristãos*, Lisboa, Centro de Estudos Históricos Ultramarinos, 1969, pp. 235-6.
11. Jose Wicki, *Documenta Indica* (hereafter *DI*), 18 vols., Roma, 1949-88, vol. V, Document 97, p. 665; S. Jeyaseela Stephen, 'Economic Change, Institutional Development and Urbanization in Santhome, 1507–1676', in *Portuguese Presence in India During the Sixteenth and Seventeenth Centuries*, ed. Yogesh Sharma and Jose Leal Ferreira, Delhi, 2008, p. 7.
12. Lúcio de Sousa, 'Slave Networks and their Expansion through Macao to Europe and America', *Revista de Cultura*, no. 35, July 2010, pp. 84-94, see p. 89.
13. Ibid.
14. *DI*, vol. I, p. 65, Letter of Miguel Vaz to Dom João III in Portugal in 1545.
15. *DI*, vol. I, pp. 297-8. Letter of Henrique Henriques to Igantius Loyola from Vembar on 31 October 1548.
16. *DI*, vol. X, pp. 125-9. Letter of Nicolao Lancillotto from Kollam to Ignatius Loyola in December 1550.
17. *DI*, vol. X, pp. 129-30.
18. Ibid.
19. *Monumenta Ignatiana*, Series Prima, Tomus Quartus, Madrid, Gabriel Lopez del Horno, 1906, ep. 2371, pp. 116-19.
20. Public Library of Évora, Portugal, *O Primeiro Concilio Prouinçial çelebrado em Goa, no anno de 1567*, Goa, João de Endem, 1568.
21. António da Silva Rêgo. Documentação para, vol. X, p. 343.
22. *APO-CR*, IV & V (II), p. 178.
23. *DI*, vol. VIII, p. 409.
24. *DI*, vol. X, pp. 214-15, 266.
25. *DI*, vol. X, pp. 638-9.
26. *DI*, vol. XVII, p. 88.
27. *DI*, vol. X, pp. 361-3.
28. *APO-CR*, pp. 135-7.
29. *APO-CR*, pp. 142-3.

30. *APO-CR*, pp. 177-8, 183-4.
31. *APO-CR*, p. 267.
32. *APO-CR*, pp. 267-8.
33. *APO-CR*, p. 51.
34. *APO-CR*, pp. 269-70.
35. Pedro Chirino, *Relación De Las Islas Filipinas*, Manila, Historical Conservation Society, 1969, pp. 141-2.
36. Archivo General de la Nación (hereafter AGN), Mexico City, Seccion Historia, 406, fls.187r-191v (1616).
37. AGN, Seccion Jesuitas, 4-26.2 (1620).
38. W. Ph. Coolhas, ed., *Generale Missiven van de Gouverneurs-Generaal en Raden Aan Heren XVII der Verenigde Oostindische Compagnie*, 9 vols., 'S Gravenhage, 1960-84, vol. I, p. 175, see also, p. 791.
39. Denys Lombard, *Memoires d'un Voyage aux Indes Orientales; Un Marchand Normand a Sumatra*, Paris, 1996, pp. 120-30.

CHAPTER 4

Slaves from the Tamil Coast to Long Distant Foreign Markets: Portuguese Slave Trade with Manila and Spanish Slave Trade with Mexico, 1616-1704

Political changes took place in Tamil country after the defeat of the Vijayanagara ruler in the battle of Talikota in 1565. Further, new political developments also took place in Portugal after the death of King Dom Sebastiao in 1578. Philip II, the King of Spain also became the King of Portugal in 1580. As a result he introduced new policies for global trade. At this juncture, significant commercial development took place both in the East and in the New World. The Iberian union remained till 1640 when the Braganza dynasty in Portugal, was ushered in with the 1640 revolution against the Spanish Habsburgs. Joao IV became the new King of Portugal in December 1640. As a result, international trade around the world developed, reaching new heights between 1580 and 1640.

The European contact with Manila began as early as 1521 and Miguel Lopez de Legazpi, after the establishment of the Spanish colony, in his letters of 1568 and 1569 to Philip II, the King of Spain, praised the abundance of timber in the Philippines.[1] Andres de Mirandaola in his letter of 1574 and Andres de San Nicolas, Luis de Jesus and Juan de la Conception in their accounts of 1624 commended highly the fertile forest in the Philippines, the prevalence of cinnamon trees, brasil-trees, small pomegranate trees and orange trees that had delicious fruits, besides the abundance of incorruptible woods, such as ebony, cedar, cypress and cedar.[2] Andres de Mirandaola's letter of 1574 and Francisco de Sande's letter of 1576 mentioned the availability of suitable wood for shipbuilding in the Philippines for the naval purposes of the Spanish king.[3] Juan Pacheco Maldonado wrote in his letter to King Philip II in 1575 that there was enough timber to construct three to four galleons each year, since Spain needed ships to defend her new possessions in the East.[4] Santiago de Vera from Manila mentioned in 1586 that Filipinos had proven skill in building ships of all kinds owing to abundance of wood.[5] Several ships were built at Masbate, Marinduque, Camarines and Albay while new shipyards came to be established at Cavite and Oton. By 1616, six out of the seven galleons stationed in Manila for its defense, were built in the Philippines. These large ships required continual repair due to wartime losses and frequency of the shipwrecks that took place. There was also the need to replace timber in the tropical waters.[6] The large scale endeavour of shipbuilding and repairs in the Philippines had therefore to be carried out by a vast amount of labour that was required. The municipalities had begun to provide people to work in the shipyards.[7] Hernando de Los Rios Coronel in 1621 mentioned that manpower was required in the Philippines and the masts of one galleon involved the efforts of 6,000 Filipinos for 3 months, simply to supply and transport the wood.[8]

In the wake of the circumstances stated above, the royal officials recommended the purchase of slaves from India to Manila, in as early as 1584 and again 1597, who could serve as caulkers and carpenters for the King's ships. This was viewed in a way to save huge expenditure incurred on the salaries paid.[9]

PRIVATE PORTUGUESE TRADERS AND SLAVE TRADE FROM NAGAPATTINAM TO MANILA, 1616-1689

Spanish records provide some notions of slavery, slave trade being conducted direct especially with physical contact. The sellers and buyers shared their ideas of servitude, rights and obligations. This writer has carefully avoided the slaves who had been exported from Goa, Cochin and Bengal in India, who were in Manila and later found their way to Mexico.[10] One has included only the slaves hailing from the Tamil Coast. It is very easy to trace since Portuguese merchants and other slavers have often applied the region and caste names and also applied to the port of embarkation of slaves. Slaves were brought from the port and Portuguese settlement of Nagapattinam to Spanish Manila.

On 26 August 1616, Luis Danga, a resident of Dilao, purchased Jacinto, a Tamil slave captured during warfare by Benito Ferreira, a Portuguese man.[11] Manuel Mamadu (Mohammed), a Tolucan (Muslim) slave who was Christianized had also been sold into slavery during the famine and he was shipped in 1622 along with slaves belonging to the caste of Reddis and other Tamils from Nagapattinam to Manila.[12] The public defender of the slaves in Manila was able to persuade the court that Manuel's captivity was illicit, while the other Tamil slaves who accompanied him in the ship to Manila posed no problems.[13]

Spanish records very often mention the castes of the Tamil slaves brought to Manila. One finds mention of paraiyar caste slaves.[14] The records of 1619 mention the slaves of the valayars, the fishermen caste on the Tamil coast.[15]

In Nagapattinam the Portuguese private traders were able to acquire supplies of slaves from the area because some natives sold themselves into slavery due to famines. One has the testimony of a Hindu male of the paraiyar caste named Mani (Meney in the record), who admitted that he had been forced to sell himself in 1620 to Francisco Macedo, a Portuguese merchant and captain, due to hunger. He revealed that he entered into slavery through the efforts of a Portuguese broker called Joto Carin. The vicar general of the church of Our Lady of Immaculate Conception in the Portuguese settlement of Nagapattinam wrote that he examined the slave named Meney 25 years old and was fully convinced the sale was good. The missionary had then cleared the buyer's conscience and gave him a license to sell Meney as a slave.[16] It is a fact that slave traders began to use such a process that was ostensibly meant to provide slaves with some legal recourse to their advantage.

The status of slaves brought from Nagapattinam to Manila had been settled by the court authorities in Manila. Andres Annaya, a 18-year old slave of paraiyar caste, was sold by a Portuguese trader to Diaz who lived in Manila. It was found in 1622 that Diaz was arguing before a judge in Manila defending the slaves he had purchased. He said that Andres Annaya was equal to others who belonged to the same caste of paraiyars and all of them including Andres Annaya were captured during war and made slaves. The judge in Manila delivered judgement and he confirmed the slavery of Andres Annaya.[17]

Spanish records mention the slaves of the Tamil communities in addition to migrants from Telugu country who had settled in the Tamil region under the nayaks of Vijayanagar empire. Manuel Reddi who spoke Telugu but also knew Tamil, having lived in the hinterland of Nagapattinam, had been purchased as a slave and was brought to Manila in a ship in 1631 along with the load of slave cargo that included Tamil men of vellalas (valala) caste.[18]

A record mentions that slaves were destined to reach Manila along with textile cargo under the Portuguese. The same ships returned carrying rich and large cargo of silver ingots which came from Mexico to Manila. In one instance in 1631 a Portuguese ship was captured by the Dutch and the rich cargo of silver bullion had become the property of the Dutch East India Company since the booty was not returned.[19] Thus one finds slave trade was highly profitable.

The Portuguese missionaries were not in favour of slave trade and so the Portuguese viceroy in Goa took steps to control and he banned the slave trade. An order was issued in this regard prohibiting the sale of slaves in Nagapattinam and Tuticorin since 28 June 1632.[20] However, slave trade by private Portuguese traders thrived secretly.

The Portuguese slave traders and their Spanish clients made more specific references to the social groups of slaves, mentioning particularly the castes. One finds continued references to Reddis and Vellalar slaves exported to Manila even during the year 1634.[21]

The caste names of Chettis are mentioned in Spanish records of 1634 and their ships had been also recorded. These traders were not slaves but whether they brought slaves or textiles had not been clear.[22] Records continue to mention Tamil merchants trading in Manila even in the year 1685.[23]

The slaves brought from Nagapattinam were employed but their job description had been largely unknown. We find mention of serangs (saranguis) reaching Manila in 1634.[24] Another record states that serang Dila and twelve lascars had reached Manila through the ship of Luis Dias a Portuguese merchant from Tamil Coast. On arrival in the Philippines they worked in the port of Cavite. It is found that the port officials had compensated Luis Dias for the work of the lascars. The inquisition officials boarding the ships had inspected them and they took note of heretical materials mentioning the religious affiliation of the lascars. It is found that a few of them belonged to the caste of paravars, the Christians of the pearl fishery while some of them were Muslims and Hindus.[25] It had been mentioned that these maritime workers had brought to the Philippines a long tradition of seafaring and all of its associated and accumulated knowledge of sailing that they gained over the centuries. The tradition of lascar recruitment and service to staff the shipping necessitated the demand for employees in Manila. Vellalar slaves had continued to arrive in Manila in 1647 and they were used as slave labour.[26] Antonio a Tamil slave brought from Nagapattinam in 1644 was sold for 318 pesos in Manila. The slave was found collecting forest products for the master.[27]

The Dutch Company officials on the Coromandel Coast pointed out the distinction between the slaves captured during the naval battles and wars fought between the Portuguese and the Dutch and the illegal kidnapping and stealing of men and women by the Portuguese private traders in Nagapattinam. In 1651, Carel Reniers (1650-3) the Dutch Governor General and his Council in Jakarta condemned the unbecoming Christian practices of the Portuguese in Nagapattinam who stole slaves from the hinterland of the ports at the dead of night. They also committed open robbery with the connivance of some natives around Nagapattinam who profited from slave trade. Taking these cases well in mind and on high moral grounds, the Dutch officials felt at that time that they should never imitate this great sin of the Portuguese who were stealing and kidnapping slaves even if the Dutch were to acquire more of them.[28]

Slaves abducted and captured were purchased and sold time and again owing to profit in slave trade. The slaves were exported by the Portuguese private traders from Nagapattinam to Manila. According to a report, there was a married Tamil male who came from Madurai to Nagapattinam exploring the possibility of finding some means of livelihood and employment to support his family. Having found some job at Nagapattinam he asked leave of absence after a month from the person with whom he was serving to go to Madurai and fetch his wife and children in 1662. After obtaining leave and necessary permission he proceeded and reached Madurai. There he learnt that the neighbour in Nagapattinam to whom he had entrusted his family had abducted them, telling the wife that her husband had sent for her. When he returned to Nagapattinam he learnt that his wife and sons were already sold and taken to Tranquebar and were resold treacherously to the Portuguese vicar-general for 30 *pagodas* and members of his family were not aware of it. In the end he came to the Danish settlement of Tranquebar and made efforts to recover them. When approached, the Portuguese priest at once resisted and reported the matter to Eskild Andersen the Danish Governor (1655-72). Further, the man himself was captured so that he could make no further attempts for his own release. Later, when he was released from the prison, the poor man lodged a complaint to the Bishop of Mylapore, but a hearing was refused out of regard for the said Portuguese priest. He submitted a petition then and prayed that he might at least have permission to re-marry, since the said priest had already bought his wife and sons. In the meantime, he learnt that his family members had again been sold for 60 *pagodas* and were ready to sail for Manila. At this time, all members of his caste assembled and undertook to pay the sale price of his wife and sons within one month, since this Tamil was a poor man. Even this did not work. The Governor had earlier decided that resold slaves should not be embarked in the ships leaving for Manila, thereupon the Portuguese priest was forced to take the wife and sons away. The priest had again managed to send them for re–sale elsewhere into the hands of the Hindu traders. The husband in desperation, changed his faith and returned to Hinduism, since he was unable to secure justice from the Christians.[29] Thus one finds crimes committed in slave trade against public decency, morality and disorderly conduct and also against public justice and breach of trust. The distinction between legal means and illegal kidnapping and robbery of slaves by the Portuguese private traders in Nagapattinam was thus flexible in theory and practice.

Manila was under the ecclesiastical jurisdiction of Mexican inquisition and not under the Portuguese inquisition in Goa. The port officials in the Philippines had to verify the legal and illegal traffic as per rules. The officials checked for the forbidden materials being brought in the incoming ships. Portuguese private merchants in many cases who transported slaves illegally to the Philippines brought the slaves before an ecclesiastical judge in Manila, testifying that they had lost their titles. The cleric drew up a slave license, which the merchant then took to the secular flexible to further legitimize his enslavement.[30]

It is noticed that the Portuguese private traders who brought slaves from Nagapattinam in 1689 had brought with them the necessary papers showing that the slaves had been taken in the time of wars, which they presented to the competent judge on arrival in Manila.[31] They were very shrewd in business because the Spanish legal system had a process by which a master or a slave could demand to review the legality of the enslavement at court. The governor appointed official in the Philippines titled 'Defender general of the slaves brought to the city of Manila from India and other parts' did not know the intricacies involved in the slave trade of the Portuguese since he was charged with merely presenting the petitions against their enslavement before the *Alcalde Ordinario* (mayor).

Portuguese presence in China was intensified with the founding of Macau, a Portuguese settlement by merchants between 1554 and 1557. In the following decades, Macau was gradually incorporated by the Portuguese crown. Some Tamil slaves were taken by the Portuguese to Macau. Ignacio Morales was a Portuguese merchant in Macau and he had purchased a Tamil slave called Antonio of the Shanar caste (casta Sena). Morales came to Manila later with his slave and in 1674, he sold his slave Antonio to Francisco Fresno, a Spaniard.[32]

Some Spaniards also commenced to trade with the ports of Coromandel. Spanish captains sent their ships to Madras and Porto Novo to obtain woven textiles owing to demand. Tamil merchants also visited the Philippines. In 1701, the royal treasurer of the Philippines in Manila granted a license to sail and return to a Tamil Muslim ship captain and merchant who hailed from the Coromandel Coast to bring textiles and slaves.[33] Slave trade continued in Coromandel Coast as late as 1703, when a ship anchored in Manila Bay with a load of 70 Tamil slaves and some Bengali slaves.[34]

TAMIL SLAVES IN MANILA EMPLOYED IN COCONUT PALM CULTIVATION, 1646

It is important to ask why the slaves were brought to Manila. This was owing to labour demand. Slave trade that commenced and flourished between the Philippines and Tamil ports resulted in the residence of a significant slave population of Tamils who were employed in positions that involved various types of odd jobs in central Luzon.

The Spaniards in Manila had introduced usage and cultivation of coconut palms.[35] Sebastián Hurtado de Corcuera, the Spanish Governor in 1646, mandated the growing of abaca and coconut palms in all communities with the proper growing conditions. Abaca palms provided fibre for cordage and rigging used on the naval craft of the Philippines. Coconut palms provided oil for illumination and the production of pitch, as well as fibre and toddy. Slaves came to be employed in agriculture and horticulture. The slaves imported by the Portuguese were exempted from tax and the governor stipulated that these slaves would not even be written down on the list. Additionally, the mayor needed to verify that those officially exempted from tribute really earned this classification.

Tamil slaves also embraced Christianity over a period of time and they were converted. Baptism was administered to Juan and Joseph, the two adult (black Malabar) Tamil slaves on 15 April 1623. One finds Don Bernardino Balinguit the master of the slaves had served as the (padrino) godfather. Several Tamil slaves continued to be admitted to the Roman church as one finds in the parish records of Lubao between 1622 and 1648.[36]

Interestingly, one finds infant baptisms recorded only with the names of the mothers of the slaves. It suggests the possibility of illicit sexual activity, and even as concubines of masters. In a record of 3 October 1638, Juan de Ávalos served as the godfather of Rafael, the son of Lady Juana of Tamil origin. However the record does not mention the name of an unknown father.[37] On 2 November 1648, Lazaro Gonzalo and Inés the Tamil lady sponsored the baptism of Simón, the son of Pedro a Tamil slave and María Vanalangin.

SPANISH TRADE FROM MANILA AND TAMIL SLAVES TO COLONIAL MEXICO, 1527-1704

Slaves were exported from India to Portugal in the early days after the advent of Vasco da Gama. One finds mention of Tamil slaves who had reached Lisbon. It is found that the

Spaniards who sailed to the West had taken the assistance and help of some of these persons and employed them as interpreters and cooks who had hailed from the port of Calicut located on the west coast of India.

TAMIL SLAVE WORKERS EMPLOYED BY THE SPANIARDS, 1527-1551

In the course of sailing to the Americas it is mentioned that Megallan had commissioned Álvaro de Saavedra Cerón in 1527 to set sail from Zihuatanejo (present-day state of Guerrero) to cross the Pacific to land in Moluccas. He died at sea trying to find the route back to the Americas.[38] It is mentioned that Cortés a native of Calicut had served Saavedra as an interpreter in Asia.[39] This man was one of the few Asians who had been to Mexico before the establishment of the Galleon trade began by the Spaniards from Manila to Acapulco.

According to a document of 1540 which lists the possessions of Juan de Zumarraga, the first Bishop of Mexico (New Spain), one finds mention of his cook, a slave called Juan Núñez owned by the Bishop who came from the port of Calicut.[40] It is also found that Antonio de Mendoza, first viceroy of New Spain had owned a slave from India in 1551.[41]

TAMIL SLAVES CROSSING THE PACIFIC AND EMPLOYED IN COCONUT PALM TREE PLANTATIONS IN MEXICO, 1619

With the establishment of the Manila Galleon sailing to Mexico, migration and slave trading activities had come to be widely developed. Initially slaves from India who were sent to Manila, found their way to New Acapulco in Mexico. Anton Thomas a Tamil slave was taken in the ship from Manila to Acapulco in 1602.[42] Luis de Astete, a surgeon in Mexico City purchased Gaspar a Tamil slave. In 1614, there were 8 slaves who lived in Mexico City (besides 5 slaves from Cochin, 4 from

Colombo and one from Gujarat). Many slaves had the same names and so they should not be confused. The masters who purchased them and the years when the transactions took place had to be seen carefully. We find the presence of many Asians arriving in Mexico with the development and the spread of plantations of coconut palm trees. Many free men had also come to work in the plantations of these trees, which eventually supplanted the traditional economy in Mexico. In one of the plantations which belonged to a Filipino immigrant in 1619, it is found that 5 Indians were employed.[43]

SALE AND RESALE OF TAMIL SLAVES IN MEXICO

Captain Juan Chavaria the captain of the ship 'San Luis' purchased Andres a Tamil slave in Manila from a Portuguese trader for 57 *pesos* in 1622. The slave was taken to Mexico and he was sold in 1635 in Acapulco to Simon Lopez for 200 *pesos*.[44] Manule Joao Alcantra, the sailor of the ship 'Nuesta Senora del Rosario' (Our Lady of Rosary) had purchased a Tamil slave named Gaspar in Manila in 1643. He sold the slave to Captain Pablo de Carrascosa who was sailing to Acapulco. Later one finds that the slave was sold again to Francisco de Araujo on arrival at Acapulco. Gaspar was again sold to Luis de Astete for 250 pesos. Thus sale and resale of slaves had often been conducted and it is a feature very common in Manila and Mexico.[45]

SALE AND RESALE OF A TAMIL SLAVE OF UDAIYAR CASTE IN MANILA AND MEXICO, 1643

The Spanish Philippines had a diverse slave population, war captives and foreign slaves from as far away as Portuguese India. On arrival in Mexico, slave owners and Spanish officials grouped them together, overlooked their social and linguistic differences and categorized them all as chinos. But in the records one finds mention of slaves with the mention of the word Malabar, since they spoke Tamil language besides caste name of the slaves. Most of the persons who entered colonial New Spain, including western Mexico, were slaves. The Spanish residents of Colima and western Mexico purchased these slaves in the city of Mexico and Acapulco.

A document from the municipal archives of Colima records that Juan de Venegas a Spanish captain in Manila purchased Ignacio a Tamil slave of Udaiyar caste (casta Vadoya). He took the slave with him when he travelled from the Philippines to Colima in Mexico. Ignacio was thereafter sold to Alonso de Valderrama, who travelled with the slave to Acapulco. Valderrama, in turn, sold Ignacio to Tomás García de Lozada. Finally Juan Beltrán de Allende, a resident of Mexico City purchased Ignacio after paying money to Tomás García de Lozada in 1643. Thus it is surprising to note that sale of Ignacio for the first time was held in Manila and resale of the same slave had been conducted thrice in Mexico.[46]

Vadugar slaves were transported from Manila to Mexico in 1643. They were employed at Colima.[47] Thiyagu (Diego) a Tamil slave living in Mexico City asserted his condition as a subject of India and he was unlawfully enslaved. His owner claimed he had purchased Diego first in Goa and he presented several Portuguese witnesses who testified that all the natives from Portuguese India were slaves.[48] Thus some exemplary evidences set the stage for the Mexico slave market and its nature of sale and resale passing slaves into many hands.

TAMIL SLAVES EMPLOYED IN TEXTILE WORKSHOPS IN MEXICO

Tamil slaves worked mainly as domestic servants or in textile workshops (obrajes). Tamil slaves lived and died in Mexico and one finds information in the ecclesiastical notaries of death. The notary of the parish of the Sagrario in 1708 had documented the death and burial of Luis Pera, the Tamil (Malabar) black slave owned by Don Juan de Garay

Coechea.[49] The transpacific slave trade ended in 1672-3 with the prohibition of Asian slavery. As a result the number of Tamils and other Asian slave transportation from Manila to Mexico decreased.

To conclude, it may be said that the prisoners of war, declared as slaves were brought from Nagapattinam and sold in Manila by Private Portuguese merchants. However legal stamp as slaves were given by the Jesuit ecclesiastical authorities in Nagapattinam for transport overseas. The Spanish authorities in Manila also examined the status of the slaves at the time of purchase and sale in the court because they promoted the slave trade. Manila slave market gave further way to voyages of slaves to Mexico. The great ships of the Manila Galleon thus linked the Spanish Philippines to the rest of the empire. During the seventeenth century countless slaves from culturally diverse communities including Tamils were brought in the ships of the Manila Galleon to Mexico.

NOTES

1. Miguel Lopez de Legazpi's letter dated 26 June 1568 to King Philip II, in Emma Helen Blair, James Alexander Robertson, eds., *The Philippine Islands, 1493-1898*, 55 vols., Arthur H. Clark Company, Cleveland, Ohio, 1903-7 (hereafter Blair and Robertson), vol. II, pp. 232-43, see p. 242; Miguel Lopez de Legazpi, 'Relation of the Philippine Islands dated 7 July 1569', in Blair and Robertson, vol. III, pp. 54-61, see p. 59.
2. Andres de Mirandaola's letter dated 8 January 1574 to King Philip II, in Blair and Robertson, vol. III, pp. 223-9, see p. 225; Andres de San Nicolas, Luis de Jesus, and Juan de la Conception, 'General History of the Discalced Augustinian Fathers', in Blair and Robertson, vol. XXI, 1624, pp. 111-318, see pp. 197, 227.
3. Andres de Mirandaola's letter dated 8 January 1574 to King Philip II. Ibid., p. 225; Francisco de Sande, 'Relation of the Filipinas Islands', written from Manila dated 7 June 1576, in Blair and Robertson, vol. IV, pp. 21-97, see p. 59.

4. Juan Pacheco Maldonado's letter of 1575 from Manila to King Philip II, in Blair and Robertson, vol. III, pp. 295-303, see p. 303.
5. Santiago de Vera, 'Memorial to the Council by Citizens of the Filipinas Islands from Manila dated 26 July 1586', in Blair and Robertson, vol. VI, pp. 157-233, see p. 206.
6. Sebastian de Pineda, 'Philippine Ships and Shipbuilding', in Blair and Robertson, vol. XVIII, 1619, pp. 169-88, see pp. 173, 180; Juan de Medina, 'History of the Augustinian Order in the Filipinas Islands', in Blair and Robertson, vol. XXIV, 1630, pp. 29-182; Sebastian Hurtado de Corcuera's letter to King Philip II dated 11 July 1636, in Blair and Robertson, vol. XXVI, pp. 265-90.
7. San Pablo, 'Compulsory service by the Indians', in Blair and Robertson, vol. XIX, 1620, pp. 71-6; Nicholas Cushner, *Spain in the Philippines: From Conquest to Revolution*, Quezon City, 1971, pp. 117-26.
8. Hernando de Los Rios Coronel, 'Memorial y Relacion para su Magestad, Madrid', in Blair and Robertson, vol. XIX, 1621, pp. 183-298, see p. 203.
9. Archivo General de Indias (hereafter AGI), Seville, Spain, Seccion Filipinas, 29-50, 230r-232v (1584), AGI, Filipinas, 29-63, 427r-428v (1597), Carta de los oficiales de la Real Hacienda de Filipinas . . . proponen sustituir a los calafates y carpinteros de naos por esclavos de la India que sepan esos oficios, para ahorrar el salario que se les paga.
10. AGI, Filipinas, 10, R. 1, N. 25 (Masulipatnam, 1672); Archivo General de la Nación de México—Distrito Federal, México (hereafter AGN), Historia, 406, fls. 188r-191v (1616, 1674, Cochin); National Archives of the Philippines, Manila, Protocolo de Manila, SDS 19763 (Sale of slave Diego purchased by Miguel de Salazar), fls. 14b-15 (1674).
11. AGN, Historia, 406, fls. 187r-192r (1616).
12. AGN, Civil, 680, N. 2, passim (1594); AGN, Jesuítas, IV-68, fl. 1r (1 August 1622, 31 August 1622).
13. AGN, Indiferente Virreinal, caja 1355, exp. 34, fls. 2r-3r (1631).
14. AGN, Jesuitas, IV-68, exp. 1, fls. 1r-1v (1616); Family History Library Genealogical Society of Utah—Salt Lake City, USA (hereafter FHLGSU), MF, no. 1126936, Lubao, Bautismos, item 1, fl. 44r (1629).
15. AGN, Historia, 407, fl. 274r (1619).
16. AGN, Seccion Jesuitas, 4-26.2 (1620).

17. AGN, Seccion Jesuitas, IV-50.
18. AGN, Indiferente Virreinal, caja (hereafter c.), 1355, exp. 34, fls.1r, 3r (1631).
19. Nationaal Archief (hereafter NA), Den Haag, MSS VOC, 1094, fls.79-79v, 88.
20. Historical Archives of Goa, Panaji (hereafter HAG), Mss Moncoes do Reino, Livro 19C, 67-70/5-2, fls. 95-6.
21. AGN, Indiferente Virreinal, c. 1355, exp. 36, fls. 1r-1v (1634).
22. AGN, Indiferente Virreinal, c. 1355, exp. 37, fls. 1r-1v (1634).
23. AGI, Contaduría 1245, Tercera Pieza, fl. 599v (1685).
24. AGI, Contaduría 1216, fl. 294v (1634).
25. AGN, Inquisición, v. 355, exp. 44, fl. 501r (1626) and AGI, Contaduría, 1233, 2a pieza, fl. 118r (1658).
26. AGI, Escribanía de Cámara, 441B, fl. 7825v (1647).
27. Déborah Oropeza, *Los 'indios chinos' en la Nueva España: La inmigración de la nao de China, 1565-1700*, Tesis de doctorado en historia, El Colegio de México, 2007, p. 126.
28. W. Ph. Coolhas, ed., *Generale Missiven van de Gouverneurs-Generaal en Raden Aan Heren XVII der Verenigde Oostindische Compagnie*, 9 vols., 'S Gravenhage, 1960–84 (hereafter *GM*), vol. II, p. 479.
29. Nicolao Manucci, *Storio do Mogur or Mogul India*, 4 vols., ed. William Irvine, repr., New Delhi, 1981, vol. III, pp. 128-9.
30. AGN, Historia, 407, fls.162r-164r (1616).
31. AGI, Filipinas, 25-1-46 (1689).
32. Consejo Superior de Investigaciones Científicas-Instituto Histórico (hereafter CSIC-IH), MF, no. 3534, unnumbered (18 September 1674).
33. AGI, Filipinas, 124, N. 10, fls. 13v-14v (1701).
34. AGI, Filipinas, 127, N. 17, fls. 3r-4r. fs. 30v-33v (1703).
35. AGI, Filipinas, 84, N. 46, fl. 1r (1585).
36. FHLGSU, MF, no. 1126936, Lubao Bautismos, San Agustín, 1621-48, 1660-1736, 1738-51, 1757-65, item 1, fl. 4r (1622); For Balinguit, FHLGSU, MF, no. 1126936, item 1, fl. 9v (1623); FHLGSU, MF, no. 1126951, Lubao Matrimonios, San Agustín, 1622-75, 1695-1835, item 1, fl. 4v (1622). For the marriage of Lindavin and Tayomin, see ibid., fl. 5r (1622). For Sebastián, FHLGSU, MF, no. 1126936, Lubao Bautismos, San Agustín, 1621-48, item 1, fl. 27r.
37. Juana Malabar, see FHLGSU, MF, no. 1126936, Lubao Bautismos, San Agustín, 1621-48, item 1, fl. 100r (1638); FHLGSU, no.

1126951, Lubao Matrimonios, San Agustín, 1622-75, 1695-1835, item 1, fl. 5v (1623); FHLGSU, MF, no. 1126936, Lubao Bautismos, item 1, fl. 41r (1628); FHLGSU, MF, no. 1126951, Lubao Matrimonios, item 1, fl. 51r (1634).

38. Martín Fernández de Navarrete, *Viajes y descubrimientos españoles en el Pacífico: Magallanes, Elcano, Loaysa, Saavedra*, Madrid, Maxtor, 2011, originally published in 1919, pp. 204-54. See also, Ione S. Wright, *Voyages of Álvaro de Saavedra Cerón, 1527-29*, Coral Gables, University of Miami Press, 1951.
39. Juan Gil, *La India y el Lejano Oriente en la Sevilla del Siglo de Oro*, Seville, Biblioteca de Temas Sevillanos, 2011, pp. 150-1.
40. Joaquín García Icazbalceta, *Fray Juan de Zumárraga: Primer o bispo y arzobispo de México*, Buenos Aires, Espasa-Calpe, 1952, p. 221.
41. Déborah Oropeza, Los indios chinos, p. 13.
42. AGI, Contaduria, 901-1601-2 fl. 57v.
43. Oropeza, Los indios chinos en la Nueva España, p. 98. It is found that there were also 115 slaves including 21 from Manila, Cebu, Pampanga, Cagayan, Zambales, and other places in the Philippines, 2 from Terrenate, and 2 from Papua.
44. AGN, Jesuitas, IV-50.
45. AGN, Historia, V-406, fl.74r-74v; V-407 fl. 274; V-407, fl. 327.
46. Archivo Histórico del Municipio de Colima, Colima, México (hereafter AHMC), sección B, c. 23, exp. 5, fls.1r-1v (1643).
47. AHMC, sección B, c. 23, exp. 4, f. 1f (1643).
48. Juan Gil, La India y el Lejano Oriente, pp. 240-1.
49. FHLGSU, MF, no. 35770, Asunción Sagrario Metropolitano, Defunciones de castas 1707-33, item 1, fl. 35r (1708).

CHAPTER 5

Being and Becoming Dutch Company Slave: Transportation from Pazhaverkadu to Jakarta, 1621-1665

Slave trade and traffic to overseas countries developed on the Tamil coast after the advent of the Europeans. It is necessary and important to examine why the slave trade developed overseas, what circumstances prompted the presence and growth, how it was conducted, where the slaves were transported, who were involved in these activities and what was the role and policy of the state and the rulers. In historical research, data driven methodologies have gained ground. Hence integrating it would be valuable, and allow for new types of research questions and analyses.

Pazhaverkadu (called Pulicat) an entrepôt located on the Coromandel Coast developed long distance trade under the rulers of Vijayanagar. It had a direct international trade route with the ports of Melaka, Pasai and Pedir of Malay-Indonesian archipelago. Since several regional trade routes converged, it had the added advantage of commanding an entire sector of maritime commerce under the Portuguese where private merchants of Mylapore settled at Santhome and were very active in the nearby region.[1]

The Dutch East India Company (formed in 1602) and its traders first sailed and reached South East Asia. As the textiles of Coromandel were exchanged for pepper and spices, they came from the port of Banten to Pazhaverkadu in 1606. They began their negotiations with the local ruler seeking permission to trade but it broke off. They succeeded the next time, obtaining permission from Venkatapatidevaraya II (1586-1612) the ruler of Vijayanagar in May 1610. He allowed them for two years and it was stipulated that a tax of 2 per cent had to be paid on all imports and exports. Hans Marcelis, the Dutch chief, resided at Pazhaverkadu with four of his employees.[2] He purchased and exported a variety of textile goods to Jakarta in Indonesia which served as the Dutch commercial headquarters in Asia.[3] The Dutch Company gradually incorporated the purchase of slaves into its maritime trading network. It is mentioned in the documents that slave trade from Pazhaverkadu was more profitable than the cloth trade.[4] Capital for investment in slave purchases had been found inadequate as was reported.[5] This article therefore looks into the slave trading activities of the Dutch Company in Pazhaverkadu and its links with Jakarta. It is hoped that such an exercise in statistics would enable one to revisit to the old and fascinating history from a different perspective shedding new light on the topic. The study is based chiefly on the statistics culled from the primary sources, both manuscripts and printed documents in Dutch language.

Tapan Raychaudhuri was the first to mention the Dutch slave trade in Coromandel in his work published in 1962.[6] Sanjay Subrahmanyam in his work in 1990 had failed to assign importance to Dutch trade in slaves at Pulicat.[7] Scholars who have studied in general about the Dutch slave trade have not laid emphasis on geographical origin of slaves. Such pointers are important within the vast trading ocean to note the specificities of individual coastal zones in slave trade which contrasted with each other.[8]

It is well reported in the Dutch records that the first and the earliest shipment of slaves of 124 boys and girls from Masulipatnam had arrived on the ship *Gouden Leeuw* at Jakarta in 1622.[9] This clearly points to the fact of the geographical origins of slaves in addition to the Telugu-speaking linguistic group. Hence in this study, one has carefully excluded the Telugu, Oriya and Bengali-speaking slaves purchased and brought from Maulipatnam, Pipili and Arakan to Pazhaverkadu for shipping to Jakarta that had been recorded in the documents. It is highly necessary to treat this subject separately. Only the purchase of slaves at Pazhaverkadu port and its immediate hinterland including places like Ponneri, Gummidipoondi, Aarampakkam, etc., has been included. The Dutch East India Company was directly involved in the slave trade at Pazhaverkadu. The records mention only the company slaves and not the slaves owned by various individuals. The company slaves after purchase were branded on the right thigh or arm with the logo (VOC) of the Dutch Company. This was done to make clear distinction from those owned by privateers.

The Dutch Company purchased slaves and it is reported that both the sale deed and the purchase deeds were executed. The sale must have been conducted through public auction which was the practice in Tamil country as the native records mention. Price was fixed at that time and payment was immediately made. The names of the writer of the deed and the witnesses present were also recorded. The native agents and brokers were doing the business and they assisted the Dutch. These slaves who were bought, were lodged in the Dutch trading factory. They were fed and waited for transport in Dutch ships to Jakarta. They were obtained mainly to serve the Dutch Company needs owing to labour scarcity that prevailed in Jakarta.

TABLE 5.1: EXPORT OF SLAVES IN DUTCH SHIPS FROM PAZHAVERKADU TO JAKARTA, 1621-1624

Year	*Month Date*	*Name of the Ship*	*Slaves (men, women)*
1621	June	*Schoonhoven*	150
1622	December	*Nieuw Seelandt*	1,167
1623	March	*Tholen*	514
1623	June	*Witte Beer*	150
1623	November	*Tholen*	200
1624	2 February	*Wapen van Rotterdam*	730
TOTAL			2,911

Source: See Note.[10]

TABLE 5.2: EXPORT OF SLAVES IN DUTCH SHIPS FROM PAZHAVERKADU TO JAKARTA, 1625

Year	*Month Date*	*Name of the Ship*	*Slaves (men, women)*
1625	January	*Wapen van Rotterdam*	600
1625	June	*Vreede*	80
1625	November	*Delfshaven*	100
1625	December	*Edam, Tanasserij*	100
TOTAL			880

Source: See Note.[11]

TABLE 5.3: EXPORT OF SLAVES IN DUTCH SHIPS FROM PAZHAVERKADU TO JAKARTA, 1627-1631

Year	*Month Date*	*Name of the Ship*	*Slaves (men, women)*
1627	June	*Medemblick*	200
1627	September	*Medemblick*	173
1628	January	*Medemblick*	200
1629	13 April	*Waepen van Hoorn*	150
1629	May	*Cameel*	160
1629	5 September	*Jager*	30
1630	August	*Waepen van Hoorn*	44
1630	December	*Hoorn*	100
1631	February	*Warmond*	25
TOTAL			1,082

Source: See Note.[12]

It had been ordered from Jakarta in September 1628 that slaves as old as some of those sent in the previous years should not be purchased and transported. According to Dutch records of Pazhaverkadu slave trade was not very regular. The Dutch had not exported slaves during the years 1618-20, 1626, 1632-3, 1635, 1638-9, 1649-50 and 1652-9.

It had also been said in December 1630 that the Dutch in Pazhaverkadu purchased slaves lest they starve to death. Therefore the ship *Hoorn* sailed to Jakarta with 100 slaves.

In 1634 it was stated that there were only few slaves who could be purchased in Pazhaverkadu due to the exceedingly high mortality rate among the native population. The seven slaves purchased at that time were far more expensive than those bought in the previous years.[13]

TABLE 5.4: EXPORT OF SLAVES IN DUTCH SHIPS FROM PAZHAVERKADU TO JAKARTA, 1634-1637

Year	*Month Date*	*Name of the Ship*	*Slaves (men, women)*
1634	September	*Zeeland*	7
1636	July	*Wapen of Rotterdam*	59 (57 men and women, 2 female children)
1637	February	*Wessaenen*	21
TOTAL			87

Source: See Note.[14]

The Dutch Company servants in Pazhaverkadu were instructed in June 1635 not to buy many women and girls in the near future. Further, in November 1635 they were also instructed to purchase in the ratio of one female slave for every two male slaves.

Dutch records report that the slave voyages from Pazhaverkadu to Jakarta normally took the duration of one month. In 1636 it had been stated that owing to adverse weather conditions, the voyage of Pazhaverkadu to Jakarta with slaves took over three months (3 July–9 October 1636). Four Tamil slaves died en route in addition to 26 Dutchmen. Arent Gardenijs in his letter of 14 February 1643 wrote that a storm in Pulicat had delayed the departure of the ship carrying slaves for some days.

During the years of famine, drought and failed crops slaves were available in abundance. In 1646 (May to December) the Dutch ships transported a total of 2,117 slaves when a severe famine raged throughout the Coromandel region. Slaves were

TABLE 5.5: EXPORT OF SLAVES IN DUTCH SHIPS FROM PAZHAVERKADU TO JAKARTA, 1640-1645

Year	*Month Date*	*Name of the Ship*	*Slaves (men, women)*
1640	March	*Wijdenes*	19
1641	January	*Cappelle*	14
1641	February	*Orangieboom*	37 (31 men, 6 women)
1642	May	*Duijff*	29
1642	October	*Nieuw Rotterdam*	21
1643	February	*Petten*	109 (87 men, 16 women, 6 female children)
1644	May	*Haen*	9 (women)
1645	March	*Broeckoord*	8
1645	May	*Nieuw Rotterdam*	7 (women)
1645	August	*Maeslant*	12 (2 men, 8 women, 2 female children)
TOTAL			265

Source: See Note.[15]

said to be very cheap and they were abundantly available for purchase.[16] The famine situation did not improve and in the next year (1647) one finds 1,915 slaves were purchased and exported from Pazhaverkadu to Jakarta.[17]

TABLE 5.6: EXPORT OF SLAVES IN DUTCH SHIPS FROM PAZHAVERKADU TO JAKARTA, 1646

Year	*Month Date*	*Name of the Ship*	*Slaves (men, women)*
1646	16 May	*Lis*	81
1646	7 June	*Maeslant*	36
1646	20 June	*Heemstede*	200
1646	3 September	*Haan*	450
1646	12 October	*Salamander*	300
1646	1 December	*Nieuw Amsterdam*	600
1646	12 December	*Heemstede*	100
1646	20 December	*Schiedam*	350
TOTAL			2,117

Source: See Note.[18]

TABLE 5.7: EXPORT OF SLAVES IN DUTCH SHIPS FROM PAZHAVERKADU TO JAKARTA, 1647

Year	*Month Date*	*Name of the Ship*	*Slaves (men, women)*
1647	March	*Zeerob*	172 (130 men, 42 women)
1647	April	*Dolphijn*	135
1647	April	*Grijpskerck*	164 (82 men, 82 women)
1647	June	*Lillo*	105 (70 men, 35 women)
1647	July	*Petten*	126 (90 men, 36 women)
1647	August	*Bergen op Zoom*	601
1647	August	*Meerman*	80
1647	August	*Maesland*	200
1647	August	*Haen*	150
1647	November	*Gulden Gans*	72 (40 men, 32 women)
1647	November	*Snouck*	110
TOTAL			1,915

Source: See Note.[19]

TABLE 5.8: EXPORT OF SLAVES IN DUTCH SHIPS FROM PAZHAVERKADU TO JAKARTA, 1648 & 1651

Year	*Month Date*	*Name of the Ship*	*Slaves (men, women)*
1648	March	*Lis*	28 (13 men, 1 male child, 12 women, 2 female children)
1651	July	*Witte Paert*	28
TOTAL			56

Source: See Note.[20]

The Dutch in Pazhaverkadu fought naval battles against the Portuguese who were rivals in trade. When ships were seized, those on board were made captives and enslaved. These slaves captured by the Dutch Company were also transported in Dutch ships from Pazhaverkadu to Jakarta.

It is mentioned that many slaves died during the voyages from Pazhaverkadu to Jakarta. Those who died on the voyage

TABLE 5.9: EXPORT OF SLAVES IN DUTCH SHIPS FROM PAZHAVERKADU TO JAKARTA, 1660-1665

Year	*Month Date*	*Name of the Ship*	*Slaves (men, women)*
1660	March	*Ter Elburgh, Nieuwpoort*	506
1660	December	*Walvisch, Ulysses*	295
1661	August	*Leerdam*	20
1661	August	*Vogel Phenix*	80
1662		*Ulysses*	141
1664	February	*Raethuys*	8
1665	March	*Nieuwpoort*	9
TOTAL			1,059

Source: See Note.[21]

TABLE 5.10: EXPORT OF PERSONS CAPTURED IN PORTUGUESE SHIPS DURING NAVAL SIEGE AND MADE SLAVES AND TRANSPORTED IN DUTCH SHIPS FROM PAZHAVERKADU TO JAKARTA, 1630-1643

Year	*Month Date*	*Name of the Ship*	*Slaves (men, women)*
1630	December	*Hoorn*	54
1633	September	*Warmond*	26
1643	November	*'S-Hertogenbos*	18
TOTAL			98

Source: See Note.[22]

were thrown into the sea. In 1624 the vessels for making kanji (rice-gruel) were in poor shape due to heavy use and so the slaves were fed with half-cooked rice. As a result 45 slaves died during the voyage.[23] One finds 572 slaves did not survive in the voyage from Pazhaverkadu to Jakarta during May-December 1646 because of a pestilential disease of bubonic plague.[24] Again 137 slaves, who had been transported in ships from Pazhaverkadu to Jakarta in 1647 died. It is sad to note that 293 purchased slaves died in Pazhaverkadu before transportation to Jakarta.[25] Thus in total 430 slaves had died in that year incurring a heavy financial loss to the Dutch Company.

The Dutch records just furnish the classification of company slaves such as men, women, boys, girls and infants. In some cases the total number of slaves alone had been stated. The price paid for the slave had been sometimes recorded. According to records the price of one slave ranged during famine period between 18 reals and 20 reals (1 real = ten panams). However during other times it was high and the price varied between 27 Dutch guilders to 40 Dutch guilders. During the famine, the price of one slave fell as low as 4 Dutch guilders.[26] The records do not speak of the age of the slave, the caste and the name of the agents or brokers who sold them.

In short, the Dutch in Pazhaverkadu had purchased 10,470 slaves in and around the port for export to Jakarta between

TABLE 5.11: DEATH OF SLAVES EXPORTED IN DUTCH SHIPS DURING THE VOYAGE FROM PAZHAVERKADU TO JAKARTA, 1622-1648

Year	*Month Date*	*Name of the Ship*	*Slaves (men, women)*
1622	December	*Nieuw Seelandt*	237 (69 men + 168 women)
1624	2 February	*Wapen van Rotterdam*	100 (45 men + 55 women)
1625	December	*Edam*	30
1636	3 July-9 October	*Wapen of Rotterdam*	4
1646	May	*December*	572
1647	March	*Zeerob*	72
1647	April	*Grijpskerck*	12
1647	June	*Lillo*	5
1647	July	*The Petten*	16
1647	November	*Gulden Gans*	32
1648	March	*Lis*	6
TOTAL			1,086

1621 and 1665. The death of slaves transported was 1,086. Hence 9,384 slaves had reached Jakarta and they were employed in pepper and nutmeg gardens, animal husbandry and fortification works.[27] Slaves from Pazhaverkadu were also re-exported to Amboina and Banda and did various jobs assigned. The Hindu rulers of Tamil country had banned the export and transport of slaves to countries overseas. The Dutch did not respect the orders issued by the native rulers. No one seems to have bothered about the condition of the slaves and this is the historical truth. The Dutch purchased slaves secretly with the connivance of many native intermediaries and indulged in unlawful human trade and traffic. The slave trade in Pazhaverkadu declined during 1658-69 because the Dutch had brought plenty of labourers from China to Jakarta. Further, slaves from Makassar, Bali, Timor and Kalimantan were brought to Jakarta to meet the labour demand.

NOTES

1. S. Jeyaseela Stephen, *Expanding Portuguese Empire and the Tamil Economy: Sixteenth-Eighteenth Centuries*, Manohar, New Delhi, 2009, pp. 165-6.
2. S. Jeyaseela Stephen, *From European Dwelling Settlements to Global Cities: Ports of the Tamil Coast and the Colonial Modernity*, Primus, 2021, pp. 172-3.
3. S. Jeyaseela Stephen, *Oceanscapes: Tamil Textiles in the Early Modern World*, Primus, 2014, p. 194.
4. Om Prakash, *The Dutch Factories in India: A Collection of Dutch East India Company Documents Pertaining to India, 1617-1623*, New Delhi, Munshiram, 1984, vol. I, p. 191.
5. W.Ph. Coolhas, ed., *Generale Missiven van de Gouverneurs-Generaal en Raden Aan Heren XVII der Verenigde Oostindische Compagnie*, 9 vols., 'S Gravenhage, 1960-84 (hereafter *GM*), p. 175 (24 October 1624).
6. Tapan Raychaudhuri, *Jan Company in Coromandel, 1605-1690: A Study in the Interrelations of European Commerce and Traditional Economies*, The Hague, 1962, pp. 165-6.

7. Sanjay Subrahmanyam, *The Political Economy of Commerce: Southern India, 1500-1650*, Cambridge, 1990.
8. S. Arasaratnam, 'Slave Trade in the Indian Ocean in the Seventeenth Century', in K.S. Mathew, ed., *Mariners, Merchants and Oceans: Studies in Maritime History*, New Delhi, Manohar, 1995, pp. 195-208; Markus Vink, 'The World's Oldest Trade: Dutch Slavery and Slave Trade in the Indian Ocean in the Seventeenth Century', *Journal of World History*, vol. 14, no. 2, 2003, pp. 131-77.
9. Jan Pietersz Coen, *Beschiden Omtrent Zijn Bedirjf in Indie*, 7 vols., ed. H.T. Colenbrander, The Hague, 1919-34 (hereafter *Bescheiden*), vol. I, pp. 706, 708, vol. III, p. 177.
10. Nationaal Archief (hereafter NA), Den Haag, Mss VOC 1073, fl.53v; W. Ph. Coolhas, ed., *Generale Missiven van de Gouverneurs-Generaal en Raden Aan Heren XVII der Verenigde Oostindische Compagnie*, 9 vols., 'S Gravenhage, 1960-84 (hereafter *GM*), 9 July 1621; *GM*, 1 February 1623, p. 121; VOC 1077, fl.21v; Jan Pietersz Coen, *Beschiden Omtrent Zijn Bedirjf in Indie*, 7 vols., ed. H.T. Colenbrander, The Hague, 1919-34 (hereafter *Bescheiden*), vol. I, pp. 780-1; VOC 1079, fl.10v, *GM*, 3 January 1624; Coen, Bescheiden, vol. I, p. 781; VOC 1077, fl.21v, *GM*, 20 June 1623, Jan Pieterszoon Coen, *Bescheiden*, vol. I, p. 780; VOC 1079, fl.10v, *GM*, 3 January 1624; VOC 1087, fls. 181-181v, NA, Pulicat's Dagregister, 2 February 1624; J.A. Van der Chijs, et al., *Dagregister Gehouden int Casteel Batavia vant Passerende daer te Plaatse als Over Geheel Nederlandts-India, 1628-1682*, 31 vols., The Hague-Batavia, 1887-1928 (hereafter *DR*), 8-11 March 1624, p. 33; VOC 1082, fl.214, Batavia to Marten Ysbrantsz in Pulicat, 26 March 1624; VOC 1082, fl.135, *GM*, 27 January 1625.
11. NA, VOC 1087, fl.198v, NA, Pulicat's Dagregister, 22 January 1625; VOC 1087, fl. 204v, Pulicat's Dagregister, 15 June 1625; VOC 1087, fl.174v-175, Marten Ysbrantsz in Pulicat to Batavia, 5 December 1625; VOC 1090, fl. 28, Marten Ysbrantsz in Pulicat to Batavia, 27 January 1626; *GM*, 3 February 1626, p. 185; VOC 1087, fl. 211-212, Pulicat's Dagregister, 28 November 1625; VOC 1086, fl. 2, VOC 1089, fl.1v, *GM*, 3 February 1626.
12. NA, VOC 1091, fl. 2v, Marten Ysbrantsz in Pulicat to Batavia, 27 June 1627; VOC 1095, fl.39v, NA, Pulicat's Dagregister, 10 July 1627; VOC 1091, fl. 6v, VOC 1092, fl. 269v, VOC 1095, fl.141, *GM*, 9 November 1627; VOC 1094, fl. 91v, Marten Ysbrantsz in Pulicat to Batavia, 24 January 1628; VOC 1095, fl.41v, Pulicat's

Dagregister, 31 January 1628; VOC 1097, fl.34v, *GM*, 15 December 1629; VOC 1097, fl.464, Marten Ysbrantsz in Pulicat to Batavia, 23 May 1629; VOC 1097, fl.34v, *GM*, 15 December 1629; VOC 1100, fl.100, Marten Ysbrantsz in Pulicat to Batavia, 24 August 1630; VOC 1100, fl.135, Marten Ysbrantsz in Pulicat to Batavia, 4 December 1630; VOC 1103, fl.135, Marten Ysbrantsz in Pulicat to Batavia, 12 July 1631.

13. NA, VOC 1113, fl. 327v, Letter of Marten Ysbrantsz in Pulicat to Batavia, 20 September 1634; J.A. Van der Chijs, et al., *Dagregister Gehouden int Casteel Batavia vant Passerende daer te Plaatse als Over Geheel Nederlandts-India, 1628–1682*, 31 vols., The Hague-Batavia, 1887–1928 (hereafter *DR*), p. 445 (4 December 1634).
14. NA, VOC 1119, fls. 1172-1173, Wapen of Rotterdam's bill of lading, 5 July 1636; *DR*, 9 October 1636, pp. 240-1; VOC 1122, fl.620, Carel Reijniersen in Pulicat to Batavia, 10 February 1637; VOC 1122, fl. 672v, Wessaenen's bill of lading, Pulicat, 10 February 1637; *DR*, 14 March 1637, p. 87.
15. NA, VOC 1133, fl. 429, Arent Gardenijs in Pulicat to Batavia, 3 March 1640; VOC 1134, fl. 294, Batavia to Arent Gardenijs in Pulicat, 14 April 1640; VOC 1135, fl. 312, Arent Gardenijs in Pulicat to Batavia, 16 February 1641; *DR*, 19 February 1641, p. 183; VOC 1135, fl. 311v, Orangieboom's bill of lading, 16 February 1641; *DR*, 31 March 1641, p. 215; VOC 1138, fl. 742, Arent Gardenijs in Pulicat to Batavia, 3 May 1642; VOC 1138, fl. 449, VOC 1138, fls. 843-843v, VOC 1143, fl.657, Arent Gardenijs in Pulicat to Batavia, 10 October 1642; *DR*, November 1642, p. 307; VOC 1151, fls.748, 751v-752v, Arent Gardenijs in Pulicat to Batavia, 17 February 1643; VOC 1143, fl.670, Petten's bill of lading, Pulicat, 14 February 1643; Arent Gardenijs in Pulicat to Batavia, 14 February 1643; VOC 1151, fl.753, Arent Gardenijs in Pulicat to Batavia, 8 March 1643; *DR*, 17 April 1643, p. 251; *DR*, April 1643, pp. 258-60; VOC 1147, fl. 594v, Arnold Heussen in Pulicat to Batavia, 4 May 1644; *DR*, 21 June 1644, p. 290; VOC 1156, fl.342v, Arnold Heussen in Pulicat to Batavia, 27 March 1645; VOC 1156, fl. 346, Broeckoord's bill of lading, 28 March 1645; VOC 1158, fl.196v, general reports on the Coromandel Coast 1644-1645; *DR*, 6 May 1645, p. 334; VOC 1152, fl. 14v, *GM*, 9 July 1645; VOC 1156, fl. 255v, Arnold Heussen in Pulicat to Batavia, 2 May 1645; VOC 1156, fl.243, Nieuw Rotterdam's bill of lading, Pulicat, 19 May 1645; VOC 1152, fl.17v, *GM*, 9 July 1645; VOC 1156,

fl.237, VOC 1157, fl.761v, Arnold Heussen in Pulicat to Batavia, 16 August 1645; VOC 1156, fl. 244, Maeslant's bill of lading, Pulicat, 16 August 1645; *DR*, 17 September 1645, p. 350.

16. NA, VOC 1160, fl. 9; *GM*, 15 January 1647.
17. NA, VOC 1163, fl. 67; *GM*, 31 December 1647.
18. NA, VOC 1161, fl. 804v, Arnold Heussen in Pulicat to Batavia, 28 February 1646; VOC 1161, fl. 939, Castle Geldria's Journal, Pulicat, 28 February 1646; VOC 1161, fl. 826v, Arnold Heussen in Pulicat to Batavia, 3 May 1646; VOC 1161, fl. 953, Castle Geldria's Journal, Pulicat, 4 May 1646; VOC 1161, fl. 799, Arnold Heussen in Pulicat to Batavia, 9 June 1646; VOC 1161, fl. 963, Castle Geldria's Journal, Pulicat, 9 June 1646; VOC 1161, fl. 974, Castle Geldria's Journal, Pulicat, 17 August 1646; VOC 1161, fl. 986, Arnold Heussen in Pulicat to Batavia, 16 August 1646; VOC 1161, fl. 838, Arnold Heussen in Pulicat to Batavia, 24 August 1646; VOC 1161, fl. 974v, Castle Geldria's Journal, Pulicat, 24 August 1646; VOC 1161, fl. 779, Arnold Heussen in Pulicat to Batavia, 28 September 1646; VOC 1160, fls. 9, 13, GM, 15 January 1647.
19. NA, VOC 1164, fl. 703v, Arnold Heussen in Pulicat to Batavia, 5 March 1647; VOC 1164, fl. 706, Zeerob's bill of lading, Pulicat, 5 March 1647; VOC 1164, fl. 708; VOC 1164, fl. 690, Arnold Heussen in Pulicat to Batavia, 17 April 1647; VOC 1163, fl.33, *GM*, 31 December 1647; VOC 1164, fl. 687, Grijpskerck's bill of lading, Pulicat, 20 April 1647; VOC 1164, fl. 765, Arnold Heussen in Pulicat to Batavia, 1 June 1647; VOC 1164, fl.762, Lillo's bill of lading, Pulicat, 1 June 1647; VOC 1164, fl. 757, Arnold Heussen in Pulicat to Batavia, 27 June 1647; VOC 1164, fl.748, Petten's bill of lading, Pulicat, 28 July 1647; VOC 1164, fl. 684v, Arnold Heussen in Pulicat to Batavia, 2 August 1647; VOC 1164, fl. 686, Bergen op Zoom's bill of lading, Pulicat, 2 August 1647; VOC 1168, fls. 523-523v, Arnold Heussen in Pulicat to Batavia, 5 October 1647; VOC 1168, fls.494–495, VOC 1168, fl. 514, the Gulden Gans's bill of lading, Pulicat, 6 November 1647; VOC 1168, fls.523-523v, Arnold Heussen in Pulicat to Batavia, 5 October 1647; VOC 1168, fls.494-5, VOC 1168, fl.514.
20. NA, VOC 1168, fl. 490, Arnold Heussen in Pulicat to Batavia, 3 March 1648; VOC 1168, fl.503, Lis's bill of lading, Pulicat, 3 March 1648; *DR*, 3 May 1648, p. 72; VOC 1168, fl. 556, Arnold Heussen in Pulicat to Batavia, 25 May 1648; VOC 1184, fl. 233v, Laurens Pit in Pulicat to Batavia, 6 July 1651.

21. NA, VOC 1232, fls. 73-73v, *GM*, 16 December 1660; VOC 1232, fl.428, *GM*, 26 January 1661; *GM*, 26 January 1661, p. 355; VOC 1236, fl.594, Laurens Pit in Pulicat to Batavia, 4 August 1661; VOC 1234, fl.130, Laurens Pit in Pulicat to Heeren XVII, 15 September 1661; *DR*, 18 October 1661, pp. 312-13, 325; VOC 1234, fl.99, *GM*, 22 December 1661; VOC 1236, fl. 600, Laurens Pit in Pulicat to Batavia, 4 August 1661; VOC 1236, fl. 648, VOC 1234, fl. 130, Laurens Pit in Pulicat to Heeren XVII, 15 September 1661; VOC 1234, fl. 92, *GM*, 22 December 1661; VOC 1238, fl. 190, *GM*, 26 December 1662; *DR*, 12 May 1664, p. 152; VOC 1245, fl.333, Cornelis Speelman in Pulicat to Heeren XVII, 3 September 1664; VOC 1252, fl.359, Cornelis Speelman in Pulicat to Batavia, 5 March 1665; *DR*, 2 May 1665, p. 96.
22. VOC 1100, fl.135, Marten Ysbrantsz in Pulicat to Batavia, 4 December 1630; VOC 1109, fl. 316v, Marten Ysbrantsz in Pulicat to Batavia, 21 September 1633; *DR*, November 1642, p. 302.
23. NA, VOC 1083, 6 June 1624; NA, VOC, 1082, fl. 214.
24. NA, VOC 1160, fl. 9; *GM*, 15 January 1647.
25. NA, VOC 1163, fl. 67; *GM*, 31 December 1647.
26. S. Jeyaseela Stephen, *Subaltern Lives, Tamil History and Society from Medieval to Early Modern Age*, Kalpaz, New Delhi, 2019, p. 151.
27. Jan Pietersz Coen, Beschiden, vol. III, p. 294.

CHAPTER 6

Dutch Slave Trade and Shipping from Pazhaverkadu, Devanampattinam and Porto Novo to Syriam, Jakarta, Aceh and Banten, 1624-1688

The main reason that induced the Dutch East India Company to obtain slaves from the Tamil Coast was to employ them at the various Dutch factories established in Myanmar. Mattheus Leendersz at Syriam in Myanmar in his letter dated 10 February 1638 to the Dutch factor in Pulicat wrote that 'Do not forget to send, at the earliest, the slaves that were ordered and an additional 20 slaves if possible, because without them the Dutch Company's affairs would be severely hindered. Moreover, when you send them, please make sure to include several strapping fellows who could be put to work on any task at Syriam.'[1] The Dutch factor in Pulicat was placed under heavy pressure to find the required slaves for export. The large scale export was dependent chiefly upon the local availability and supply through the local agents and merchants. Therefore he contacted several persons to arrange for slaves.

In the records of 1641 one finds that some slaves sent from Pulicat were used by the Dutch factor of Syriam to bribe the Burmese officials. Two young slave girls were sent as gifts to Homoor, a broker in Syriam whose help and assistance the Dutch Company chiefly relied upon for developing commerce.[2] The next year (1642) a ship arrived from Pulicat and brought slaves. But after one month, five men and women slaves were found incapacitated for any work and so they were deported back to Pulicat.[3] It is interesting to find in the letter of the Dutch factor of Pulicat to Dutch Governor-General in Jakarta dated 30 April 1642 that the price of the returned slaves had been valued (collectively to a total amount of 103 guilders) which they had earlier paid in Pulicat in the Dutch Company account.[4]

The Dutch factor in Pulicat continued to purchase slaves. Four ships that sailed on 3 March 1644 and another four ships that left on 5 October 1644 carried a total of 7,100 slaves.[5] He could obtain plenty of slaves at that time because of the famine that continued to prevail as late as in 1646. The Dutch settlements on the Tamil Coast also remained having a large permanent slave population. There was a continuous interaction among different groups of people interested in slaves. The Dutch had kept many slaves for their own use in the various factories without exporting. Pulicat had 440 slaves as on 17 September 1644 and they were all doing various jobs in the factory of the Dutch Company.[6]

The Dutch factor in Pulicat could export only 19 slaves on 21 May 1652 since the bad famine conditions were over. As a result there were no slaves available for export.[7] In 1654, children were enslaved on a large scale in the English settlement of Madras and they were transported silently to the Dutch factory at Pulicat. This facilitated the slave trade of the Dutch Company greatly.[8]

According to the letter of the Dutch factor of Pulicat to Jakarta dated 10 July 1664, the slaves of the Tamil Coast constituted the major population in the Dutch factories of Syriam and Ava in Myanmar.[9] There had been 826 slaves in Syriam and 1,199 at Ava in 1664.[10] Slaves exported from Pulicat had to work in the fields and gardens in Syriam during their spare time. This was enforced by the Dutch in order to help pay and compensate for their upkeep and thus found a way to supplement their maintenance. It is reported by the Dutch factor of Syriam vide his letter dated 18 December 1663 to the factor in Pulicat that the Tamil slaves had sowed a large paddy field which yielded approximately 1,000 *cesters* (48,000 lb) of rice per season.[11] Since the slaves were put to work tirelessly without proper rest, many also absconded, escaped and deserted. It had been reported in the Dutch document that the whereabouts of three such runaway Tamil slaves in 1663 could not be traced in Syriam.[12] Many slaves had also fallen ill and they often became sick and a general observation on the health condition of the Tamil slaves had been furnished by the Dutch factor of Ava vide his letter dated 14 November 1663 to the Dutch factor at Pulicat in detail.[13]

The slaves transported from Pulicat had performed an endless variety of chores in Syriam obviously to the economic advantage of the Dutch Company. The main task of the slaves had been concerned with the maintenance of Dutch ships. There were many carpenters and blacksmiths who were employed in shipbuilding works. A letter of the Dutch Governor-General of Jakarta dated 10 June 1666 to the Dutch factor at Pulicat, mentions four Tamil Muslim sawyers requested to be dispatched in 1666. These men were sent to teach the slaves of the Dutch Company in Syriam to select the quality timber variety for shipbuilding, training to saw timber and also supply the planks required. Thus unskilled slaves had come to be productively employed in shipbuilding and repairing the Dutch Company ships in Syriam.[14] According to the letter of the Dutch factor of Syriam dated 18 December 1663 to the factor in Pulicat, Tamil slaves in Syriam had assisted the Dutch on their river voyages to and from Pegu.[15] Some slaves trained in wood cutting in Pulicat had also been exported. A mention of this is found in the letter of the Dutch factor of Pulicat to the factor at Syriam dated 17 September 1671. He also stated that these slaves could be sent to the forest in Syriam for chopping wood.[16] In the same letter, other transported slaves who were already well trained and employed at the gunpowder factory in Pulicat had also been mentioned. He added that these slaves could be properly employed to refine saltpetre in the Dutch factory at Ava.[17]

The Dutch factor in Syriam continued to ask for slaves to be supplied from Pulicat. He also mentioned the need to replace those in Syriam who were aged and became sick or were otherwise incapacitated. But it was not always that easy to obtain slaves and so the Dutch factor in Pulicat answered in the negative.[18] Owing to a dearth of slaves for export to Syriam, the Tamil slave population at the Dutch factory had dwindled.[19] There were only six Tamil slaves in Syriam, four in Ava and two in Pegu as on 12 February 1679.[20]

It may be worthwhile to ask a question as to why the Dutch in Myanmar desired to have the Tamil slaves. The reason was that the Dutch factories at Syriam, Ava and Pegu in Myanmar were placed under administrative control of the Dutch Governor of Coromandel in Pulicat. The Dutch Company devised a policy with the view to transport slaves from distant places because the greater the distance from their homelands, the less the possibility of slaves absconding from any situation they found intolerable. It is noticed that even this did not work because Tamil slaves had often escaped in Myanmar.

RULES FRAMED FOR SLAVE TRADE BY THE DUTCH EAST INDIA COMPANY

The Dutch Company attempted to define the master slave relations. It framed certain rules and regulations for the smooth governance of slave trade overseas being introduced from the Tamil Coast. Jan Pietersz Coen, the Dutch Governor was the chief architect in this regard. According to the rules, slave traders must ensure the physical fitness and health of the slaves before finalizing sale to the Dutch Company. One does not know whether this provision was introduced with the motive based on the humanitarian grounds or by commercial considerations. Traders who sold a slave suffering from venereal disease if noticed and reported later, had to refund the full price.[21] A slave could be purchased and sold only in the presence of a notary and two independent witnesses. Manumission or freeing of a slave could also be done only in the same manner. These provisions were considered very necessary by the Dutch Company since the purchase and sale of slaves came widely to be conducted illegally on the Tamil Coast. Masters who tortured and ill-treated the slaves had to forfeit them. However, there had been no mention as to the slaves thus forfeited and whether they were freed or taken over by the Dutch Company. Anyone who debauched the slave of another was liable to punishment but there was no prohibition on the debauching of a slave by the master himself. Anyone who caused physical injury, harm and murder of a slave was also awarded severe punishment.[22]

Local customs and manners prevalent on the Tamil Coast were faithfully followed before export of slaves overseas. Runaway slaves of the Dutch Company were whipped and shut up in cells. Those slaves who harmed or shamed their masters and mistresses were also dealt with similarly. A slave who killed his master or mistress was sentenced to death.[23] A slave could complain to a judge against the cruelty meted out to him by his master. A slave left in misery by his own master could be freed by a judge.[24] Even if a bold slave had complained one is not sure whether there was any possibility of a fair enquiry. Further, how far the rights of the slaves were protected is a big question. A freed slave was expected to show respect for his master and his descendants at all times. He should take care of his master in case the latter had met with an economic crisis. If the freed slave died without any near blood relatives, the master was entitled to receive one-fourth of his property. These characteristics indicate that the manumitted slaves enjoyed only nominal freedom. Manumission had been thus used by the Dutch East India Company to extract the services and income in perpetuity from the slaves.[25] When the Dutch finally closed down the factory in Myanmar the only eleven remaining Tamil slaves (both men and women) were shipped to Jakarta on 28 March 1679.[26]

THE DUTCH COMPANY SLAVE TRADE FROM THE NAYAKA KINGDOM OF GINGEE AND THANJAVUR

The ports of Aalamparavai and of Kunimedu, located ten miles south of it, were important ports of the Nayaka kingdom of Gingee. Devanampattinam (situated 25 miles south of Kunimedu) was the main port settlement of the Portuguese from where they exported saltpetre to Goa.[27] The Dutch arrived at Devanampattinam in 1608 and obtained permission from Krishnappa Nayak of Gingee (1597-1624) on 15 October 1608 to trade for two years. The import and export duties were fixed at 4 per cent. The contract was renewed on 29 March 1610 and the payment of customs duties were reduced to 2 per cent on all imports and exports.[28] Devanampattinam had a flourishing textile trade connected with the hinterland weaving centres and also within the complex of nearby place called Cuddalore which was located close by, within two miles. Devanampattinam therefore developed extensive overseas trade with many Asian ports and the capital city of Gingee could be reached by two days journey from the port.

It was reported by the Dutch that owing to the famine in November in 1618, three or four children could be purchased for one pagoda at Tirupapuilyur in the environs of Devanampattinam.[29] The Dutch began to buy slaves available in the region since 1624 and brought them to Devanampattinam Kunimedu and Aalamparavai. These slaves were transported to the port of Pulicat for export to Jakarta in Indonesia.[30]

Slaves were not available for purchase since famine conditions improved. As a result the Dutch in Devanampattinam could not export slaves from 1631 to 1634.

Slaves were easily available for export from Devanampattinam though there was a heavy demand for slave labour in Jakarta. The Dutch decided to approach the nayak ruler of Gingee in 1643 to seek official permission to purchase slaves and export them. Philip Baldeaus, the Protestant missionary was sent as envoy to the court. He requested the nayak for permission to purchase and export slaves in the ships of the Dutch East

TABLE 6.1: EXPORT OF SLAVES IN DUTCH SHIPS FROM DEVANAMPATTINAM TO JAKARTA, 1624-1630

Year	*Month Date*	*Name of the Ship*	*Slaves (men, women)*
1624	February	*Wapen van Rotterdam*	400
1625	January	*Wapen van Rotterdam*	100
1626	June	*Sampan*	20
1626	June	*Jager*	31
1626	July	*Duijf*	38
1626	March-October	*Sampan*	98
1627	January	*Duijf*	200
1627	February	*Valcq*	275
1627	March	*Revengie*	100
1628	January	*Medemblick*	100
1628	August	*Vlielandt*	42
1628	September	*Schiedam*	73
1630	August	*Sampan*	206
TOTAL			1,683

Source: See Note.[31]

TABLE 6.2: PURCHASED IN KUNIMEDU AND EXPORT OF SLAVES IN DUTCH SHIPS FROM DEVANAMPATTINAM TO JAKARTA, 1624-1627

Year	*Month Date*	*Name of the Ship*	*Slaves (men, women)*
1626	September	*Cleijn Delft & Jonge Leeuwinne*	224
1627	January	*Duijf & Valcq*	200
1627	March	*Revengie*	37
TOTAL			461

Source: See Note.[32]

India Company. Since slave trade was banned on the Tamil Coast, the nayak flatly refused, adding that transporting slaves overseas was considered the greatest sin by the Hindus.[33] From Dutch records it is evident, however that the company silently purchased a small number of slaves in 1651 and exported them to Jakarta.

TABLE 6.3: PURCHASE AND EXPORT OF SLAVES IN DUTCH SHIPS FROM DEVANAMPATTINAM TO JAKARTA, 1635-1636

Year	*Month Date*	*Name of the Ship*	*Slaves (men, women)*
1635	June	*Hoorn*	35
1635	June	*Der Veer*	91 (80 men, 11 boys)
1635	November	*Maastricht*	45 (12 men, 33 women)
1636	October	*Leeuwarden*	26 (17 men, 9 women)
TOTAL			197

Source: See Note.[34]

TABLE 6.4: PURCHASE AND EXPORT OF SLAVES IN DUTCH SHIPS FROM DEVANAMPATTINAM TO JAKARTA, 1651

Year	*Month Date*	*Name of the Ship*	*Slaves (men, women)*
1651	May	*Koe*	11
1651	October	*Os*	16
TOTAL			27

Source: See Note.[35]

It is found in Dutch records that the company could not purchase slaves nearly for a decade. They managed to purchase slaves in 1660-2 and exported them to Jakarta.

There is a mention that the Dutch ships sailed from Pulicat to Jakarta. Hence slaves procured from the ports of the kingdom of the nayak of Gingee were transported in boats from Devanampattinam, Aalamparavai and Kunimedu to Pulicat. On arrival the ship loaded slaves and sailed away to Jakarta.

TABLE 6.5: PURCHASE AND EXPORT OF SLAVES IN DUTCH SHIPS FROM DEVANAMPATTINAM TO JAKARTA, 1660-1662

Year	*Month Date*	*Name of the Ship*	*Slaves (men, women)*
1660	March	*Nieuwpoort*	61
1661	August	*Leerdam*	22
1662	February	*Goederhede*	59 (men)
1662	April	*Sampan*	24
TOTAL			166

Source: See Note.[36]

The Dutch wished to trade at the ports of the Nayaka kingdom of Thanjavur. In 1649 they were permitted when approached by Vijaya Raghava, nayak of Thanjavur (1634-74) to trade at the ports of Tirumullaivasal located at the mouth of river Kollidam. It had access to the immediate hinterland of Sirkali where paddy and rice was available in abundance for export. The Dutch were permitted to trade there and payment of customs duties were fixed by the nayaka ruler at 2½ per cent.

The Dutch mainly explored the purchase of slaves and they bought slaves successfully at the port of Tirumullaivasal in 1644. Though the place of origin of slaves had been from the nearby hinterland villages of Tirumullaivasal, the transportation and boarding in ships had been at Pulicat and the ultimate destination was Jakarta.

The Dutch aimed to participate in slave trade in and around the hinterland of the port of Adirampattinam and Nagapattinam in 1644 since slaves were available for export and it was conducted largely by the private Portuguese traders. According to Dutch Company records, mention had been made that the purchase price of a slave in Adirampattinam and Nagapattinam region in 1645 had become so cheap to the tune of ¾ *pagodas* and this had lured them mainly to conduct trade. The Dutch managed to purchase slaves easily from

TABLE 6.6: PURCHASE AND EXPORT OF SLAVES IN DUTCH SHIPS FROM TIRUMULLAIVASAL TO JAKARTA, 1644

Year	*Month Date*	*Name of the Ship*	*Slaves (men, women)*
1644	July	*Broeckoord*	47
1644	August	*Lis*	8
1644	October	*Nieuw Amsterdam*	78
TOTAL			133

Source: See Note.[37]

Adirampattinam area and exported 2,118 slaves to Jakarta in 1645-6 by nine ships. It is also mentioned that 572 slaves had died on the way at that time because of plague.[38]

The port of Karaikal located on the banks of Arasalar was another significant port that flourished under the nayak of Thanjavur and it was located 21 miles south of Tirumullaivasal. The Dutch were permitted to trade there and payment of customs duties was fixed by the nayaka ruler at 2½ per cent. They purchased slaves on a large scale owing to the famine during 1646 and 1647 and sent them in boats to Pulicat for export to Jakarta.

It was found difficult by the Dutch to buy slaves in the region as they were not available. They managed to purchase in small number in 1651 and sent them to Pulicat.

TABLE 6.7: PURCHASE AND EXPORT OF SLAVES IN DUTCH SHIPS FROM TIRUMULLAIVASAL TO JAKARTA, 1646

Year	*Month Date*	*Name of the Ship*	*Slaves (men, women)*
1646	February	*Lis*	79
1646	September	*Grijpskerck*	52
1646	September	*Schiedam & Heemstede*	598
TOTAL			729

Source: See Note.[39]

TABLE 6.8: PURCHASE AND EXPORT OF SLAVES IN DUTCH SHIPS FROM KARAIKAL TO JAKARTA, 1646-1647

Year	*Month Date*	*Name of the Ship*	*Slaves (men, women)*
1646	February	*Sampan*	40
1646	March	*Sampan*	15
1646	May	*Grijpskerck*	400 (312 men, 88 women)
1646	May	*Haen*	374
1646	June	*Sampan*	100
1646	June	*Salamander*	250
1646	June	*Heemstede*	381
1646	June	*Sampan*	100
1646	July	*Grijpskerck*	300
1647	October	*The Gulden Gans*	16
TOTAL			1,976

Source: See Note.[40]

TABLE 6.9: PURCHASE AND EXPORT OF SLAVES IN DUTCH SHIPS FROM KARAIKAL TO JAKARTA, 1651

Year	*Month Date*	*Name of the Ship*	*Slaves (men, women)*
1651	April	*Zeerob*	13
1651	May	*Koe*	5
1651	October	*Os*	13
TOTAL			31

Source: See Note.[41]

LOCAL RULER'S RESISTANCE TO SLAVE TRADE OF THE DUTCH FROM DEVANAMPATTINAM AND CUDDALORE TO JAKARTA, 1688

After the death of Krishnappa Nayak, the kingdom of Gingee passed into the hands of the Marathas. Shivaji, the ruler noticed the active slave trade of the Dutch East India Company and he banned the export of slaves from the ports of Devanampattinam, Cuddalore and Porto Novo. He issued a *cowle* (a written order) in March 1678 and strictly prohibited the Dutch from engaging in slave trade. He stated that under the Sultan of Golconda in Masulipatnam on the Telugu Coast it had been lawful for the Europeans to buy men, women and children as slaves. But so long as he was the master of the land in the Tamil Coast, the Dutch would not buy or transport any men, women and children as slaves.[42] Thus it is evident that the Hindu rulers of the coast came to regard transporting Tamil slaves to the overseas as being at odds with Hinduism and against their own conception of human rights. Hence they raised objections and banned the slave trade based on the religious and humanitarian grounds, losing no time to translate it into decisive action. Slave trading by the Dutch had elicited severe reactions from the local government and was found as late as in 1688 on the Tamil Coast.[43]

SLAVE TRADE OF THE DUTCH FROM PORTO NOVO TO ACEH IN SUMATRA AND BANTEN IN JAVA, 1640-1647

Marakkayars began their trade with Aceh in Sumatra in 1640 when they were encouraged by Sultan Iskander Thani (1636-41) the ruler. The Dutch who traded with Porto Novo had also participated in slave trade. During September 1640 5 ships carried a cargo of 150 slaves besides 540 packets of textiles, 20 bales of raw cotton.[44] Slave trade also flourished from Porto Novo and one reads about a ship sailing to Aceh with 37 slaves in 1641.[45] The slave trade conducted by the Dutch Company gave a boost to the *marakkayars* to purchase and assist in the export of slaves. Different business strategies came to be pursued by the native slave agents and brokers and these demonstrate how the commerce in human beings was fragmented.

An agent of the Dutch Company was in-charge of bringing slaves from the interior villages of the hinterland of Porto

Novo, while another sold them to Dutch, who in certain cases, was in-charge of transportation and held responsible till the ships departed from Porto Novo. It is equally interesting to note the response of the Tamil Muslim merchants.[46] The export of slaves had largely continued in 1646 owing to famines. Maxmillan Bowman, an Englishman witnessed the arrival of Tamil slaves in ships to Aceh during the famine and he recorded in October 1646, 'There came upon this small vessel upward of 400 slaves so hunger starved that they were scarcely able to crawl when they brought them ashore. They were sold at five to six *taels* (a Chinese weight for silver) per head, at a discount for half the usual price, due to their wretched physical condition.'[47] Ships also sailed away to Banten in Java from Porto Novo with 100 slaves in 1646 and the owner of the ship was Ahmad *marakkayar*. He was exempted from the payment of export duty on the slaves. Meerjung *marakkayar* a slave dealer who lived at Sirkazhi in the hinterland had arranged for the purchase of slaves. Trade in slaves continued in 1647 and a ship sailed away from Porto Novo to Aceh with many slaves in 1647.[48] Thus it to be noted that the port of departure of the ship which transported slaves need not necessarily indicate the place of origin of the slaves.

Maritime scholars opine that documents related to slave trade in the regions of Asia and in the Indian Ocean are scattered and available here and there.[49] Hence, the exact nature of slave trade like that in the Atlantic region could not be known and is now therefore called into question. It is certainly possible to know the long term effect of slave trade and human migration in Asia if proper analysis is made by collecting the statistical data from the Dutch records.

The Dutch documents on the Coromandel Coast do not contain details such as age and caste of the slave, the details of the agent or broker who sold the slaves. The price paid had rarely been recorded. It is mentioned that 143 slaves died on the way from Karaikal to Pulicat during transport in a rented vessel in February 1646. Therefore one could understand the pitiable health condition and misery of the slaves. The chapter explains the importance of the particular regions and the individual countries in understanding the specificities of the Indian Ocean slave trade and slavery that need to be highlighted and contrasted with each other, something which had not been highlighted in the numerous works of historians. Slaves were both imported and exported solely for the purposes of slave labour. Before embarking on a comparative study it is therefore necessary to have an understanding of the historical context of the establishment of slavery and the migration of the people in coastal areas through the slave trade. The Dutch in Kunimedu and Devanampattinam had purchased and exported 2,533 slaves for export to Jakarta. They exported 862 slaves from Tirumullaivasal, 2,118 from Adirampattinam and 2,007 slaves from Karaikal. These 7,620 slaves in total had reached were forced to work as labourers in pepper and nutmeg gardens, animal husbandry and fortification works in Jakarta. Slavery in the early modern age was thus a natural and widely accepted institution among human beings. The people were unaware of its moral wrongs until the abolitionist movement that emerged later. A mode of Dutch East India Company slave production had emerged and it was different from the former slavery that was domestic, applied mainly to the slaves owned by the inhabitants. The roles of the Dutch Company slaves were by no means domestic and were crucial to the subsistence, profit and defence of the Dutch settlements. The company was certainly concerned to maximize the productivity of slaves.

NOTES

1. Nationaal Archief (hereafter NA), Den Haag, Mss VOC 1127, fls.190–90v.
2. NA, VOC 1135, fl. 345v, letter of Arent Gardenijs in Pulicat to Hendrick Molijn in Myanmar dated 10 May 1641; VOC 1135, fl. 370 letter of the Dutch factor of Pulicat to Jakarta dated 8 June 1641.

3. NA, VOC 1138, fl.749v.
4. Ibid.
5. NA, VOC 1156, fl. 279; VOC 1147, fl. 574.
6. NA, VOC 1248, fl. 2254.
7. NA, VOC 876, fl. 281.
8. Henry Davison Love, *Vestiges of Old Madras, 1640-1800: Traced from the East India Company's Records Preserved at Fort St. George and the India Office, and from Other Sources*, 3 vols., John Murray, London, 1913, vol. I, pp. 127-8, 130-1, 135, 147, 149.
9. NA, VOC 1248, fl. 2030.
10. NA, VOC 1245, fl. 447v.
11. NA, VOC 1242, fl. 726.
12. Ibid.
13. Ibid., fl. 719.
14. NA, VOC 890, fl. 247.
15. NA, VOC 1242, fl. 726v.
16. NA, VOC 1274, fl. 771.
17. Ibid., fl.775.
18. Ibid.
19. NA, VOC 1333, fl. 604v.
20. NA, VOC 1332, fl. 484v.
21. Jan Pietersz Coen, *Beschiden Omtrent Zijn Bedirjf in Indie*, 7 vols., ed. H.T. Colenbrander, The Hague, 1919-34, vol. 1, pp. 706-8.
22. Pieter van Dam, *Beschryvinge van de Oostindische Compagnie*, ed. F.W. Stapel and C.W. Th. Van Boetzelaer, 7 vols., 'S Gravenhage, 1927-54, repr., 1977, see vol. II, pt. II.
23. Sudeshna Chakravarti, 'The Dutch East India Company and Slave Trade in Seventeenth Century India: An Outline by Pieter van Dam, An Advocate of the Company', *Journal of the Asiatic Society of Calcutta*, vol. 39, no. 2, 1997, pp. 73-99.
24. Ibid.
25. Ibid.
26. NA, VOC 1348, fl. 1220v.
27. S. Jeyaseela Stephen, *Expanding Portuguese Empire and the Tamil Economy: Sixteenth-Eighteenth Centuries*, Manohar, New Delhi, 2009, pp. 265-8.
28. Tapan Raychaudhri, *Jan Company in Coromandel, 1605-1690: A Study in the Interrelations of European Commerce and Traditional Economies*, The Hague, 1962, p. 19.

29. Om Prakash, *The Dutch Factories in India: A Collection of Dutch East India Company Documents Pertaining to India, 1617-23*, New Delhi, Munshiram, 1984, vol. I, p. 80.
30. S. Jeyaseela Stephen, *From European Dwelling Settlements to Global Cities: Ports of the Tamil Coast and the Colonial Modernity*, Primus, 2021, pp. 247-50.
31. NA, VOC 1087, fls. 181-181v, NA, Pulicat's Dagregister, 2 February 1624; *DR*, 8-11 March 1624, p. 33; VOC 1082, fl. 214, Batavia to Marten Ysbrantsz in Pulicat, 26 March 1624; VOC 1082, fl.135, *GM*, 27 January 1625; VOC 1087, fl. 198v, Pulicat's Dagregister, 22 January 1625; VOC 1090, fl. 245v, Marten Ysbrantsz in Pulicat to Batavia, 4 June 1626; VOC 1095, fl. 31, Pulicat's Dagregister, 21 June 1626; VOC 1095, fl.31v, Pulicat's Dagregister, 18 July 1626; VOC 1090, fl.113; W.Ph. Coolhas, ed., *Generale Missiven van de Gouverneurs-Generaal en Raden Aan Heren XVII der Verenigde Oostindische Compagnie*, 9 vols., 'S Gravenhage, 1960-84 (hereafter *GM*), 13 December 1626; VOC 1095, fl. 35, Pulicat's Dagregister, 9 January 1627; VOC 1095, fl. 36v, Pulicat's Dagregister, 4 February 1627; VOC 1095, fl. 37, Pulicat's Dagregister, 17 March 1627; VOC 1094, fl. 91v, Marten Ysbrantsz in Pulicat to Batavia, 24 January 1628; VOC 1095, fl. 41v, Pulicat's Dagregister, 31 January 1628; VOC 1095, fl. 46, Pulicat's Dagregister, 15 August 1628; VOC 1095, fl.17, VOC 1100, fl.100, Marten Ysbrantsz in Pulicat to Batavia, 24 August 1630.
32. NA, VOC 1095, fl. 33, Pulicat's Dagregister, 20 September 1626; VOC 1095, fl. 35, Pulicat's Dagregister, 9 January 1627; VOC 1095, fl.37, Pulicat's Dagregister, 17 March 1627.
33. NA, VOC 1151, fl.764r; VOC 1324, fl. 2r.
34. NA, VOC 1117, fl. 666, Marten Ysbrantsz in Pulicat to Batavia, 19 June 1635; VOC 1117, fls. 667-668, Marten Ysbrantsz in Pulicat to Batavia, 19 June 1635; VOC 1117, fls. 681v, 685v, Carel Reijniersz in Tegenepatnam to Batavia, 2 November 1635; VOC 1119, fl. 1170, Maastricht's bill of lading; VOC 1119, fl. 1175, 8 October 1636, Leeuwarden's bill of lading; J.A. Van der Chijs et al., *Dagregister Gehouden int Casteel Batavia vant Passerende daer te Plaatse als Over Geheel Nederlandts-India, 1628-1682*, 31 vols., The Hague-Batavia, 1887-1928 (hereafter *DR*), 31 October 1636, p. 262.
35. NA, VOC 1184, fls. 233-233v, Laurens Pit in Pulicat to Batavia, 6 July 1651; VOC 1184, fl. 172, VOC 1184, fl. 346, Os's bills of lading, Pulicat, 5 October 1651.

36. NA, VOC 1233, fls. 24-24v, Laurens Pit in Pulicat to Batavia, 24 March 1660; VOC 1233, fl. 33, Laurens Pit in Pulicat to Batavia, 6 May 1660; VOC 1232, fl. 381, Laurens Pit in Pulicat to Heeren XVII, 9 August 1660; VOC 1236, fl. 594, Laurens Pit in Pulicat to Batavia, 4 August 1661; VOC 1234, fl. 130, Laurens Pit in Pulicat to Heeren XVII, 15 September 1661; *DR*, 18 October 1661, pp. 312-13, 325; VOC 1234, fl.99, *GM*, 22 December 1661; VOC 1240, fl. 382, Laurens Pit in Pulicat to Batavia, 9 February 1662; VOC 1240, fl.355, Laurens Pit in Pulicat to Batavia, 8 April 1662.
37. NA, VOC 1156, fl. 276, Arnold Heussen in Pulicat to Batavia, 5 October 1644; VOC 1156, fl.281, Arnold Heussen in Pulicat to Batavia, 5 October 1644; VOC 1156, fl.286, Arnold Heussen in Pulicat to Batavia, 5 October 1644; VOC 1156, fl. 298, Nieuw Amsterdam's bill of lading, Pulicat, 6 October 1644; VOC 1156, fl. 303.
38. NA, VOC 1160, fl. 9; *GM*, 15 January 1647.
39. NA, VOC 1161, fl.935v, Castle Geldria's Journal, Pulicat, 19 February 1646; VOC 1161, fl.975, Castle Geldria's Journal, Pulicat, 8 September 1646; VOC 1164, fl. 731v, Schiedam's bill of lading, Pulicat, 29 September 1646.
40. NA, VOC 1161, fl. 941, Castle Geldria's Journal, Pulicat, 9 March 1646; VOC 1161, fl. 941, Castle Geldria's Journal, Pulicat, 16 March 1646; VOC 1161, fl. 952v, Castle Geldria's Journal, Pulicat, 1 May 1646; VOC 1161, fl. 826, Arnold Heussen in Pulicat to Batavia, 3 May 1646; VOC 1161, fl. 956, Castle Geldria's Journal, Pulicat, 19 May 1646; VOC 1161, fl. 962, Castle Geldria's Journal, Pulicat, 6 June 1646; VOC 1161, fl. 965v, Castle Geldria's Journal, Pulicat, 10 June 1646; VOC 1161, fl. 795, Arnold Heussen in Pulicat to Batavia, 9 June 1646; VOC 1161, fl. 798, Arnold Heussen in Pulicat to Batavia, 9 June 1646; VOC 1161, fl. 971, Castle Geldria's Journal, Pulicat, 26 July 1646; VOC 1168, fl. 515v, Arnold Heussen in Pulicat to Batavia, 5 October 1647.
41. NA, VOC 1184, fls. 261, 276, Laurens Pith in Pulicat to Batavia, 18 April 1651; VOC 1184, fl. 233, Laurens Pit in Pulicat to Batavia, 6 July 1651; VOC 1184, fls. 233-233v, Laurens Pit in Pulicat to Batavia, 6 July 1651; VOC 1184, fl.172, VOC 1184, fl. 346, Os's bills of lading, Pulicat, 5 October 1651.
42. K.A. Nilakanta Sastri, 'Shivaji's Charters to the Dutch on the Coromandel Coast', *Proceedings of the Indian History Congress*, Third Session, Calcutta, 1936, pp. 1156-65.

43. British Library (hereafter BL), London, *Oriental and India Office Collection*, (hereafter *OIOC*), G/19/5, fl. 43r; *OIOC*, MSS Eur. Mackenzie General 55, fls. 46-7; Records of Fort St. George, *Diary and Consultation Book, 1672-1746, 1749-57*, ed. C.M. Schmidt, J.J. Cotton, A.V. Venkatarama Ayyar, B.S. Baliga et al., 90 vols., Madras, 1910-53, The Diary & Consultation Book of the Honble Elihu Yale Esq President Governour & Councill their proceedings & transactions for the affairs of the Rt. Honble English East India Company in the Presidency of the Coast of Choromandell & the Bay of Bengala, Consultation of 14 May 1688.
44. *Dagregister, 1640-1*, p. 206.
45. Ibid., p. 215. The ship also carried gunpowder, sugar and rose water.
46. Ibid., pp. 204-7.
47. William Foster, ed., *The English Factories in India: A Calendar of Documents in the India Office, British Museum & Public Record Office*, vol. I (1618-21), vol. II (1622-3), vol. III (1624-9), vol. IV (1630-3), vol. V (1634-6), vol. VI (1637-41), vol. VII (1642-5), vol. VIII (1646-50), vol. IX (1651-4), vol. X (1655-60), vol. XI (1661-4), vol. XII (1665-7), vol. XIII (1668-9), Oxford, 1906-27 (hereafter *EFI*), vol. VIII, pp. 54-5.
48. BL, *OIOC*, *Factory Records of Fort. St. George*, no. 20, see the letter of English East India Company servant John Davis, Ralph Ingeram and Wilson written from Cuddalore dated 14 May 1687; Thomas Bowrey, *A Geographical Account of the Countries around the Bay of Bengal, 1669-79*, ed., Sir Richard Temple, Cambridge, 1905, pp. xxxi-xxxiii.
49. S. Arasaratnam, 'Slave Trade in the Indian Ocean in the Seventeenth Century', K. S. Mathew, ed., *Mariners, Merchants and Oceans: Studies in Maritime History*, New Delhi, Manohar, 1995, pp. 195-208, see p. 195.

CHAPTER 7

Dutch Slave Trade from Nagapattinam to Colombo, Banten, Jakarta, Melaka, Cape Town and the Social Realities of the Enslaved, 1655-1791

Portuguese private traders in Nagapattinam developed slave trade with Melaka and Manila towards the end of the sixteenth century and it continued till 1658 when the Dutch captured and occupied the Portuguese settlement.[1] The individuals made profit from their personal small scale slave trade, particularly because they had access to the same transportation network in which they could sell their slaves at sites where they could obtain higher prices. The Dutch Company's slave trade was different from private Portuguese slave trade. The Dutch Company had legalized slave trade at Nagapattinam which developed between the nodes of Jakarta which functioned as the Capital of the Dutch East India Company and with Colombo and Galle in Sri Lanka that had emerged as part of a larger grid of migration of the Dutch maritime empire. The Dutch developed a new type of slaves, called company slaves which differed from existing modes of bondage in the coastal Tamil area in which private slaves were owned by individuals. The Dutch East India Company used mobility and coercion which were the key elements in mobilizing labour and maintaining an order.

THE EARLY SLAVE TRADE BY THE DUTCH IN NAGAPATTINAM AREA, 1655-1656

The Dutch explored the possibilities to purchase slaves in Nagapattinam area and they could manage to transport slaves on a large scale in 1655 to Colombo in Sri Lanka.[2]

TABLE 7.1: PURCHASE AND EXPORT OF SLAVES IN DUTCH SHIPS FROM NAGAPATTINAM TO COLOMBO, 1655-1656

Year	*Month*	*Slaves (men, women)*
1655	January	3,695
1656	January	500
TOTAL		4,195

Source: See Note.[3]

These slaves were employed in the fortification works at Colombo in the Dutch factory. Thus the Dutch purchased and exported 4,195 slaves from Nagapattinam area between 1655 and 1656.

TRANSPORTING WAR PRISONERS DECLARED AS SLAVES FROM NAGAPATTINAM TO JAKARTA, 1658

The Dutch were very much desirous to attack and occupy the Portuguese settlement of Nagapattinam. On 20 July 1658 they made attempts and after three days Nagapattinam fell into the hands of Major Van der Laan. Many Portuguese residents fled from the place. After two days (25 July 1658), the Dutch ship *Leeuwin* sailed away, 50 people mostly married, including women and children from Nagapattinam to Jakarta were captured as war prisoners and declared as slaves.[4] On 2 September 1658 war prisoners were again transported from Nagapattinam to Bengal in *Avondster* the ship for onward transmission to Jakarta but the actual number of persons had not been mentioned.[5] After two days (4 September 1658), the sloop *Narasapur* sailed away from Nagapattinam carrying 100 worthless people and again another sailing vessel called *Piply* took 70 worthless persons to Jakarta.[6]

On 9 September 1658 it is mentioned that 210 people from Nagapattinam who were mostly women and children, including taupases and slaves were taken to Jakarta.[7] On 27 October 1658 a sailing vessel called *Piply* took 73 persons and *Avondster*, another ship carried 200 Portuguese prisoners of war and slaves from Nagapattinam to Jakarta.[8] One has no idea as to the fate of all these war prisoners and slaves, whether they were further transported elsewhere to Dutch trading settlements in South East Asia or employed in Jakarta itself.

THE GROWTH OF SLAVE TRADE AT NAGAPATTINAM UNDER THE DUTCH, 1658-1661

The Dutch were permitted by the nayak of Thanjavur to reside and trade in Nagapattinam for three years only. The contract was renewed on 5 January 1662 and the company was permitted to pay half per cent toll on all goods imported and exported.[9] The officials of the Dutch East India Company in Jakarta instructed the Dutch in Nagapattinam to buy and transport slaves since there was demand for labour in Amboina in 1659-60. The company officials in Amboina reported that the small pox epidemic that had broken out in 1660, had caused deaths and so there was a shortage of labour to look after the new plants of cloves. Further it has also been stated that the rebels had destroyed the plants and there was need to plant new trees because the existing plants had become 5 to 30 years old.[10]

The invasion of Bijapur army on the kingdom of Thanjavur made it impossible for the purchase of slaves during that period. The Dutch factor of Nagapattinam was instructed to supply slaves to Sri Lanka in 1659 and he arranged with the help of local agents and traders. The purchase price of a slave in Nagapattinam then was stated to be one *real.* As the price was very cheap, 5,000 slaves were purchased and transported on 11 September 1659 from Nagapattinam to Colombo in Sri Lanka.[11] It was at this time that the VOC had also issued an order on 27 June 1659 prohibiting the transport of slaves by the Tamil merchants in their ships from Nagapattinam to Sri Lanka.[12] Following the ban, slave trade by private merchants came into operation in a clandestine fashion. However, the Dutch made all attempts to curb the private trade in slaves. The company made attempts to purchase and it transported slaves on 14 August 1660. Most of the slaves were peasants from the region of Thanjavur.[13]

It is reported that out of the 5,000 slaves transported, 3,000 persons were considered absolutely worthless in Sri Lanka by November 1660.[14] As a result 425 workers hailing from Thanjavur were sent back in ships to Nagapattinam and the costs of the return transport had to be borne by the agents.[15]

There were plenty of slaves owned by Europeans in Colombo and these slaves were employed in private houses. Dutch burghers sailed to Nagapattinam and they purchased slaves. Prospective native traders also carried many slaves to Colombo in ships which is reported on 2 April 1660.[16] Slaves transported were branded with a small company mark (VOC) on the right thigh or arm. This was done so that company slaves could not be sold several times. It was also used as a means to differentiate between private slaves and the free labourers who were also transported from Nagapattinam to Colombo.

Those slaves and free labourers who arrived were not familiar with the building construction works in Colombo because they were farmers, weavers and artisans. Some died in a year. Many slaves hailing from Thanjavur area were released and they were allotted land for cultivation. It is reported that more than 900 slaves were employed in cultivating the lands around Colombo by 1662.[17]

In a record of 26 January 1661 one finds mention of 400 slaves waiting for the transport in the ships of the Dutch Company from Nagapattinam.[18] War and famine had brought misery to people in the region of Nagapattinam. Many came forward to sell themselves as slaves and this facilitated the slave trade. The Dutch exported 6,793 slaves from Nagapattinam to Colombo between 1659 and 1661. These ships sailed carrying slaves in the period between January and April during the north-east monsoon.

TABLE 7.2: PURCHASE AND EXPORT OF SLAVES IN DUTCH SHIPS FROM NAGAPATTINAM TO COLOMBO, 1659-1661

Year	*Month Date*	*Slaves (men, women)*
1659		5,000
1660	1-14 January	1,393 (500 men, 860 women, 33 children)
1661	July	400
TOTAL		6,793

Source: See Note.[19]

The Dutch purchased a total of 1,461 slaves at Nagapattinam in 1660 they exported to the ports of Banten, Melaka and Jakarta and the details are given as follows.

TABLE 7.3: PURCHASE AND EXPORT OF SLAVES IN DUTCH SHIPS FROM NAGAPATTINAM TO BANTEN, 1660

Year	*Month Date*	*Name of the Ship*	*Slaves (men, women)*
1660	May	*Kabelijau*	46

Source: See Note.[20]

TABLE 7.4: PURCHASE AND EXPORT OF SLAVES IN DUTCH SHIPS FROM NAGAPATTINAM TO JAKARTA, 1660

Year	*Month Date*	*Name of the Ship*	*Slaves (men, women)*
1660	March	*Nieuwpoort*	54
1660	30 March-9 August	*Many ships*	700
1660	May	*Kabelijau*	77
1660	July	*Hercules*	220
1660	July	*Leeuwin*	151
TOTAL			1,202

Source: See Note.[21]

TABLE 7.5: PURCHASE AND EXPORT OF SLAVES IN DUTCH SHIPS FROM NAGAPATTINAM TO MELAKA, 1660

Year	*Month Date*	*Name of the Ship*	*Slaves (men, women)*
1660	July	*Hercules*	54
1660	July	*Leeuwin*	99
1660	November	*Rode Leeuw*	60
TOTAL			213

Source: See Note.[22]

An eyewitness account of Nagapattinam in 1661 vividly portrayed the situation. It was depicted that the famine had worsened to such an extent that entire villages, hamlets and settlements had been depopulated, leaving hardly anyone. Dead bodies were lying scattered in dry tanks, along common roads, indeed, even on the streets of the city of Nagapattinam. Those who had survived, resembled lifeless corpses more than living people. They cried along the fields and roads for a single meal to fill their empty stomachs before dying. In short, the account ended saying that the miseries and sufferings were such, that no pen could describe the extremity of the situation.[23]

At that time the Dutch Company officials began to portray their participation in the slave trade and traffic as a work of Protestant Christian charity. Laurens Pit the Dutch Governor of the Coromandel Coast (1652-63) informed the Directors of the Company in August 1660 that it was indisputable that the purchase of these poor people was a work of compassion since they would perish otherwise, as happened to those who were turned away.[24] Elaborating on Pit's Christian humanitarian theme, Johan Maetsuycker (1653-78) the Dutch Governor-General and his Council mentioned in Jakarta in November 1660 that their intention was that the purchase of slaves of both the elderly and the young would continue indiscriminately, especially when they were members of a single family as was often the case. If the Dutch Company accepted only the young and turned down the old, the latter would perish, which had already occurred quite often. This would not conform to the Christian compassion because to accept the children and leaving the parents to die in their presence, or to accept the men and turn down the women, would be harsh. He finally ended saying that it would be also unacceptable to the Lord God.[25]

The Portuguese missionaries being Catholics, noted the Dutch slave trading methods and activities and so criticized them. Antão Proença (1625-66) the Portuguese Jesuit reported and condemned the Dutch for buying slaves in exchange for rice at Nagapattinam in 1662. He wrote that it was shameful and eternal shame to the Dutch, who had the cruelty to speculate on the misery of the Tamils. The Dutch attracted the natives to the port of Nagapattinam on the coast by using abundant nourishment as bait. When the slave numbers were considerable in the godowns, they transported slaves silently in Dutch ships to various places.[26] Antão Proença also referred to the widespread famine in the region, which he attributed to the vagaries of war and the failure of the monsoon. He stated that the mortality was so great that corpses were heaped up in great piles.[27] The Dutch also explored the purchase of slaves at Sadurangapattinam and the slaves bought in 1663 were sent to Nagapattinam for export to Melaka.

TABLE 7.6: PURCHASE AND EXPORT OF SLAVES IN DUTCH SHIPS FROM SADURANGAPATTINAM TO MELAKA, 1663

Year	*Month Date*	*Name of the Ship*	*Slaves (men, women)*
1663	June	*Cabelijauw*	5

Source: See Note.[28]

A Dutch record of 21 September 1668 states that customs duty on slaves was exempted at Melaka for Dutch ships. The non-Dutch ships had to pay 20 per cent customs duty. Slaves were made duty free to provide the much-needed labour in Melaka.[29] In 1687, it was reported that 100 slaves had been transported from Nagapattinam on the Coromandel Coast to Melaka, because the scarce coolies were too expensive, costing 8 *stuivers* per day.[30]

REDISTRIBUTION OF NAGAPATTINAM SLAVES BY THE DUTCH COMPANY FROM COLOMBO IN SRI LANKA IN SHIPS TO JAKARTA IN INDONESIA, 1678-1683

Dutch records often mention that the slaves of Nagapattinam transported to Sri Lanka had been re-transported to South East Asia. In 1679 slaves from Nagapattinam who reached Sri Lanka numbering 100, were sent to Melaka costing 3,153 *florins*. It is reported that 11 slaves died during the voyage.[31] In the same year (1679) it is mentioned that 900 slaves of Nagapattinam were transferred from Sri Lanka to Jakarta.[32] The Dutch East India Company in Jakarta found it difficult to procure slaves from Timor and so these slaves numbering 1,000 hailing from Nagapattinam were sent to Jakarta. As these slaves were mainly women and children, they were not suitable for work in the mines.[33] The next year (1678) 360 slaves of Nagapattinam were sent from Colombo to

Jakarta and 900 slaves were shipped again in 1679 from Colombo to Jakarta.[34] It was reported in March 1683 that in Colombo in Sri Lanka there were no longer any surplus Company slaves for re-transportation to Jakarta in Indonesia. There were 1,160 male and female slaves that could still work, while 307 slaves were unable to work due to old age and infirmities, 209 slaves were practically worn out, 15 slaves had absconded and 99 slave children attended schools besides 123 infant slaves.[35]

Rijkloff van Goens the Dutch Governor of Sri Lanka (1662-3, 1665-75) reported in his various letters of 1661-2 to the Governor-General in Jakarta and also to the Directors of the Dutch East India Company in Amsterdam in 1675, 1676, 1677 and 1680 that divine providence had made the slaves come to Sri Lanka in order to repopulate the lands there and to support the Dutch Company's designs.[36] Dutch export of slaves continued from Nagapattinam and one finds weavers and artisans who had been exported to Jaffna on 29 March 1667.

Besides slaves one finds many free labourers who were also purchased and sent to Colombo due to labour shortage there. It is mentioned in Dutch sources that the Sinhalese were too lazy and not greatly disposed to take up fortification work and also to dig the earth and do other related irrigation works.[37] In 1674 the Dutch Company in Colombo abolished the use of hired labour in Colombo. Hence a number of hired workers had not been transported from Nagapattinam and their number dwindled.[38] Dutch records mention that the practice of coolies and hired workers who were brought to Colombo to work at the fortifications had been stopped and discontinued since 1674.[39]

When Ekoji I (1674-84) became the ruler of Thanjavur in 1675 the Dutch were allowed to continue their trade at Nagapattinam. They continued to buy slaves and exported them. The Dutch Company planned to utilize those textile worker slaves who had been skilled exported from Nagapattinam to Colombo. They were asked to weave cloth, also engaged in textile dyeing and helped in the organization and production of cloth in Sri Lanka.[40]

The Dutch private traders were prohibited to trade in slaves in 1685. The reason was that the Dutch Company itself was the main slave trader.[41] Incoming coolie workers and slaves reached illegally in ships from Nagapattinam through private traders to Colombo where they were detected in 1692. They were confiscated and put to work at fortifications in Colombo.[42] During 1690-91 slave purchase at Nagapattinam also came to a halt because the famine situation had improved.

THE SLAVE PURCHASES AND TRADE AT NAGAPATTINAM UNDER THE DUTCH, 1694-1704

The Dutch purchased 5,000 slaves in 1694 when slaves were available for sale at the rate of one *real* per head at Nagapattinam. In 1695 one finds 3,500 slaves were imported to Jaffna and the traders paid the import duties. Hendrick Zwaardecroon the commander of Jaffnapatnam noted that import of more people meant more mouths to be fed, while rice was more dear than labour at the time. He stated explicitly that he would have preferred if traders had brought in rice rather than humans.[43] Again 3,859 slaves were purchased by the Dutch in Nagapattinam and exported by 30 November 1696. Thus the relationship between rice and slave market is also an interesting line of enquiry. The Dutch continued to purchase and transported 1,741 slaves from Nagapattinam to Colombo in 1697.[44] Thus the Dutch had exported 14,100 slaves in total from Nagapattinam between 1694 and 1697.

The Dutch continued to purchase and transport slaves whenever available and possible from Nagapattinam to Colombo. It had transported 1,582 slaves in 1704 when crops failed in the region.[45] Thus famines, warfare and crop failure had largely helped to the export of slaves to Sri Lanka.

The Dutch East India Company shifted its trading headquarters on the Coromandel Coast from Pulicat to Nagapattinam in 1690. The Dutch continued to purchase slaves in Nagapattinam whenever possible. The poverty of people and famines in the region facilitated. The Dutch Company built slave lodges in the trading settlements on the Coromandel Coast to facilitate export. The plan of the Dutch fort of Nagapattinam in 1700 by Issack de Graff the map-maker shows the slave rooms, halls and also secret chambers where slaves were lodged and fed before transportation in ships.[46] The plan and drawing of the Dutch factory of Saduranga-pattinam in the seventeenth century by Issack de Graff also mentions the slave cottages where slaves stayed before export.[47] The plan of the Dutch factory at Porto Novo in 1700 drawn by Issack de Graff refers to slave cottages built where the purchased slaves were lodged.[48] The plan of the Dutch fort of Geldria at Pulicat in 1708 prepared by Jan Christianensz Toorzee refers to the chambers of the slaves kept for export.[49] Thus one finds extensive arrangements were made at Dutch settlements for the stay of the slaves before shipping overseas.

SLAVE EXPORTS FROM NAGAPATTINAM TO AFRICA, 1705-1739

The Dutch Company exported slaves to Cape Town and used slave labour widely. It ordered that slaves who were found on the ships returning to the Netherlands were not to become free, but were sentenced to remain as slave for the rest of their lives in the possession of the company.[50] Such measures were meant chiefly to target the slave owners who brought the slaves illegally on board the homeward bound ships. Hence slaves were compelled to be sold before sailing to the Netherlands from Cape Town.

The Dutch Company also brought convict labour in large numbers as slaves to be employed in Cape Town. It included company servants, exiled criminals and political prisoners. They were used to labour on the public works. Some slaves kept by the Company were distributed to burghers on credit, and were privately owned. There were around 300 privately owned slaves in Cape Town in 1690s.[51]

A 10 years old boy named Chinnan was sold by his mother in Nagapattinam because of her utter poverty and lack of means for livelihood to an employee of the Dutch Company. Slave supplies from Nagapattinam were plentiful during the period of economic crisis. In 1705 Chinnan the slave and his sister had reached Cape Town as exported. One finds that Chinnan was owned by a farmer in the Stellenbosch district. He ran away to the place of his sister in Cape Town when he could no longer endure ill-treatment.[52]

The directors of the Dutch East India Company asked the opinion of M.P. de Chavonnes in their letter dated 24 June 1716, regarding the governor of Cape and his Council on a range of issues relating to coal, agricultural production, trade and labour. In terms of labour, the directors wanted to know whether the immigration of free European labour would be preferable to the then current reliance on slaves. The Governor believed that free European farm labour would be more expensive and troublesome than slaves. He reported that wages would have to be covered for all work done not only in the fields but also for the daily work done by slaves. He said that doing manual work could not be demanded from the Europeans in this weather. He added that the Dutch Company would find it more useful and cheaper to keep slaves than European farm labour. Further, as wine and other strong drinks were fairly cheap, all workmen and the lower classes were addicted to drink, it would be extremely difficult to restrain them and keep them confined to their duties. He said that the Dutch Company had already been provided amply with drunkards in the Cape and their hands had been not free.[53]

C. van Beaumont and J. Cruse the Dutch officials opined on 10 February 1717 that Europeans would not be found nearly as much of use as slaves, particularly in the case of daily menial tasks. They said that it had been more fitting for the slaves rather than Europeans who could be used.[54]

Slaves exported from Nagapattinam and the miserable life of the young Tamil slaves exported to Cape Town had been revealing. Suppudu (Cupido) was a slave in Cape Town and he was brought to trial in 1739. According to records he could no longer bear the loneliness of being the only slave employed in the household. He struggled very much to adapt himself to the new cultural context.[55] He told his mistress that he was not used to wearing the clothes that she gave. He complained that he had worked alone for two years. While attempting to stab his mistress he declared that 'it would be better if I murder you, your husband and your child, and that I flay you open like flecked fish, and then do me as well'.[56] Suppudu had felt alienation and loneliness strongly.

PURCHASE AND SALE OF SLAVES BY THE NAVAL OFFICERS OF THE DUTCH COMPANY ON THE COROMANDEL COAST, 1737-1743

Some slaves from Coromandel Coast had been found sold to the middle level officers of the ships and also to high ranking officials of the Dutch Company during 1737 and 1743. Januarij a male slave of the Coromandel Coast was sold in 1737 by an unknown person (name not recorded) to Constantia Amalia Falk at 50 *rix* dollars. Joseph, another male slave of Coromandel Coast was sold in 1740 by Jan Jacobsz Gouda, a nurse of a returning ship to Adam Amie, another nurse on a ship at 60 *rix* dollars. Sisnander a male slave of Coromandel Coast was sold in 1741 by joint owners (a surgeon at the company's hospital and an assistant) to the captain of a ship for 150 Arcot rupees. October, a male slave in 1743 was sold by a junior merchant to another junior merchant of the Dutch Company at 250 Arcot rupees.[57]

SLAVES EXPORTED FROM NAGAPATTINAM TO CAPE TOWN, 1763-1775

It is found that old names of the slaves were changed and new names like Januarij and October had been given when sale was made from one person to another. This suggests creating a new identity in the minds of the slave owners. Chinna

Thaai the female slave hailing from Nagapattinam was sold thrice and she finally reached Cape Town. She ended up with the Christian name called 'Rosa'. In Cape Town she was employed in 1763 at Groot Constantia's wine estate located outside the suburbs of the town.[58] Again one notices that Seena a young girl was sold into slavery in Nagapattinam in 1768 and she was exported to Cape Town. She was also called by the name Rosa in 1775 at Cape Town.[59]

SLAVES EXPORTED TO SRI LANKA, 1720-1791

Slaves continued to be exported from Nagapattinam and Tuticorin to Sri Lanka. A deed mentions that Louis de Saram Maha Mudaliyar purchased a boy called Maden, renamed Lourens, on 30 December 1728, from a seller called Joan chetti for the price of 12 *rix* dollars in Tuticorin.[60] Unruly slaves in Sri Lanka were exposed to public abuse. The slave offenders were formerly locked by the neck and wrists into wooden framework. Many slaves standing in the pillory died in 1723. The Tamil slave list includes Maalathi, Ayyapan, Chinna Pillai, Latchumi, Muthu, Namasivaayam, Savarimuthu, Chinnakutti, Muthusamy, Karuppan and Kittu.[61]

The Dutch in Nagapattinam exported slaves to Sri Lanka particularly to Colombo and Galle. A deed signed at Nagapattinam in 1766 had mentioned Spadille, one of the 16 slaves. She was emancipated by Anna Maria Giethoorn and the certificate was signed in 1769.[62] A certificate had been signed in Nagapattinam where a slave called Lakshmi (Lechumee in record) belonging to a dealer named Kadhiravan (Cadieraavan). She was freed finally in Sri Lanka in 1787. Thus the legal status and fate of some of the slaves who gained freedom had come to light.[63]

The prices of slaves purchased by the Dutch on the Coromandel Coast had been mentioned in records. The Tamil male cook Cupido was sold for 70 *rix* dollars.[64] The slave woman called Aurora in 1751 had been referred to as old maid, and so she was sold at a low price of 30 *rix* dollars.[65]

Thus the individual variations in salve prices are important to be taken into account.

SOCIAL LIFE OF THE TAMIL SLAVES IN CAPE TOWN

Slave trade was nominally a Danish company monopoly after 1732, but this was also an illegal trade. Slaves were evidently sent to the Cape for official sale for some years after 1737, but these transactions were on a limited scale. This was a period of labour shortage in the Dutch colony for the heavy work involved on company projects. Slaves brought from Pazhaverkadu, Pondicherry, Tranquebar, Nagapattinam, and Manapaadu to Cape Town got married to slaves who had come from Jaffna in Sri Lanka and from Makassar, Timor and Amboina in South East Asia. These slaves gave birth to slave children. Johanna of Madras was born at Cape in 1709. Johannes de Jong was the daughter of Moses of Pazhaverkadu and she was born in 1752 at Cape Town.

TABLE 7.7: MARRIAGES OF TAMIL SLAVES IN CAPE TOWN, 1702-1788

Year	*Male*	*Female*
1702	Arend of Coromandel	Helena from Makassar
1702	Arend of Coromandel	Maria of Nagapattinam
1709	Classen of Coromandel	Catharina of Nagapattinam
1721	Antony of Pazhaverkadu	Esperanca of Nagapattinam
1721	Claas of Coromandel	Helena of Timor
1725	Classen of Coromandel	Johanna de Ryk of Bengal
1732	Moses of Pulicat	Cecilia of Jaffna
1746	Francis of Coromandel	Agatha of Java
1746	Francois Pondicherry	Rosalie from Pondicherry
1774	Frederick of Coromandel	Johanna of Tranquebar
1787	Nicholaas Christophe	Magdalena of Nagapattinam
1788	Adam of Manapaadu	Catharina Maria of Amboina

Source: Hans F. Heese, *Cape Melting Pot: The Role and Status of the Mixed Population at the Cape, 1652-1795*, trs. Delia Robertson, Cape, 2015, pp. 27-8, 96, 101-2, 219-21, 224-5, 230.

The Dutch continued to obtain and export slaves as late as 1791-2. The letter of Sir Charles Oakley, the English Governor at Madras in 1792 pointed out that the traffic in slaves for export had received great encouragement by the permission granted by the Dutch Company to the contractors. As a result, numerous intermediaries had been found active and doing the purchase and transported slaves under the Dutch banner.[66]

To conclude, it may be said that the Dutch records allow one to have glimpses of slaves as human beings with their own emotions and personalities. One finds how slaves have fallen prey to enslavement including slavery prevalent including prisoners of war. The slave labour differed substantially from period to period, as a result of changes that occurred in the system in tune with the global regime of slavery. Slaves and slavery had great shifts in response to the socio-economic order.

The Dutch Company increasingly used slavery, the main form of coerced labour, as an effective mode of production and also more as part of labour-intensive routes to economic development. Slavery had been an integral and dynamic part of a permanently developing Dutch empire in Asia, globally connected and increasingly capitalist economic system. This study points out that slavery as a modern, dynamic economic system of production and the coercion was not the only key element crucial to the systems of labour, especially for slave labour, it was increasingly accepted that transportation and mobility was one of the crucial elements underpinning the systems. Within the Dutch shipping network, the port of Colombo was second in importance only to Jakarta. Famines and warfare supplied slaves from Nagapattinam for transport to Colombo. The slave traffic between the Coromandel Coast and Colombo was particularly significant. The Dutch Company in Nagapattinam had purchased and exported 28,136 slaves in total to Sri Lanka between 1655 and 1704. They re-exported 2,160 slaves of Nagapattinam in ships from Colombo to Jakarta in 1679. There were 1,913 slaves hailing from

Nagapattinam who were employed at a Colombo factory in 1683. The slaves of Nagapattinam who were brought to Colombo were sent to Galle, Jaffna, Trincomalee and Negombo to meet the labour needs of the Dutch Company. Such minute details could not be traced from records. These Dutch Company slaves of Nagapattinam had also worked on fortifications and in the agriculture sector there.

What one finds here on the history of labour relations is important. One finds subdivisions into reciprocal, tributary, independent, slave and wage-labour relations. Wage labour has been especially associated with free wage labour, in the form of casual wage labour as neatly recorded in Dutch records. The form of contract labour (indentured) has been absent in Dutch Company records of Nagapattinam. Free persons have been referred to in Dutch records and they performed casual wage labour side by side with slaves. According to Dutch records the term coolie pointed out to wages and associated with the person employed. It is not associated with unskilled and menial labour. The term is of Tamil origin in etymology and confronted the creation of social underclass, neither slaves nor clients of patrons in the seventeenth century. The meaning of the term coolie changed later and it became a synonym for contract labour both the formally and informally bonded.

Slaves in Tamil society were integrated to the household and there was a move from household slaves to workers to be employed in the Dutch factories overseas. Debt slavery developed in times of catastrophes like famines and there was no link or association of slavery with race in Tamil country. Thus the study has emphasized the historical role of other labour relations beyond the European binary of slavery and free wage labour. Bringing together all forms of bondage and coercion (slavery, debt bondage, etc.) in European and colonial contexts, indicate the commonalities between these different groups of workers while not preventing a detailed analysis of their particularities, and making it possible to acknowledge the combined role of multiple coercive labour relations in shaping the modern world. There was definitely an absence of freedom and equality and it would be interesting to know how the idea of heaven had been constructed and shaped in the Hindu religion and Tamil society. Ignoring the moral implications of the slave trade by the Dutch, it is concluded it was a trade, as compared with other trades. The slave traffic and trade from the Tamil Coast played a strategic role in the Asian commercial system. The Dutch procured the necessary labour, in the form of coerced human strength, for the production in Indonesia and Sri Lanka. This means that an approach based on a calculation of the 'alternatives' or the 'opportunity costs' cannot be applied. This approach is grounded in the idea that the production factors that were put into the slave trade would also have contributed to the economy of the Netherlands, had they been invested in other sectors.

NOTES

1. S. Jeyaseela Stephen, *Subaltern Lives: Tamil History and Society from Medieval to Early Modern Age*, Kalpaz, New Delhi, 2019, pp. 144-7.
2. Tapan Raychaudhri, *Jan Company in Coromandel, 1605-1690: A Study in the Interrelations of European Commerce and Traditional Economies*, The Hague, 1962, p. 166.
3. Nationaal Archief (hereafter NA), Den Haag, Mss VOC 1232, fl. 382; VOC, 1231, fl. 795.
4. NA, VOC 1227, fl. 289v, Letter of Van Goens from Jaffna to Jakarta.
5. NA, VOC 1231 fl. 155.
6. NA, VOC 1231, fl. 174, Letter of Laurens Pit from Pulicat dated 4 September 1658.
7. NA, VOC 1227 fl. 94, Letter of Van Goens to Laurens Pit from Pulicat dated 9 September 1658.
8. NA, VOC 1227, fl. 194, Letter of Ougly dated 27 October 1658.
9. S. Jeyaseela Stephen, *From European Dwelling Settlements to Global Cities: Ports of the Tamil Coast and the Colonial Modernity*, Primus, Delhi, 2021, p. 117.
10. W. Ph. Coolhas, ed., *Generale Missiven van de Gouverneurs-Generaal en Raden Aan Heren XVII der Verenigde Oostindische Compagnie*,

9 vols., 'S Gravenhage, 1960-84 (hereafter *GM*), vol. III (1655-74), p. 315 (16 December 1660).
11. NA, VOC 1231, fl. 795.
12. L. Hovy, *Ceylonees Plakkaatboek: Plakkaten en Andere Wetten Uitgevaardigd door het Nederlandse Bestuur op Ceylon, 1638-1796*, 2 vols., Hilversum, Verloren, 1991, vol. I, pp. 46-8.
13. *GM*, vol. III, p. 175, pp. 335-66 (24 October 1655-6); NA, VOC 1232, fl. 382.
14. NA, VOC 1233, fls. 171-8, fls. 174-5 (22 November 1660).
15. Sri Lanka National Archives (hereafter SLNA), VOC Archives, Record group 1, Inventory number 9, fls. 238v-239, Minutes of the Governor and Council in Colombo dated 16 November 1660.
16. NA, VOC 1233, fls. 157-8.
17. NA, VOC 1234, fls. 25r-v; SLNA, 2712, Colombo Diary, fl. 57.
18. *GM*, vol. III, p. 335 (26 January 1661).
19. NA, VOC 1232, fl. 382; VOC 1233, fls. 25v-26, Laurnes Pit in Pulicat to Batavia, 24 March 1660; VOC 1232, fls. 382-3, Laurnes Pit in Pulicat to Heeren XVII, 9 August 1660; NA, VOC 1236, fls. 576, 600.
20. NA, VOC 1233, fls. 41v-42.
21. NA, VOC 1233, fls. 23-4; VOC, 1232, fls. 382-3, Laurnes Pit in Pulicat to Heeren XVII, 9 August 1660; VOC 1233, fls. 41v-42; VOC 1233, fls. 45, 46, 46v; VOC 1233, fls. 50v, 53.
22. NA, VOC 1233, fls. 45, 46, 46v; VOC 1233, fls. 50v, 53; VOC 1232, fl. 82; *GM*, 16 December 1660.
23. *GM*, vol. III, pp. 355-6, see Maetsuyker and Council, 26 January 1661.
24. NA, VOC 1232, fl. 383, Letter of Governor Laurens Pit and his Council of Coromandel to the Directors in Amsterdam dated 9 August 1660.
25. NA, VOC 884, fl.703, Letter of Governor Van Goens and his Council in Colombo to the Directors in Amsterdam dated 4 November 1660.
26. Letter of Antão Proença to Paul Oliva, the superior-general of the Society of Jesus, from Tiruchirapalli in 1662, in Joseph Bertrand, *La Mission du Madure d' après de Documents in Edits*, 4 vols, Paris, 1847-54, see vol. III, pp. 124-5.
27. Joseph Bertrand, *La Mission du Madure*, vol. III, pp. 129-30.
28. NA, VOC 1232, fl.1263, fl. 682v.
29. Matheson Library, Monash University, Australia, Microfilm Records, Amsterdam Chamber, VOC 1266.

30. *GM*, vol. V, p. 133.
31. *GM*, 11 December 1679, p. 367.
32. Ibid., p. 354.
33. Ibid., p. 370.
34. *GM*, vol. IV, p. 294, p. 354 (11 December 1679); SLNA, Minutes of the Governor and Council in Colombo, 21 November 1678, fl. 61v-62.
35. *GM*, 19 March 1683, p. 569.
36. NA, VOC 1234, fl.125v, Letter of Van Goens from Colombo to Jakarta, 5 April 1661; See 'Beschrijvinge van de staat en gelegenheid van het eijlant Ceijlon door Van Goens, dated 24 September 1675', in F. Valentijn, *Oud en Nieuw-Oost-Indien*, Dordrecht-Amsterdam,1724-6, vol. V, pp. 204-45; NA, VOC 1315, fls. 3306-312, 'Overgeleverd advies dir.-genl. Van Goens met betrekking tot de toestand van Ceijlon, dated 7 November 1676'; NA, VOC 1351, fls. 2539v-2550r, Vertoog van den toestand des gouvts Ceijlon door oudgouvr Van Goens de Jonge van Ceijlon, dated 25 February 1680; P.A. Leupe, Vertooch wegens den presenten staet van de generale Nederlantse Geoctroijeerde Oost-Indische Compe bij Rijckloff van Goens, extr ord raed van India ende commandeur over de retourvloot van Ao. 1655, *Bijdragen tot de Taal-Land-en Volkenkunde*, 1856, pp. 141-80.
37. *GM*, vol. III, p. 793 (31 January 1672).
38. SLNA, 1/20, Minutes of the Governor and Council in Colombo, fl.27v-28 (29 October 1674), fls. 35r-36 (3-26 November 1674).
39. SLNA, 1/20, Minutes of the Governor and Council in Colombo, fl.27v-28, fls. 35v-36.
40. NA, VOC 891, fl. 142.
41. L. Hovy, Ceylonees Plakkaatboek, vol. I, pp. 227-8 (5 December 1685).
42. NA, VOC 1506, fls. 1604-5 (31 May 1692).
43. Sophia Pieters, trs., *Memoir of Hendrick Zwaardecroon, Commandeur of Jaffnapatam, 1697*, Colombo, 1911, pp. 6-7.
44. Knaap Gerrit, 'Europeans, Mestizos and Slaves: The Population of Colombo at the end of the Seventeenth Century', trans. Robert Ross, *Itinerario*, vol. V, 1981, pp. 84-101, see p. 96.
45. Ibid.
46. NA, *Verzameling Buitenlandse Kaarte, Leupe* (hereafter *VEL*), no. 1083.
47. NA, *VEL* 1087.
48. Ibid.

49. NA, *VEL* 1089,
50. J.A. Van der Chijs, *Nederlandsch-Indisch Plakaatboek*, 17 vols., Batavia/ S. Gravenhage, 1885-1900, vol.1, pp. 409-10.
51. J. Armstrong and N. Worden, 'The Slaves, 1652-1834', in Elphick and Giliomee, eds., *The Shaping of South African Society*, pp. 109-83; N. Worden, *Slavery in Dutch South Africa*, Cambridge University Press, London, 1985, p. 9.
52. N. Worden and G. Groenewald, *Trials of Slavery: Selected Documents Concerning Slaves from the Criminal Records of the Council of Justice at the Cape of Good Hope*, 1705-94, Van Riebeeck Society, Cape Town, 2005, Criminele Verklaringen, 1702-49, pp. 3-4.
53. M.P. De Chavonnes, *The Reports of Chavonnes and his Council, and of Van Imhoff, on the Cape*, Van Riebeeck Society, Cape Town, 1918, pp. 87-8.
54. Ibid., pp. 101, 112.
55. Western Cape Archives (hereafter WCA), Council of Justice (hereafter CJ), 786 *Sententiën*, 1736-43, fls. 263-70, translated in Worden and Groenewald, *Trials of Slavery*, pp. 165-8.
56. Ibid., CJ 786, *Sententiën*, 1736-45, fls. 236-70, 1739, Cupido van Mallabar, translated in Worden and Groenewald, *Trials of Slavery*, p. 167.
57. Tamil Nadu State Archives (hereafter TNSA), Chennai, *Kantoor Bengalen te Chinsura en Rechtsopvolgers*, Boxes 1677A, 1677B, 1679A, 1679B, 1694, 1696 and 1715.
58. WCA, Cape Town, Miscellaneous File, N 49, Serrurier Papers, Transfer deeds of slaves, 1763-6.
59. WCA, Miscellaneous File, M 49, Serrurier Papers.
60. Nira Wickramasinghe, *Slave in a Palanquin: Colonial Servitude and Resistance in Sri Lanka*, Columbia University Press, New York, 2020, p. 60.
61. Ibid., p. 47.
62. SLNA, MSS 1/4146, 21 August 1784, Anna Maria Giethoorn and Spadille.
63. SLNA, MSS 1/4146, 17 April 1787, Cadieraavan and Lechumee.
64. Arsip Nasional Republik Indonesia (ANRI), Jakarta, *Vendutiekantoor*, 1, 1751-01-01, 1751-03-30.
65. ANRI, Vcndutickantoor, 1, 1751-04-29.
66. British Library, Oriental and India Office Collections, P/252/76, fl.791, Letter of Charles Oakeley to Jacob Eilbracht dated 14 February 1792.

CHAPTER 8

Slave Trade and Traffic in Tuticorin under the Dutch to Colombo, Cape Town and the Netherlands, 1660-1791

The Dutch East India Company transported both slaves (unfree labourers) and free labourers during the famines in the Tamil country in the years around 1660 to Sri Lanka and Jakarta because the trade in humans was found to be very lucrative. Dutch burghers (free traders) sailed to Tuticorin and they purchased slaves. Prospective native traders also carried many slaves to Colombo in ships which is reported on 2 April 1660.[1] The slaves transported were branded with a small company mark (VOC) on the right thigh or arm. Those who arrived were not familiar with the building construction work in Colombo and some died in a year. Many slaves hailing from Thanjavur area were released and allotted land for cultivation. It is reported that more than 900 slaves were employed in cultivating the lands around Colombo by 1662.[2]

The Dutch factor in Tuticorin was asked to procure slaves during 1670-1. Besides slaves one finds that many free labourers were also purchased and sent to Colombo due to labour shortage there. It is mentioned in Dutch sources that Sinhalese were too lazy and not greatly disposed to fortification works and also to digging the earth and other irrigation related works.[3]

In 1674 the Dutch Company abolished the use of hired labour in Colombo. Hence the number of hired labourers and coolies from Tuticorin were not transported and their number dwindled.[4] Dutch records mention that slaves, coolies, peons and footmen (free and hired servants) were brought from Tuticorin to Colombo to work at the fortifications. This practice was discontinued in 1674.[5]

It is reported that 1,839 free labourers and also slaves were transported between 1673 and 1677 from the port of Tuticorin and Manapaadu to Sri Lanka. Regulations were modified for slave trade and an order was passed on 2 December 1676, which stated that ships could sail with slaves from Tuticorin to Sri Lanka with only a Dutch sailing permit.[6] 360 slaves transported to Colombo from Tuticorin in 1678 were transferred to Jakarta followed by another 800 slaves in 1679. It is stated that only slaves employed in the loading and unloading of cargoes in the ships in Colombo were retained.[7]

The Dutch factory at Colombo in 1681 had 1,993 Tamil slaves and later 1,570 in 1685. The strict control of maritime traffic to Sri Lanka by the Dutch Company acted as counter interest to slave trade. Often the main sources for slaves ran dry and the Dutch Company found not a single slave for purchase in Tuticorin in 1684.[8]

An ordinance promulgated by the Dutch in 1685 can easily be misunderstood that forbade the import of slaves from Tamil Coast to Sri Lanka.[9] Pragmatism ruled and the document itself explains that the Dutch Company dearly needed the slaves. Rules and regulations about slave trade and imports have always been misunderstood in the light of interrelated stakes at the Dutch factories. In 1685 the company prohibited the import of slaves from Malabar and Tuticorin only by the private citizens. The reason was that the Dutch Company itself was the main slave trader.[10] An order was passed on 6 December 1685 by the Dutch forbidding those on board the Company ships and private sailing vessels to carry the slaves of the nayak kingdom of Madurai from the port of Tuticorin as the ruler was against slave trade.[11] After three years (in 1688) the ban was lifted and slaves were exported from the port of Tuticorin and Manapaadu. Trade in humans continued in 1688, 1689 and 1690.[12]

The Dutch in Colombo received slaves from Tuticorin and had 1,520 in 1688. Later the number increased to 1,787 by 1694. Incoming workers and slaves reached illegally in ships through private slave traders to Colombo were detected in 1692. They were confiscated and put to work at fortifications in Colombo.[13] The Dutch Company had allowed the export of 3,859 slaves by the private merchants from the Tamil Coast to Sri Lanka during 1694-6. In 1695 3,500 slaves were imported to Jaffna and the traders paid the import duties. Hendrick Zwaardecroon the commander of Jaffnapatnam noted that import of more people means more mouths to be fed, while rice was dear rather than labour at the time. He explicitly stated that he would have preferred if traders had brought in rice rather than humans.[14] Thus the relationship between rice and slave market is also an interesting line of enquiry.

The Dutch continued to transport slaves to Colombo and had 1,741 in 1697 and 1,582 slaves in 1704.[15] The slaves who reached were employed at Galle, Jaffna, Trincomalee and Negombo to meet the labour needs of the Dutch Company. However, the company could not compete with the Dutch private traders in purchasing and transporting slaves from Tuticorin.[16] The nayak ruler of Tamil country often opposed slave trade but famines, warfare and crop failure in 1707 had very favourably responded to export of slaves.[17]

THE TRANSPORT OF SLAVES FROM TUTICORIN TO CAPE TOWN IN SOUTH AFRICA AND TO THE NETHERLANDS, 1694-1734

It had become a custom by the Dutch Company higher officials while returning to The Netherlands to take with them their slaves for their personal assistance. Therefore it was ordered that these slaves brought to The Netherlands should be sent back to their respective countries. In 1644 the Dutch Council in Jakarta mentioned that on the orders of the Directors of the Dutch East India Company in Amsterdam, it stated that the Dutch had not been allowed to transport slaves from India to The Netherlands. Slaves if transported would be confiscated without any further judicial process.[18] In another ordinance in 1646, the prosecutor of the Court of Justice in Jakarta reminded that the transport of slaves to The Netherlands was punishable by a fine of 50 reals.[19] The ordinance of Jakarta in 1646 clearly mentioned that the superiors in The Netherlands were troubled with regard to the return of slaves to India. It was declared that slaves illegally transported from India would be given their freedom. In 1647, it was stipulated that the fine imposed on the transport of slaves had been fixed and increased to 100 reals. The Dutch Company officials complained that the return of slaves to India resulted in high costs. They noted that it was very important to prevent the slave trade to the Netherlands with effective means.[20] The high-ranking servants of the Dutch Company had continued to bring their slaves. In 1694, one finds two slaves called Polvist and Victoria had been transported from Tuticorin to Amsterdam by Jacob Pauw who was the owner. It is known that the slave owner had paid the transport cost and provisions for the voyage of these two slaves to the Netherlands.[21]

It is further reported that four men slaves and a woman slave from Tuticorin were carried in a ship that sailed to The Netherlands during 1695 and 1707. They were sold at Cape Town in South Africa when the ship halted. The profit made by the slave owner on his way back to The Netherlands was very high and attractive.[22]

The travel ban of slaves from India to Netherlands was just to make it more difficult to bring the slaves to The Netherlands. But these slaves came to be sold in the midway at Cape Town. Further in 1734, the regulations for the transport of slaves to The Netherlands bound voyages were sharpened, by limiting the number of slaves to four persons for every high employee of the Dutch East India Company. While this new practice was introduced one finds more slaves who were men, who were purchased and taken in a ship that sailed and on arrival at Cape Town the slaves were sold.

The slave owners received the money on their way to the voyage to The Netherlands.[23]

THE GROWTH OF SLAVE TRADE OF THE DUTCH COMPANY FROM TUTICORIN TO SOUTH AFRICA AND SRI LANKA, 1730-1780

The Dutch in Tuticorin continued to trade in slaves and the company had received many slaves from the region of Cape Comorin (Kanyakumari). These slaves were exported to Colombo and Galle. Some of them were also exported to the Cape Town on ships sailing to The Netherlands. Dutch records mention that 103 slaves (respectively, 23, 24, 15, 21, 18 and 2) from the Tamil Coast were exported to Cape Town between the years 1701, 1703, 1712, 1718, 1736 and 1739.[24]

Otto Mentzel who lived in Cape Town in 1730s had given a reasonably fair description of the range of Tamil slaves. He stated that the slaves came from Tutegrin (Tuticorin). All these slaves spoke Tamil and belonged to various castes but lived in the Cape Town together without any discrimination.[25]

The Dutch settlement of Tuticorin became the most important centre of slave shipments to Sri Lanka. Slaves were transported in ships directly from here and, as a result slavery became a way of life in the Tamil-Dutch town, attracting greedy individuals interested in profiting from the commerce in human beings. The native slave agents and merchants were able to supply a substantial number of Tamil slaves from the hinterland of Tuticorin. The Dutch settlement also had a large permanent slave population. There was continuous interaction among different groups of people interested in exporting slaves. The Dutch were compelled to take the assistance of the local agents to obtain slaves because they neither knew the local language nor the places from where they could acquire slaves for export. There were already many dealers conversant with the purchase and sale of the slaves in the inland. Dutch Company officials and servants approached such brokers for supply, who extended active support and cooperation. Dutch Company records mention that slaves for export in the ports were easily available only during the famine years because the natives sold themselves or their children in bondage because of debt and to escape starvation, though the Dutch Company needed a supply of slaves annually. Many slave dealers emerged in Tuticorin owing to the busy trade and one of the famous and the most reputed agent was called Chidambaram. He was paid large sums of money as much as 1,300 pagodas in one year by the Dutch Company for his supply of slaves.[26]

Dutch privateers in Sri Lanka continued to purchase many slaves who were transported from Tuticorin in the eighteenth century. The company also had a large slave population but they were owned by it. Slave trade and slave ownership in Tuticorin and the letters to and from Tuticorin point out the illicit trade during 1742-3.[27] One finds two declarations concerning the ownership of Wouter Gilles Trek of two Tamil female slaves. It was drawn up by Arnoldus Lunel in Tuticorin with deeds of purchase of the slaves in 1775-6. The ownership of Pieter Lambert Trek, the bookkeeper of the Dutch company at Kanyakumari, a Tamil female slave is also found and it was drawn by Arnoldus Lunel in Tuticorin in 1776. The declaration of Pieter Lambert Trek concerning sale of a female slave and her son to Johan Henridk Smith was drawn in Tuticorin in 1776. The ownership of Johannes Martinus Fruins residing at Kanyakumari as a Tamil female slave was drawn by Arnoldus Lunel in Tuticorin in 1780. Thus in the Dutch records one finds plenty of deeds of sale and purchase of the slaves from Tutcorin.[28]

MANUMISSION OF TUTICORIN SLAVES IN COLOMBO, 1739-1791

Manumission of slaves by self purchase was not a civil right under the Dutch Company. However, purchase was a route to manumission of Tamil slaves of Tuticorin used by both Dutch

Company owned and privately owned slaves in Colombo. Numerous manumissions for exchange of a slave had been recorded. A deed in 1739 refers to the company-owned slaves Petchiammaal and Elammal who were manumitted in exchange for two other slaves called Pasqual and Coridon.[29] It should be noted that the enslaved women had provided male slaves to take their place. Kittuammal, another slave was manumitted through a deed dated 13 January 1751. She got manumitted because she supplied her master with Rosetta, another female slave given in bondage in exchange.[30] Kittuammal, Petchiammaal and Elammal the slaves were freed by exchange of slaves between 1739 and 1752.

Slaves paid money for manumission to their owners too. During 1750 and 1752 the amount had varied from small to large sums. Kandan and his two children Victoria and Domingo were freed in June 1750 after paying 225 *rix* dollars. The manumission of two other male slaves called Adriaan and Muthu Karuppan was paid and their freed status had cost 100 *rix* dollars each. Four slaves (two men and two women) were freed for 50 *rix* dollars each. Further, Maria and her six children were manumitted for a sum that averaged out to 36 *rix* dollars per person.[31] All the slave owners demanded the full replacement value of their slave considering that the administrative cost of manumitting a slave which was very high including payment to the church which was 10 *rix* dollars. It is likely that the sum received by slave owners was intended only to cover the administrative costs.

Philippus Matteus Trekels the slave owner of Achilles was paid an enormous sum of 250 *rix* dollars in 1779.[32] Adriana Elisabeth Luders received 30 *rix* dollars for the manumission of her slave called Cardoes in 1791.[33] Variation in price thus depended perhaps on a number of factors, including the slave's age, level of skill, and relationship with slave owner. The sum paid for manumission by purchase was surely set by the slave owner. A generous master could have been more open to the idea of a slave buying himself out of bondage and so he had set a very reasonable price.

Kasthuri and her daughter Thavasi the slaves were together manumitted for 138 *rix* dollars. One finds their freed status from Manuel Adam Fernando the slave owner on 20 February 1786.[34] Wilhelmina Elisabeth Schreuder manumitted her slave Deepa in March 1786. Deepa had paid the value of herself. The exact amount is not mentioned in the record.[35] No clear pattern emerges from some records regarding the differences in the value of male and female slaves.

It is interesting to observe the *bewijs* (emancipation deeds of slaves) that prove the fact that they preceded the owner's renunciation of rights over the slave. It thus leads to the conclusion that it was a legal necessity to prove the rightful ownership of a slave before being able to renounce those rights through manumission. To prove that the individual emancipating the slave was the legal owner, he had to present the details of which—the clerks' names, the date and place where the emancipation deeds had been signed—all that were then noted in the records. Geetha a Tamil slave was freed in 1751 when she presented Rosetta to become a slave in her place in Colombo. The deed points to the fact that Geetha was a privately owned slave. Another example of Dutch Company owned slaves being manumitted in exchange for others took place in March 1739.

In one record, one finds the deed signed at Negombo in Sri Lanka in 1696. But the slave was freed after 56 years, i.e. only in the year 1752. Eight deeds of emancipation of Tamil slaves included references to the certificates signed in Tuticorin. Johanna Obrack, the widow of Pieter de Moor, the *kapitein militair* (military captain) freed the male slave named Alexander in 1750. The certificate proved that Johanna Obrack was Alexander's legal owner and signed in Tuticorin in 1724. In this case he served as a slave for 26 years.[36] Three other slaves belonging to Michiel Symans who were freed in 1781 also had the certificates signed in Tuticorin in 1724. In this case the slaves had served for 57 years.[37] These evidences prove that the slaves were mainly children when picked up and transported from Tuticorin to Sri Lanka. Dutch records from 1774 to 1781 mention the ships that annually sailed from Tuticorin to Colombo and Galle carrying slaves and there was a large scale slave migration.[38]

The death of Tamil slaves from Tuticorin in Sri Lanka between 1771 and 1775 had been recorded. In Colombo, between March and August 1771 ten Company slaves died and seven of them were recorded as Tamils from Tuticorin.[39] The following year, between March and June a total of eight slaves died, and four of them had been transported from Tuticorin.[40] The list from December 1775 had been the longest, enumerating 19 deaths between March and August of that year.[41] The nine slaves named in the list were transported through Tuticorin. In four cases the slave was listed as the son or daughter of a transported slave.

SLAVERY IN TUTICORIN: THE DOMESTIC SLAVES AND THEIR PATHETIC LIVES, 1681-1746

Slaves were purchased at Tuticorin and the Portuguese artillery men on the west coast in Cochin had employed them in their houses. The dynamics of slave mobility and control had been noticed dealing with interactions that took place in a market. In early April 1681, Sangu the slave named Anthonij (Antony), of 14 years owned by Emmanuel Pereira, the taupas (artillery men) had walked through the bazaar located outside the city of Cochin. He was sent by his master to sell a number of goods.[42] While in the market, he was approached by Pedro, who had himself been a slave earlier but ran away several years ago. Pedro had asked Antony whether he wanted to go back to Kallikulam near Tuticorin his birthplace. Antony replied that he did not. Pedro persisted, by asking him time and again whether he wanted to go anywhere else. Antony replied that he was interested in going and visiting the city of Calicut. He further added that though he was interested he could not do so. Pedro agreed to bring a boat near the house of Emmanuel Pereira, his master, on the following Friday. Finally, on Sunday Pedro moored his boat near Emmanuel Pereira's house and Antony climbed aboard. Just as Pedro was about to sail away, Antony jumped back ashore and told Pedro that he had forgotten to take some of his belongings from the house. He went into the house but, much to Pedro's surprise (instead of the Antony returning), Pereira came running with weapons drawn, yelling 'thief'.[43] Two nearby taupas men heard Pereira's voice and they rushed to help while Pedro tried to sail quickly away. But the three jumped into a boat nearby and caught him up while Pedro drew his sword and shield but was quickly overwhelmed by the three pursuers. A quick blow hit his shield, another hit him on the arm, and the last blow made him throw his weapon overboard and surrender. This event happened because Pereira had told Antony sometime ago that if anyone ever tried to tempt him to run away, he should agree to go and immediately tell Pereira, in order to capture that person as a slave thief.[44] It is thus known that Antony the slave had a relatively high degree of mobility. Emmanuel Pereira his owner, trusted him and often sent him to the bazaar to engage in economic transactions.

Pedro Gomez the Christian Mukkuvar owned a tavern at Puththanthurai in 1746. He ran the business by employing his slave called Cruz who went early in the morning everyday to open the tavern and he remained there the whole day until its closure in the evening. Cruz was mainly responsible for the daily running of the tavern. On a Sunday evening, Paandi a native of Tuticorin aged 20 called Anthonij (Antony) came to the tavern. He noticed that Cruz the slave was sad. When he asked the reason, Cruz cried bitterly revealing that his master Pedro Gomez had informed that he would sell Cruz to the sailors.[45] Antony at that time had suggested that if Cruz came with him he would help him reach his native place. Cruz replied that he did not know his native place. He agreed to leave with Antony if he would really find where the place was.[46] Cruz who lived in a hut close to the house of his master

Pedro Gomez and his wife Dominga, left Puththanthurai along with Antony that night. Pedro Gomez the owner of the slave was taken aback next day when the doors and windows of the tavern were closed.[47] Pedro was informed at that time by some children from the neighbourhood that they had seen Cruz and Antony talking near the water tank the previous night. Pedro immediately realized that he had threatened his slave on Sunday that he would sell him to some sailors and this had probably prompted Cruz to run away.[48] According to records, Cruz was eventually found by Pedro Gomez's relatives near Travancore. They urged him to return to his owner, which Cruz also apparently did and narrated the details.[49]

EXPORT OF SLAVES CONTINUED FROM TUTICORIN TO SRI LANKA AS GLEANED FROM THE REGISTER OF SALES, 1755-1791

Slaves were purchased from Malabar and Canara by the Dutch Company in Cochin. The purchase and sale deeds were prepared and sailing permits were issued by the Dutch authorities for export from Tuticorin. This practice had continued from 1755 to 1791.

The slaves including men and women, were purchased mainly from different places including Purakkadu in Malabar and Vengurla in Canara. These sale and purchase deeds were drafted in Cochin by the Dutch officials. The mention of castes such as Nair, Izhlava, Paraiyar, etc., were noted down. Sometimes professions like lascar, smith, etc., were also mentioned. The age of the slaves had been noted with the minimum of 16 years and maximum of 22 years. After completing the sale formalities in Cochin within ten days, the certificates for transportation were prepared for transporting them to Tuticorin. The records of 1774 as found at the Tamil Nadu State Archives in Egmore, Chennai are badly damaged. There is a separate register containing sailing permits issued for slave transportation in thonies (boats) from Tuticorin to

TABLE 8.1: SLAVES TRANSPORTED FROM THE PORT OF TUTICORIN TO SRI LANKA, 1755-1791

Period	*Number of slaves*
25 January 1755–5 August 1756	53
1758	145
1759	181
1770	92
1771	189
1772	71
1 October 1773–31 December 1773	59
5 January 1774–5 June 1774	150
1 April 1775-27 June 1775	72
3 January 1776–30 April 1776	96
19 July 1777–16 December 1777	107
1784–1785	67
1786	88
12 February 1787–20 August 1787	99
1 September 1789–27 November 1789	114
1790–1791	127
TOTAL	1,710

Source: See Note.[50]

Colombo in Sri Lanka. However, it has been found that very bad and sad things had happened as gleaned from the Dutch records preserved in the National Archives in the Hague, the Netherlands. One finds during the acts of transport with the mention of the old name of the slave, new name of the slave given, caste, gender and the age. One finds Krishnan aged 19 was renamed September. Another slave Krishnan 20 years of age, was renamed Augustus (August). Sankarappan aged 16, was now called Meij (May). Another young man Sankarappan aged 20 was renamed Maart (March). Kittu the slave aged 19, was renamed Junij (June) and Kandan the slave aged 19 was renamed October. Thus the Dutch Company had completely erased the identity of slaves before transporting them from Tuticorin to Sri Lanka.[51]

MADHAN, THE TAMIL SLAVE AND HIS TRAVEL FROM TUTICORIN TO THE NETHERLANDS, 1739-1741

An individual labelled as 'slave', a young boy, is described as being of Tamil (Malabar) origin. He had been purchased on 1 June 1739 by Christian Dober an employee of the Dutch East India Company at Tuticorin.[52] The boy was at that time twelve years old.[53] He was abducted from his father which had been stated.[54] The village he originally hailed from is unknown. He was taken away from his father and sold off as a slave at the urban centre of Tuticorin. The village did not formally fall under the authority of the Dutch Company in Tuticorin. Hence the village chiefs could not ask the Dutch Company to return the slave boy, even if they came to know about the abduction. Thus abductions normally happened in villages lying outside the Dutch jurisdiction and the slaves were brought for sale to the port. The document certifying the sale gives his name as Maden (Madhan) of the Sanas (Shanar) caste.

Christian Dober kept the slave for domestic purposes for two years in Tuticorin. Later he sailed from Tuticorin to the Netherlands in 1741 and took Madhan the slave with him. Dober had renamed the slave boy Felix. The slave was under his custody in his house even in the Netherlands.

THE TRAVEL OF THE SLAVE FROM THE NETHERLANDS TO GERMANY, 1741

Christian Dober wanted to join the Moravian Church and live with the Moravian community in Germany. The Moravian missionary movement was founded by Count Zinzendorf, a Lutheran missionary in 1722 at Herrnhut (the Lord's Watch), near Dresden in Saxony. Zinzendorf offered a part of his estate as a refuge for a group of persecuted believers from Bohemia and Moravia. From these Brethren came the first organized Protestant mission. Zinzendorf became the leader of the Church of the United Brethren (Moravians) and he launched a mission in 1732 to convert the slaves in the Danish islands in the West Indies.

It is gleaned from the diary of David Nitschman a Moravian missionary in 1741 that Christian Dober had promised the young boy Madhan/Felix as a gift to the Moravian community.[55] It is unclear from the record whether the boy was brought with the intention of handing over to the Moravian Brethren when he joined the mission or he had actually gifted the slave boy to Zinzendorf.

THE CONVERSION AND BAPTISM OF THE SLAVE IN GERMANY, 1746

According to Dutch records Madhan/Felix was introduced to the Moravians in S'Heerendiek by Christian Dober after arriving in the Netherlands on 20 July 1742.[56] Christian Dober took the slave with him to Germany. The slave boy was baptized by Zinzendorf on 10 January 1746 in Marienborn. His baptismal name was Samuel Johannes. Johan Jacob Sutor another Moravian missionary had reported and confirmed the news that the slave boy of Christian Dober was baptized and called Samuel Johannes.[57]

Countess Erdmuthe Dorothea, the wife of missionary Zinzendorf had mentioned that Christian Dober had given the slave boy to her immediately after arrival in Marienborn. Christian Dober who got admitted into the Moravian missionary community did so to enhance his reputation with the church leaders. Countess Zinzendorf kept the boy in her house and took care of him. When her husband left for British North America to expand his missionary work she sent him to an orphanage.[58]

THE SLAVE AND HIS STUDIES IN THE SEMINARY AT BARBY, 1746-1753

Countess Zinzendorf sent the slave boy to children's home in Marienborn.[59] Samuel Johannes was formally admitted into the Moravian community in 1746. According to archival records he received training as a tailor and later attended the seminary in Barby (Salzlandkreis district).[60]

SAMUEL JOHANNES AT HERRNHUT: THE RUNAWAY SLAVE, MARCH 1754

Samuel Johannes was ordered suddenly in March 1754 to come to the town of Herrnhut (Gorlitz district). The reason behind this had been traced. The authorities in the seminary had found growing dissatisfaction with the conduct of the young boy.[61] Samuel Johannes was therefore placed in the service of Baron von Schell in Herrnhut on 13 March 1754. The slave boy fled from there after staying fourteen days. Hence a report of absconding was filed. The Berthelsdorf seigniorial court when approached immediately ordered his apprehension on 27 March 1754.[62]

On the first leg of his flight, Samuel Johannes found refuge on the nearby estate Unwürde of Chamberlain Karl Gotthelf von Hund and Altengrotkau, an active freemason. The Moravian search parties learnt about the place of stay of the slave and they asked the slave to be handed over. Karl Gotthelf von Hund at that time refused to hand over the slave. Countess Zinzendorf sent a letter to Karl Gotthelf von Hund on hearing the news and requested the slave to be returned to her.[63]

This letter contains many interesting details. One finds the concepts of societal hierarchy and servitude in condensed form. Its terminology hints uncertainty regarding the legal status of Madhan/Felix/Samuel Johannes. The Countess and the Berthelsdorf seigniorial court confirmed and noted that the absconded slave was not a free person. In the very first sentence of the letter one finds mention about the slave's origin. It designated him as a runaway black Malabar. It further added that the slave was a born slave who had been gifted to the Countess. The letter attempts to assert the fundamental right of her claim of dependence and servitude of the slave.

The letter also affirmed how Christian Dober consigned the boy to Countess Zinzendorf's care and free disposition. It also proceeds to justify her authority over the runaway black Malabar through the obligations she assumed as a Christian and patron. This is further emphasized by detailing the amount of money she had spent on the slave, on the Christian baptism, education and training of the wild slave. In short, it stated that she had done everything as master, parent, and guardian could do for a serf and ward.

The position of the Countess and the runaway had been construed on two separate levels, one as mistress and slave/serf with an obligation of obedience and deference. Again it has been said that that the relationship was that of guardian and ward expecting an obligation of loyalty and gratitude. Therefore, the Countess expressed the sole right besides God to claim possession and usage of Samuel Johannes. The slave on the other hand, was not a free man since he was a true born serf to the Countess and as such was bound to remain in subservience until he received a letter of release.[64]

THE SURRENDER AND ARREST OF SAMUEL JOHANNES AT BARBY, MAY 1754

After remaining hidden for two months, on the estates of Chamberlain von Hund, Samuel Johannes made his way to Barby in April 1754 and he surrendered himself. An order to keep him under arrest was issued on 4 May 1754 on behalf of Countess Zinzendorf to the court at Barby.[65] One finds that Samuel Johannes was eventually transported from Barby to Herrnhut based on legal provisions.[66]

SAMUEL JOHANNES TRANSPORTED FROM GERMANY TO PENNSYLVANIA IN BRITISH NORTH AMERICA AND HIS DEATH, 1754-1763

Within a few months Samuel Johannes was transported in a ship to the town of Bethlehem in Pennsylvania. He was found again with the Moravians. Several enslaved Africans were employed at that time in Bethlehem. There is no information as to whether he was considered a slave or not. By crossing the Atlantic, he had entered a colonial slaving zone where slavery was widespread and obvious. Samuel Johannes was not designated a slave in the Bethlehem records. Also he was not labelled a Negro the term used to refer to slaves in the colonies. Instead, he is repeatedly referenced as a Malabar.[67]

It is found that Samuel Johannes married Magdalena Mingo, a free woman of African creole and Danish ancestry who had lived in Marienborn and Herrnhut for several years. The marriage took place at the church in a Holy Mass. This ceremony was held along with thirteen other married couples who were all Europeans.[68] Samuel Johannes spent nine years till the remainder of his life. He passed away on 24 May 1763.[69]

The case of Madhan/Felix/Samuel Johannes is especially striking because he was sold by slave owners ending up in Pennsylvania. The name had changed when was sold from one person to another, creating a new identity in the minds of his owners. One finds slavery changing from a dormant state into an actively invoked claim of legal proprietorship, thereby fraying into several categories and partly overlapping categories of dependency. The story of the slave reports say how Moravian missionaries in Europe and in North America had appreciated an opportunity to make slaves become Christians with evangelistic fervour. One also finds that individuals and Moravian community in Germany had slaves with rights of propriety. Community members claimed authority over Samuel Johannes going beyond church discipline, domestic servitude, or serfdom. In sum, slavery had been one of the major undercurrents integrating the histories of the world from the port of Tuticorin on the Tamil Coast to Europe and America. It highlighted the local contexts of the systems of bondage, as well as the long-distance connections forged by the commercialized circuits of slavery and slave trade carried out widely by both the non-Europeans and Europeans.

It may be said that the slaves were transported overseas by the Dutch Company and the trade continued and flourished during famines, droughts and failure of crops. Many of them were very poor and had no means for livelihood except selling themselves voluntarily. There were many native agents, dealers and brokers who helped the Dutch in the procurement and sale of slaves. The labour scarcity in the various Dutch settlements like Jakarta, Colombo, Galle and Cape Town was the main reason for the thriving slave transportation from the port of Tuticorin.

NOTES

1. Nationaal Archief (hereafter NA), Den Haag, VOC 1233, fls. 157-68.
2. NA, VOC 1234, fls. 25r-v; Sri Lanka National Archives (hereafter SLNA), 2712, Colombo Diary, fl. 57.
3. W. Ph. Coolhas, ed., *Generale Missiven van de Gouverneurs-Generaal en Raden Aan Heren XII der Verenigde Ossitindische Compagnie*, 9 vols., S' Gravenhage, 1960-84 (hereafter *GM*), vol. III, p. 793 (31 January 1672).
4. SLNA, 1/20, Minutes of the Governor and Council in Colombo, fl. 27v-28 (29 October 1674), fls.35r-36 (3-26 November 1674).
5. SLNA, 1/20, Minutes of the Governor and Council in Colombo, fl. 27v-28, fls.35v-36.
6. L. Hovy, *Ceylonees Plakkaatboek: Plakkaten en Andere Wetten Uitgevaardigd door het Nederlandse Bestuur op Ceylon*, 1638-1796, 2 vols., Hilversum, Verloren, 1991, vol. I, pp. 129, 196-7.
7. SLNA, 1/24, Minutes of the Governor and Council in Colombo, fl. 61v-62; *GM*, vol. IV, pp. 294, 354.
8. NA, VOC 1396, fl.66v (4 July 1684).
9. L. Hovy, Ceylonees Plakkaatboek, vol. 1, p. 227, Plakkaat 163.
10. Ibid., pp. 1227-8 (6 December 1685)
11. Ibid., pp. 117-8.
12. NA, VOC 1479, fls. 611r-627v.
13. NA, VOC 1506, fls. 1604-5 (31 May 1692).
14. Sophia Pieters, trs., *Memoir of Hendrick Zwaardecroon, Commandeur of Jaffnapatam, 1697*, Colombo, 1911.
15. Knaap Gerrit, 'Europeans, Mestizos and Slaves: The Population of Colombo at the end of the Seventeenth Century', trans. Robert Ross, *Itinerario*, vol. V, 1981, pp. 84-101, see p. 96.

16. Markus Vink, 'The World's Oldest Trade: Dutch Slavery and Slave Trade in the Indian Ocean in the Seventeenth Century', *Journal of World History*, vol. 14, no. 2, June 2003, pp. 131-46, see pp. 142-3.
17. *GM*, vol. VI, p. 496 (30 November 1707).
18. J.A. Van der Chijs, *Nederlandsch-Indisch Plakaatboek*, 17 vols., Batavia/ S'Gravenhage, 1885-1900, vol. II, p. 88.
19. Ibid., pp. 109-110.
20. Ibid., p. 118.
21. Nationaal Archief, The Netherlands, The Hague (hereafter NL–HaNa), Archief van de VOC, 1540, fls. 363-64.
22. Nigel Worden, 'Indian Ocean Slaves in Cape Town, 1695-1805', *Journal of South African Studies*, 42(3), 2016, pp. 389-408, see p. 406.
23. Nigel Worden, Indian Ocean Slaves, p. 406.
24. NA, VOC 1628, VOC 1630, VOC 1641, VOC 1651, VOC 1653, VOC 2419, VOC 2360, VOC 3843, VOC 7534 and VOC 7538.
25. O. Mentzel, *A Complete and Authentic Geographical and Topographical Description of the Famous and (All Things Considered) Remarkable African Cape of Good Hope*, Cape Town, Van Riebeeck Society, 1925, vol. II, p. 125.
26. P.M. Markus Vink, 'The World's Oldest Trade: Dutch Slavery and Slave Trade in the Indian Ocean in the Seventeenth Century', *Journal of World History*, vol. 14, no. 2, June 2003, pp. 131-77, see, p. 146.
27. Tamil Nadu State Archives (hereafter TNSA), Chennai, Cochin Records, no. 352.
28. Lennart Bes, *Plaatsingslijst van de Collectie van de familie prins–1656-Zost eeuw*, 2003, vol. II, p. 466, see document no. 50, 51, 52, 53.
29. SLNA, *Protocols of Deeds of Emancipation of Slaves*, 1/4145, VOC, fls.18r-19r (16 March 1739).
30. SLNA, 1/4145, fls. 337v-338r (13 January 1751).
31. SLNA, 1/4146, unpaginated.
32. SLNA, 1/4146 (5 September 1779).
33. SLNA, 1/4146 (5 January 1791).
34. SLNA, 1/4146 (20 February 1786).
35. SLNA, 1/4146 (22 March 1786).
36. SLNA, 1/4145, 1738-52, fls. 332r–v (31 August 1750).
37. SLNA, 1/4146, 1770-95 (24 October 1781), (24 October 1781), (9 December 1786), (9 September 1787).
38. NA, VOC 3402, fls. 516-20 (1774); VOC 3432 fls. 547-51 (1775); VOC 3457, fls. 463-4 (1776); VOC 3485, fls. 528-31 (1777); VOC 3516, fls. 523-7 (1778); VOC 3572, fls. 505-10 (1779-81).

39. NA, VOC 3324, Resoluties, 11 October 1771.
40. NA, VOC 3350, Resoluties, 15 September 1772.
41. NA, VOC 3433, Resoluties, 29 December 1775.
42. NL–HaNa, Nederlandse bezittingen India: Digitale duplicaten Chennai, 1.11.06.11, 66, Scan 75, Case ID Database CR-66-11.
43. NL–HaNa, 1.11.06.11, 66, Scan 67, Case ID Database CR-66-11.
44. NL–HaNa, 1.11.06.11, 66, Scan 75, Case ID Database CR-66-11.
45. NL–HaNa, 1.11.06.11, inv. no. 440, ff.1–39, Case ID Database CR-440-6; NL-HaNa, 1.11.06.11, 440, fl. 21; NL-HaNa, 1.11.06.11, 440, fl. 37.
46. NL–HaNa, 1.11.06.11, 440, fl. 20.
47. NL–HaNa, 1.11.06.11, 440, fl. 20; 31-2.
48. NL–HaNa, 1.11.06.11, 440, fl. 32.
49. NL–HaNa, 1.11.06.11, 440, fl. 33; S. Jeyaseela Stephen, *Tuticorin and its Trade with Asia, Africa and Europe, 1570-1880: Colonial Transformation, Human Migration and Interrelations*, Puducherry, 2022, pp. 134-5.
50. TNSA, *Cochin Records*, no. 584, sale and transfer of slaves from 25 January 1755 to 5 August 1756; no. 622, sale and transfer of slaves in 1758; no. 632, sale and transfer of slaves in 1759; no. 886, sale and transfer of slaves in 1770; no. 896, sale and transfer of slaves in 1770-1; no. 925, sale and transfer of slaves in 1772; no. 957, sale and transfer of slaves, from 1 October to 31 December 1773; no. 979, sale and transfer of slaves from 5 January 1774 to 5 June 1774; no. 1003, sale and transfer of slaves from 1 April 1775 to 27 June 1775; no. 1034, sale and transfer of slaves from 3 January 1776 to 30 April 1776; no. 1062, deeds of sale and transfer of slaves from 19 July 1777 to 16 December 1777; no. 1145, permits to export slaves from 18 February 1780 to 29 December 1787; no. 1225, sale and transfer of slaves in 1784 and 1785; no. 1266, sale and transfer of slaves in 1786; no. 1288, sale and transfer of slaves from 12 February to 20 August 1787; no. 1341, sale and transfer of slaves from 1 September 1789 to 27 November 1789; no. 1369, deeds of sale and transfer of slaves in 1790-1.
51. NA, *Akten van Transport*, VOC, 1.11.06.11, Inventory number 1062.
52. Unitats Archive (hereafter UA), Herrnhut, R.21.A.28.47, See the certificate of sale of the slave boy Maden to Christian Dober, 1 June 1739.
53. Moravian Archives, Bethlehem (hereafter MAB), Pennsylvania, USA, Diary of the Bethlehem congregation, vol. XXVI, 1763-4, pp. 93-5.

54. Alexander Volck, *Das entdeckte Geheimniss der Bosheit der Herrnhutischen Secte zu Errettung vieler unschuldigen Seelen, in sechs Gesprächen dargelegt*, Frankfurt, Heinrich Ludwig Brönner, 1750, p. 561.
55. UA, R.15.S.2, Diary of David Nitschmann's (the Syndic) and August Christian Friedrich Ellert's journey to Ceylon, vol. II, 17 August 1740- 24 November 1741.
56. NA, VOC, 6035, fol. 31.
57. Paul Peucker, 'Aus allen Nationen: Nichteuropäer in den deutschen Brüdergemeinden des 18. Jahrhunderts', *Unitas Fratrum*, vol. 59/ 60, 2007, pp. 1-35, see p. 33.
58. UA, R.6.a.A.74.4, Erdmuthe Dorothea von Zinzendorf to Chamberlain von Hund at Unwürde, 27 March 1754.
59. UA, R.8.33.b.3, The Diary of Wetterau, 2 August 1742; UA, R.4.B.V.b.3.8., Catalog Lindheim, 1744.
60. UA, R.27.291.13, The Register of Seminarians, Barby, 1750.
61. Paul Peucker, 'Aus allen Nationen', p. 21.
62. UA, R.6.a.A.74.4, The requisition for the apprehension of a Black Malabar named Samuel Johannes, 27 March 1754.
63. UA, R.6.a.A.74.4, Erdmuthe Dorothea von Zinzendorf to Chamberlain von Hund at Unwürde, 27 March 1754.
64. Ibid.
65. UA, R.6.a.A.74, Order by Siegmund August von Gersdorf on behalf of Countess Zinzendorf, Herrnhut, 4 May 1754.
66. UA, R.6.a.A.74, Pro nota regarding the extradition request from 11 May 1754; UA, R.6.a. A. 74, Passport by the bailiff of Barby, 18 May 1754.
67. MAB, Diary of the Bethlehem congregation, vol. XXVI, fl. 93.
68. MAB, Diary of the Bethlehem congregation, vol. XVII, 20 April 1757, fls. 99-01.
69. MAB, Diary of the Bethlehem congregation, vol. XXVI, fls. 93-5; MAB, ChReg 11, Bethlehem church register, 24 May 1763.

CHAPTER 9

The English Company Export of Slaves from Madras to St. Helena Colony in South Atlantic (1654-1712) and from Madras to Bengkulu in Sumatra (1682-1748)

The English settled in Chennapattinam (Madras) in 1639. The company officials noticed the active trade conducted by the Portuguese and the Dutch on the Tamil Coast and so they desired to participate in it. But the slave dealers in Madras like Kannappa had acted as an important broker of slaves for the Dutch East India Company in Pulicat.[1] Hence in the absence of native brokers it was found difficult to obtain slaves.

THE ENGLISH COMPANY EXPORT OF SLAVES FROM MADRAS TO ST. HELENA ISLAND FOR SUGAR PLANTATIONS IN SOUTH ATLANTIC, 1654-1712

St. Helena Island located in the South Atlantic had been a key port of call for European vessels making the arduous return journey from Asia because it was one of the few places where they could replenish their supplies of food and water safely. Due to the strategic importance of the island, the English Company occupied St. Helena and established an English colony there. As the island had no permanent inhabitants, maintaining a permanent settlement on this island had become a financial burden for the English Company. Therefore the English Company began experimenting with methods of colonial development as done in the English colonies of the

Atlantic world. The company struggled to attract voluntary migrants from England. The people were attracted largely towards the destinations in North America and the Caribbean.[2]

The early colonization of St. Helena by the English Company in Madras had begun in 1654. An enslaved women's involvement in medicine had been reported from Madras in 1654. A black Hindu woman from Santhome of Mylapore was brought in to St. Helena to perform an abortion of one of the English factor's wives.[3] Further the company also dispatched a party to settle at St. Helena from England in December 1658.

It is recorded that a Tamil male was forcefully brought from Fort St. George Madras to St. Helena December 1676 and finds mention. It is said that if his complaint reached the king of England, there could be problems to the English factor at Fort St. George.[4] Slaves were purchased in Madras in 1679-80 and these child slaves were employed for domestic purposes.[5]

Some of the slaves were converted in Madras and this posed problems and difficulties. In 1678 Padre Antonio Luis of Santhome of Mylapore administered baptism to a slave who belonged to Nunes Valentine who was then living in the English settlement of Madras. The missionary was asked to leave the place at the earliest and the slave boy was confined for 18 days by the English Governor and council of Madras.[6] Slave deeds in Madras were executed in Portuguese language. The scribe who wrote the sale deed in 1678 was paid two *panams* for each transaction.[7]

The directors of the English Company in London wrote in early August 1683 to their English factor in Fort St. George in Madras asking to explain why they had no thoughts of making a large sugar plantation with mills and sugar houses at St. Helena for the Company, and also a large great indigo plantation. Hence they were asked to explain the details.[8] It was believed by the English Company at that time that there would be a good market for sugar in southern Persia (Iran) and also for indigo to be produced on St. Helena.[9]

Between June 1683 and April 1684 the English Company directors instructed its overseas employees to supply planters on St. Helena with useful seeds and plants of India, horses and tools from England, bricks from southern Persia, hard wood from Bengal for use as rollers in the sugar mills, oxen from India to drive the mills and broad beans to feed the growing enslaved population.[10] The English Company directors again wrote in February 1684 to officials in Madras and said that they preferred the enslaved workers who were able to speak either English or Portuguese to be transported from Madras, the lingua franca of Madras to enable them to communicate with planters and overseers and better impart their knowledge and skills.[11]

The company directors were of the opinion that the soil of St. Helena was fit for the production of commodities of a richer nature like potatoes and yams for the company use than cattle. They ordered ten black native slaves above sixteen years old to be sent on every ship sailing from Fort St. George in Madras to St. Helena.[12] It was planned that the slaves brought were to be sold on credit to the poor planters of the island. This was to enable them to communicate with planters and overseers and better impart their knowledge and skills.[13]

The servants of the English East India Company in Madras were not willing to transport slaves owing to the existence of a ban on slave exports by the native rulers. The status quo had been maintained and it continued till 1682. However, export of slaves from Madras was sanctioned in 1683 by the English Governor and Council in Fort St. George when political conditions changed since Aurangzeb the Mughal ruler extended his rule in the region. Further one notices the discussion that had been made about the benefits of bringing the slaves to the island.[14]

A report of 1683 mentions the great number of slaves exported from Madras.[15] On 21 June 1686 one finds that 100 slaves were exported from Madras to St. Helena.[16] In September 1687 one finds that 665 slaves registered for export from Madras. An export duty of one *pagoda* on each slave was levied at that time.[17]

In 1687 the English Company directors dispatched to the authorities in Fort St. George, a 30-year old book containing

Dutch methods of commerce and governance in the East.[18] It was stolen and seized from a Dutch ship. The manual contained instructions in the Dutch design regarding new commercial and diplomatic strategies in order to push and enter the markets in the East. This was to be followed in response to English strategies with revisions in their own policies. The officials in Fort St. George acknowledged this since it helped to reformulate their policies and politics.[19]

The Directors in London sent an order in 1688 to transport slaves from Madras to St. Helena. This was made with a view to sell slaves to the free inhabitants so that plantation works could be executed.[20] Slaves from Madras and slaves received from Africa were employed in the farms in St. Helena. In one instance it is reported that an African (coffree) slave had escaped after having murdered a Tamil slave hailing from Madras. It is mentioned that the murder took place after a conflict over sticks of stolen sugar cane. The African slave could not be arrested because he had continued to live somewhere nearby, without returning to the enclosure of the African slaves. It is also said that at night he was fed secretly by the African community.[21]

The English Company records mention in 1709 that a plain near Sandy Bay on the south coast of St. Helena was fit for plantation development.[22] Tamil slaves employed in St. Helena were of good conduct and so it is mentioned that many slaves of Madras in 1712 were freed by some of their owners at their will. Further, by this time, slaves could not be obtained for export from Madras to St. Helena.[23]

THE ENGLISH COMPANY SLAVE TRADE FROM MADRAS TO BENGKULU ON THE WEST COAST OF SUMATRA FOR SHIPYARD WORKS, 1682-1748

The English East India Company established a factory at Bengkulu (Bencoolen/Benkulen) on Sumatra's west coast as part of its plan to secure supplies of pepper. The settlement was initially known as York Fort and subsequently called Fort

Marlborough. The Dutch Company factory at Priaman began to monopolize the pepper trade and this prompted the English Company directors to decide in August 1687 to concentrate their Sumatran operations at Bengkulu.

In the beginning the directors authorized the officials at St. Helena to supply slaves to Bengkulu if they had any extra ones. It is found in a record that 30 slaves had already been sent from Madras. It is also mentioned that the English had endured suffering during the voyage from Madras to Sumatra.[24] This evidence suggests that the English Company in Madras evinced interest and so it shipped slaves to satisfy the demand for labour in Sumatra.

In 1682, slave traders in Madras brought children who were stolen from the villages around in large numbers. As the female children had constituted the majority of slaves for export, the English Company decided not to export child slaves to Bengkulu.[25] According to orders issued, the English settlement of Bengkulu was subordinated to Madras in 1685. Slaves of the English Company in Madras were involved in the construction, repair, and loading of ships in Madras. The company directors in London had instructed the officials at Fort St. George in 1685 to train their slaves in carpentry in preparation to establish a large shipyard.[26] The English continued to purchase slaves as on 21 June 1686 during the time of famine.[27]

On 11 October 1686 200 slaves were exported from Madras to Acch and Kcdah.[28] Dampicr had noted that a new type of paddy cultivation had been introduced into Aceh. Hence the slaves brought from the Coromandel Coast by English traders were employed in the fields.[29]

On 8 September 1687 100 slaves were exported from Madras to Bengkulu. These slaves were obtained at a profit during a famine in the region when slaves were being sold by family members.[30] These slaves were intended to serve as soldiers in Sumatra.[31] The English Company records in September 1687 mention the export of 665 slaves in the ships that sailed from Madras to Bengkulu.[32] Slaves from Madras were sent again in a ship along with seven more coffree (African) soldiers who reached Madras in November 1693. Slaves purchased were sent in March 1694 and in January 1696 to Bengkulu.[33]

The living conditions of the Madras slaves in Bengkulu had been noticed in records. A report in 1709 stated that the slaves were very poorly clothed because varieties of cloth suitable for slaves had not reached from Madras. This prompted the English Company officials to purchase locally produced variety of ordinary ginghams as a temporary solution to sort out the problem.[34] Company officials brought slaves individually and in 1712, one finds mention of a Tamil male named January who was 25 years old, sold for $50.[35]

The local English Company officials emphasized in 1713 that both the African and Indian slaves from Madras were to be viewed like men and women and not slaves. But the directors in London pressed their company employees in Sumatra and said that their labourers were men and women though slaves. Hence they asked them to be used humanely according to their circumstances and not to be treated badly and worse than brutes.[36]

Slaves from Madras were exported to Bengkulu. One finds 60 slaves reached in 1713. Again in 1730 one finds 12 slaves shipped. Later in 1742 one finds transportation of 18 slaves and 12 slaves in 1748. The slave supplies were found inadequate in Sumatra owing to heavy demand for work at the dock. Hence in 1731 the English in Bengkulu secured the services of people including a boatman named Andrew from Madras sold for $60.[37] The lack of supply of cloth from Madras for slaves had posed serious problems. It continued, time and again reported in 1711, 1715, 1726 and 1727.[38] The much needed supplies did not arrive from Madras in 1746 which led to a reduction in slaves' monthly rice allowance.[39]

Crimes committed by slaves came to be reported. In 1735, a slave woman named Hannah was found guilty of poisoning the armourer of the fort. Hence she was sentenced to be flogged 39 times each at three places on her body. She was kept in iron chains and later exiled to Madras in a ship.[40] The Madras slave escaped owing to ill-treatment had been recorded in Bengkulu. One finds that eight Madras slaves had escaped from the fort's hospital in 1737. However these fugitive slaves were later recovered.[41]

To conclude it may be said that the English East India Company exported slaves from its trading factory of Fort St. George, Madras to Bengkulu in Sumatra and these slaves were used there. The records reveal that the company drew slaves from a catchment area to satisfy the demand for labour in its far-flung commercial empire. The policies and practices regarding the treatment of company slaves illustrate the company's role in the development of increasingly interconnected forced labour trades during the period.

NOTES

1. B. Natarajan, 'Slave Trade in Madras', *The Madras Tercentenary Commemoration Volume*, Madras, 1939, p. 249.
2. Stephen Royle, *The Company's Island: St. Helena, Company Colonies and the Colonial Endeavour*, London, Bloomsbury, 2007, p. 44.
3. British Library (hereafter BL), London, India Office Records (hereafter IOR), G/19/1, fls. 16-17, 5 May 1655.
4. BL, IOR, E/3/88, fl.180, Letter from London to Fort St. George, 15 December 1676.
5. Records of Fort St. George, *Diary and Consultation Book, 1662-1746, 1749-57*, ed. C.M. Schmidt, J.J. Cotton, A.V. Venkatarama Ayyar, B.S. Baliga et al., 90 vols., Madras, 1910-53 (hereafter *DCB*), 1679-80, p. 164.
6. *DCB*, 1678, p. 136.
7. *DCB*, 1678, pp. 61-2.
8. BL, IOR, E/3/90, fl. 95, London to St. Helena, 1 August 1683.
9. BL, IOR, E/3/90, fl. 175, London to St. Helena, 1 April 1684.
10. BL, IOR, E/3/90, fl. 83, London to Fort St. George, 13 June 1683; E/3/90, fls. 95-6, London to St. Helena, 1 August 1683; E/3/90, fl. 159, London to Bengal, 5 March 1683/84; E/3/90, fl. 174, 178-9, London to St. Helena, 5 April 1684; IOR B/37, fl. 148, 225.

11. BL, IOR, E/3/ 90, fl. 154, London to Fort St. George, 29 February 1684; E/3/90, fl. 159, London to Bengal, 5 March 1684.
12. BL, IOR, E/3/90, fl. 83, London to Fort St. George, 13 June 1683; E/3/90, fl. 91, London to St. Helena, 1 August 1683.
13. BL, IOR, E/3/90, fl. 154, London to Fort St. George, 29 February 1684.
14. BL, IOR, E/3/90, fl. 83, London to Fort St. George, 13 June 1683.
15. Basanta Kumar Basu, 'Notes on Slave Trade and Slavery in India during the Early Days of John Company', *Muslim Review*, Calcutta, vol. 4, 1930, p. 22.
16. BL, IOR, G/19/4, fl. 33.
17. Henry Davison Love, *Vestiges of Old Madras, 1640-1800*, 4 vols., London, 1913, vol. I, pp. 545-6.
18. BL, IOR, E/3/91, fl. 213r, London to Fort St. George, 28 September 1687.
19. Ibid.
20. Records of FSG, *Public Consultations, 1672-1750*, 36 vols., Madras, 1910-38, see 15 February 1688, p. 30.
21. BL, IOR, G/35/4 (not foliated), 20 October 1699.
22. BL, St. Helena Consultation, 26 July 1709.
23. BL, Collet MS D. 1153/2, fl. 44, Letter to Nathaniel Hodges dated 2 November 1712. See also, H. Yule, ed., *Diary of William Hedges*, London, 1887-9, p. cccliv.
24. BL, IOR, E/3/91, p. 378.
25. *DCB*, 1682, p. 70.
26. BL, IOR, E/3/91, fl. 35, Letter from London to Fort St. George, 16 March 1685.
27. BL, IOR, G/19/4, fl. 33, Letter dated 21 June 1686.
28. BL, G/19/4, fl. 68.
29. William Dampier, *A New Voyage Around the World*, London, 1695, p. 107.
30. BL, IOR, G/35/2, fls. 74-85v, Letter of Elihu Yale and Council at Fort St. George to Benjamin Bloome at Bencoulen, 8 November 1687.
31. Ibid.
32. *DCB*, 1687, p. 63.
33. *Letters to Fort St George*, 45 vols., Madras, 1916-32, vol. 5, 107-22 and 127-8, Letter from Bencoulen to Madras, 2 November 1693; See also, BL, IOR, G/35/3, fl. 216, 18 January 1696; H. Yule,

ed., *Diary of William Hedges*, London, 1887-9, vol. II, p. ccclvi, 6 March 1694.

34. BL, IOR, G/35/56, *Fort Marlborough Consultation* (hereafter *FMC*), 19 November 1709.
35. BL, IOR, G/35/57, *York Fort Consultation* (hereafter *YFC*), 22 May 1712.
36. BL, IOR, E/3/87, fl. 208, Letter from London to Bantam, 18 January 1670/71; BL, IOR, E/3/98, fl. 14, Letter from London to Bencoolen, 20 March 1712/13.
37. BL, IOR, G/35/61, *FMC*, 29 September 1731.
38. BL, IOR, G/35/57, *YFC*, 3 July 1711, 27 June 1715; BL, IOR, G/35/59, *FMC*, 20 August 1726; G/35/60, *FMC*, 3 May 1727.
39. BL, IOR, G/35/64, p. 312.
40. BL, IOR, G/35/61, *FMC*, 21 April 1735, 28 April 1735.
41. BL, IOR, G/35/60, *FMC*, 24 October 1727; G/35/62, 1738 section, p. 118, and 1739 section, p. 15; G/35/75, p. 132.

CHAPTER 10

Slavery and the Seascapes of Danish Slave Trade from Tranquebar to Kedah, Aceh, Colombo, Cape Town, Mauritius and Denmark, 1632-1790

In 1618 the Danish East India Company sent its first expedition and the Danes reached Tranquebar on the Coromandel Coast in 1620. After obtaining permission from Raghunatha Nayak (1600-34) the ruler of Thanjavur, a trading settlement was established in 1624.[1] It served as the headquarters for Danish trade in Asia.

Jon Olafsson the Danish traveller came to Tranquebar and he stayed there during 1624-5. He had mentioned that he had a Hindu servant boy who was 15 years old. The Portuguese missionaries in the Danish settlement had baptized him and the boy embraced Christianity. It is unclear whether the boy was a domestic slave or not. Olafsson said that the Catholic missionaries had the habit of baptizing many individuals like this. They had also purchased children from their parents and brought them close to God.[2]

The Danes in Tranquebar faced difficulties for conducting their overseas trade because of the participation of Denmark in the Thirty Years War in Europe. It led to the decline of shipping and commerce between Copenhagen and Tranquebar and so the Danes conducted trade from the port of Masulipatnam on the Telugu Coast in 1625.[3] There had been no commercial traffic between Copenhagen and Tranquebar between 1639 and 1668.[4] The Danes searched for prospects of commerce within Asian ports and began to trade with Banten in Java from Tranquebar between 1645 and 1662.

THE BEGINNINGS OF THE DANISH SLAVE TRADE IN TRANQUEBAR, 1632

Danish records mention the distinction between white men and slavery. They also differentiate between Negro slaves and the Tamil slaves in Tranquebar. Mads Rasmussen in his diary mentioned on 17 March 1632 that the Danes could get 200 Tamil slaves at Tranquebar and they were sent in the sailing vessels of Tranquebar which paid customs duty at the port. The Danes purchased slaves who were available and used them for domestic work. Some of the families who were made captives during the wars were also sold. Thus, various social conditions that prevailed permitted them to enter into slavery.[5] Brendt Pessart, the Danish Governor of Tranqubar (1636-44) had purchased slaves for domestic use.[6]

Some Portuguese traders came from Nagapattinam and settled in the Danish settlement. Joao Pinto the Portuguese renegade, became a resident of Tranquebar and came forward to offer help to the Danish company as a sailor by flying the Danish flag in the ships.[7] It had been reported in May 1639 that he extended the offer to ships for sailing to Melaka. Andrew Cogan, the English scribe in Madras reported this matter to the Agents and Council of Masulipatnam. He wondered that how this offer was taken seriously into consideration by the Portuguese Viceroy in Goa and also as to the conditions laid out in this scheme which remained secret and largely unknown.[8]

It is found in Spanish records that in Tranquebar the Danes had sent a ship that reached the Philippines. The permission to anchor the Danish ship called *Buena Esperanza* in Manila had created a furore. The issue was raised in 1645. Two royal decrees were issued in this connection to the port officials in Manila. It condemned the decision of the Spanish colonial authorities.[9]

THE PRIVATE TRADERS IN TRANQUEBAR AND THE GROWTH OF SLAVE TRADE OF THE DANISH COMPANY WITH THE PORT OF KEDAH AND ACEH IN SUMATRA IN SOUTH EAST ASIA, 1646-1647

Wilhelm Leyel (1644-54) became the Danish Governor of Tranquebar in 1644. He felt that slave trade was a means to obtain quick profits, which could then be used for gifts, tributes and outstanding debts. The Danish Company in particular sold the crews of Bengali ships, which they had seized as prize. Slave trade was widespread at that time on the Tamil Coast and the Portuguese and the Dutch had indulged in it. Leyel in his letter dated 21 September 1646, gave instructions to Hans Ekman the captain of the ship and stated that 38 slaves (both Muslims and Hindus) could be offered as gifts to the king in Kedah to develop Danish trade contacts.[10] It is known that the Danes felt the need for commercial intermediaries in order to develop trade and in 1645 the company in Tranquebar entrusted all its affairs in Kedah to a Tamil agent.

A letter from Leyel the Danish Governor dated 19 February 1647 to Jörgen Hansen, the captain of the ship called *Christianshavn*, mentioned that if Ismail Nayinar the business partner of Leyel brought slaves onboard, they should be considered Leyel's property. In the same letter, he also discussed as to how to procure provisions for the use of slaves on board.[11] Thus one finds Leyel the Danish Governor was himself a slave owner and it proves that slave trading also took place among the officials of the Danish Company.

It is found amongst the records of Wilhelm Leyel that slaves passed through the port of Tranquebar as commodities.[12] Slaves were purchased and sold locally and they were exported to the market in Aceh. This slave trade was of particular importance for the Danes at Tranquebar during the period when the Danish Company was under pressure at home and could not send ships to India during the Thirty Years War. A mention has been found that William Leyel had transported

8 slaves in August 1647, 165 slaves in September 1647 and 20 slaves in October 1647. Thus the total of 193 slaves had been purchased and sent making him a successful slave trader.[13]

The Portuguese continued to migrate from Nagapattinam and settle in the nearby port of Tranquebar. Leyel the Danish Governor therefore permitted the construction of a new Catholic church at Tranquebar in 1646. With the capture of Nagapattinam by the Dutch in 1658, a huge population of the Portuguese sought asylum under the Danes.

Mourids Christensen the Danish official in his diary entry dated 16 March 1671, had reported that the company in Tranquebar purchased and sold Tamil slaves like animals or cargo. The natives who were in need of food, sold their sons and daughters. Men and women slaves thus came to be employed on a large scale.[14]

The Danes established trading contacts with Aceh in Sumatra in 1694. It was at that time they allowed export of slaves in the ships of the Tamil merchants.[15] Missionary records mention that the marakkayars, the Tamil Muslims from Tranquebar and Poriayar, played a significant role in the trade and traffic of the Danish shipping with slaves and textiles to Aceh.[16]

The Danish trade in slaves from Tranquebar developed because the company ships took slave cargoes to Aceh. Many of the slaves transported were debt slaves who could not pay and clear their debts. Also there were slaves who were not able to meet their household expenses and therefore sold themselves and their children. Thus, the number of slaves available depended on the local conditions in Tranquebar. It is known from records that the year 1696 was said to be a good year when plenty of slaves were available. The year 1698 had been a bad one in terms of the scarcity of slaves.[17]

A second Danish East India Company was formed in 1670. The capital for trade came much later only in 1696 when two Danish ships arrived from Copenhagen to Tranquebar.[18] Tranquebar had capital for investment and steady slave trade continued till the end of the seventeenth century. Traders had to pay customs duty for shipping slaves to the Danish Company which had been earlier reorganized in 1668. The trade prospered between 1687 and 1704. When the Second Danish East India Company was dissolved and replaced by the Danish Asiatic Company in 1732, it was decided that the trade in slaves was permissible only as company trade banning the export of slaves by private traders.

THE SYSTEM OF SLAVERY IN TRANQUEBAR AND NOTICES OF THE LUTHERAN MISSIONARIES AFTER THEIR ARRIVAL

The predominance of the household economy was a major element in Danish slavery practices at Tranquebar. This was influenced more by existing local patterns. The productive activities of slaves in Tranquebar before the arrival of Danes, came to be integrated and continued to be followed with the domestic or household realm of their owners.

The Lutheran missionaries who arrived at Tranquebar in 1706 noticed the three types of slaves particularly referring to three groups of people like the Tamils, Portuguese and Muslims. On arrival in Tranquebar, Barholomäus Ziegenbalg wrote a letter to Francke on 25 September 1706 in which he suggested that the Danish Halle mission should be kick started by purchase of slaves, who should be forced to be converted to Protestantism.[19] He said that this would not be un-Christian behaviour because the parents in Tranquebar had faced financial difficulties and so they had been regularly selling their children to make ends meet.

After staying four years in Tranquebar, Ziegenbalg came to explain about slavery in his letter to Francke dated 23 December 1710. He mentioned that since the parents in Tranquebar had wished to sell their children as slaves, it would not be wrong to buy them oneself for a small amount of money so that they could be converted and brought to the fold of Protestant Church. He added that the missionaries had purchased two such slave children and they studied in the missionary school where the kids were doing well. The parents had in the meanwhile had also become Christians.[20] Ziegenbalg wrote that this was one type of slaves in Tranquebar, who spoke Tamil language and whose form of bondage did not remove them completely from their family and background, whose condition of servitude might also not be permanent and whose own offspring would not automatically become slaves as per the local custom.

Ziegenbalg continued to write in detail about slavery and he said that there was another type of slaves who were of Indo-Portuguese parentage. They spoke Portuguese language and often served as household servants. Many of them were Catholics who had been educated or converted by the Portuguese missionaries, who had come earlier to Tranquebar before the arrival of the Protestants. Here again the degree of servitude and the dividing lines between servant, serf, and slave varied, were different and negotiable and slavery was not something that could be set apart from debt-related, contractual and more voluntary forms of master-servant relationships in absolute terms.

Ziegenbalg who noticed the society carefully said that there was an important category of slaves who were of native low castes. This third social group of slaves served in the Portuguese households as domestic servants. He stated that the catechist Rayanayakkan belonged to this category and he belonged to the paraiyar caste.[21]

Ziegenbalg added that another category of slaves in Tranquebar were the Muslim prisoners sold by their captors. They were converted to Islam forcefully. He said that the slaves were brought to Tranquebar from neighbouring places for sale by slave traders.[22]

It is very clear that the Lutheran missionaries in Tranquebar did not reject slavery in all possible varieties. They wished to purchase slaves of certain categories for their own use, as they considered this to be necessary being local cultural understandings of servitude and of the way in which servants were attached to masters and households. The slaves constituted an important proportion of missionary converts. These slaves were educated in missionary school and remained slaves even after baptism.

SLAVES IN TRANQUEBAR AND THEIR CONVERSION TO CHRISTIANITY UNDER THE LUTHERAN MISSIONARIES, 1707-1708

The register of baptism maintained by the Lutheran missionaries is an important record. It contains a list of all members converted in Tranquebar since 27 September 1708.[23] The entry of 12 May 1707 particularly contains mention of 102 persons (with six exceptions), with their names, who were already baptized under Christian instruction, together with the dates of their admission and a few notes on their age, relations and their occupations.[24]

The list presents various kinds of persons such as elderly persons, children, men and women, slaves and freemen, besides those speaking Portuguese and Tamil. Two categories dominated the list. The first included household slaves (the domestic servants) of European families of high rank, especially the Danish officials and Danish pastors in Tranquebar. The second included several foster children of European families. The list refers to three servants of Sigismund Hassius, the Danish Commandant in Tranquebar.[25] A female slave of a customs officer had been also mentioned. The female slave of a clergyman's widow is referred to. The same widow had a *criagdo* (half-breed in Portuguese language—the Euro-Indian Catholic) girl whom she had brought into the Christian fold.[26] It is found that more than 25 per cent are referred to as slave or servant. The distinction between these terms is not clear. Further one notices 8 persons called *criagdo* and 17 individuals who are children under the age of fourteen, of whom some were foster children. Three members of the same family had been adopted by the Protestant missionaries since they lived in their school. Their father, also a Christian on the list, was unable to care for them. Another child is stated to have been an orphan. One child had been donated by a widow. Thus one finds that slaves had been converted largely to Protestantism in the beginning by the Lutheran missionaries.

Accusation and rumours about the Lutheran missionaries came to be spread widely in Tranquebar since the members of their church were mainly slaves, children and Catholic proselytes. It is reported in a document of 1715 written by a critic of the Danish mission under the pseudonym Christiano Aletophilo which got published much later.[27] This remark had already been reflected through the observations of Johann Georg Bovingh, a controversial co-missionary of Ziegenbalg who lived at Tranquebar from July 1709 to August 1711. Among the long list of criticism of the missionary work of Ziegenbalg one finds Bovingh (a tract printed in Europe in 1712), making comments. He stated that the poor and miserable and the defectors from the Roman Church became Christians in Tranquebar.[28] It came to be well known in Denmark (through the publication of 'Christian Friend of Truth' in 1715) that the Christian population in Tranquebar consisted largely of slaves and former Catholics, poor people and even slave children who had been purchased.[29]

Ziegenbalg wrote in his letters that many of the Catholic Christians in Tranquebar were natives and they were employed either in the service of the Company, or private servants and slaves of Danish traders.[30] The observations of the missionaries also relate a causal connection between poverty, disease and bondage. Many who could not find employment, worn out and sick from hunger and impoverishment, became slaves. Individuals in dire straits and unbearable to bear hunger, delivered either themselves or their families into slavery.[31] Ziegenbalg who observed all these various types, therefore began to plead for slave rights and he expressed these in his writings.[32]

The Lutheran missionaries sought to improve the morals of the slaves by Christianizing them and this was a missionary project. They were strongly egalitarian and their schools took in pupils from all castes in 1729, including both Tamil and Portuguese slaves (a mixed race group that persisted as a classification within the strictly segregated world). One sees paintings of these slaves doing various household work at Tranquebar in 1729 sent by the Lutheran missionaries to Halle and they are preserved at the Francke Foundation Archives.[33] On 16 October 1706 Plutschau, the missionary, had asked the people to send the domestic slaves and those slaves employed in the Danish East India Company to the schools which they had opened newly.[34] With the large scale mestico population which continued to live in Tranquebar, the missionaries made attempts to improve their lifestyle as they were denied the opportunity to move ahead in life.

The missionary education directing at Tamil slaves, pariaiyars and the Portuguese mixed-race population, supported an argument that highlighted enlightenment against the slave trade. It led to conflicts with both colonial traders and local elite interests, resulting in complaints that the missionaries made slaves stubborn and unmanageable.[35]

TRANQUEBAR MISSIONARY DESCRIPTIONS AND DISCUSSIONS ON SLAVERY

Missionaries in Tranquebar began to examine the system of prevalent slavery in depth. They described the major difference of the slavery of the Tamils then practised in Tranquebar to that of the European concept of slavery. The letter of Nikolaus Dal, Christian Friedrich Pressier and Christoph Theodosius Walther, the Protestant missionaries in Tranquebar to Michaelis in Germany dated 12 January 1727 explained it well and referred to a Tamil proverb which stated that a person who was born in one's household, gets treated like one's own child. It was mentioned that, according to Tamil law (*nach dem Recht der Malabaren*) the slave owners were not allowed to sell children of their slaves.[36]

The Lutheran missionaries in Tranquebar were questioned by the fellow missionaries in Germany. It was asked whether the slave trade had been regarded by Tamils as good. The reply furnished was that slave trade had not at all been considered ethically good by Tamils.[37]

The missionaries had added that there were mutual obligations between masters and slaves in Tranquebar. When a master was about to die, he called for his slaves who had served than obediently, granted them their freedom and provided them with whatever money might be necessary for their managing and maintaining their households and protected their dignity. If a master had many slaves not only men but also women, he allowed them to marry one another and kept on being a help to them.[38]

EXPLAINING THE VARIOUS METHODS OF SLAVE TRAPS

The missionaries mentioned that there were many ways to obtain or buy chattel slaves (leibeigenen) in Tranquebar. A person could approach another with a gush of persuasive words promising him good clothes and that he would drape him with all sorts of ornaments. In order to overcome his hesitation, he spoke to him deceptively. Afterwards he would rendezvous with him in the night, ran away to another place, and gave him a good meal and later he would sell him unscrupulously to others.

The second method was that a person threw a powder on someone to make him go out of his mind. It worked like this a person took a particular type of powder, went to a distant place looked around for potentially good and valuable slaves, sprinkled them with the powder and then backed off. As soon as the powder fell on the person, it made him go so crazy that he searched for the one who sprinkled the powder on him and voluntarily follow him like a fool. When they had gone a good distance, the imposter provided him with food, clothing and whatever else he needed and at last sold him off.

The third method was that some people, not knowing the difference between good and evil and voluntarily sold themselves, and their children also became slaves.[39]

INTERNAL MIGRATION AND SLAVE EXPORTS FROM TRANQUEBAR TO ACEH IN SUMATRA AND CAPE TOWN IN SOUTH AFRICA IN 1727-1749

Slaves were used mainly in domestic work by the Europeans in Tranquebar. Many native traders exported slaves overseas. The ship *Christianus Sextus* named after the Danish king, sailed from Tranquebar to Aceh in 1727 and it carried slaves on a Tamil merchant's account. Ships flying the Danish flag carried slaves to Aceh as slave trade flourished there. Abishegam a Hindu who worked for the Protestant missionaries had been sold as a slave in 1728. He committed a theft in the Danish settlement and as a punishment he was exiled to Aceh in the ship that sailed in 1729.[40] In Tranquebar the Danish administration officially allowed the sale of slaves for export overseas.

The internal migration of the people in Tamil country particularly from the region of Ramanathapuram (Maravar country) to the region of Thanjavur took place at that time. It had helped in a large measure to replenish the labour supply and helped to increase agricultural production during 1732-5. Some of these labour migrants to Thanjavur area who could not find adequate means to support themselves, came forward to sell themselves as slaves in Tranquebar. This had been reported by the Lutheran missionaries.[41]

The Danes and other European residents in Tranquebar purchased and sold slaves to the Dutch Company in Nagapattinam since there was heavy demand. According to missionary records the slave market in Tranquebar after 1729 did not yield any profit. So the Europeans of Tranquebar did not purchase slaves, although a slave could be bought for any amount between two *panams* and four *panams*. The main reason was that the slaves purchased did not stay alive owing to sickness and poor health and died very early.[42]

In November 1730 the missionaries had mentioned the export of slaves from Tranquebar to Cape Town. It has been said that the missionaries had given several Tamil books printed in Tranquebar to a slave to take with him to South Africa.[43]

Many slaves sold to the Dutch Company in Nagapattinam were taken from Tranquebar.[44] Engelbert, a slave was sold and he waited for export to Pegu in Myanmar in 1741. Ignasia, a slave was sold in 1747 and she was exported to Colombo in Sri Lanka. Further, Caesar and Cassander were sold as slaves and they were to be exported to Cape Town in 1747.[45] Thus Dutch slave trade at Nagapattinam came to expand through Tranquebar slave supply.

The Lutheran missionaries in Tranquebar were very much opposed to the practice of slavery because slaves exported were Christians to a large extent. Yet they could do very little against slavery and slave trade.[46] Export of slaves from Tranquebar to Cape Town had developed directly under the Danes by that time.

According to records, the conversion of slaves by a Protestant missionary in a ship is interesting to note. It has been mentioned that 17 Tamil boys and young men were sold in Tranquebar to be exported to South Africa in 1741. Nine of them were aged between 8 and 12 years, while seven of them were aged between 16 and 19 and one slave was 22 years old. The castes to which they belonged have been mentioned, while 8 of them were *paraiyars*, 5 were *vellalars*, 3 were *pallis* and one slave who spoke Telugu was of an unknown caste.[47] All these slaves were transported in a ship in which the Protestant missionary travelled to Copenhagen and in the course of voyage he gave them catechism lessons. It is mentioned that the slaves also wanted to get baptized prior to reaching Cape Town.[48]

It has also been mentioned by Benjamin Schultze, another Protestant missionary of Tranquebar in his letter from Copenhagen, dated 21 November 1743 to the Tranquebar missionaries, wherein he said that he had arrived safely to Europe but he felt very bad when two slaves of Tranquebar destined for Cape Town were whipped very badly on board the ship in which he travelled to Copenhagen.[49] Though trade in slaves had been outlawed by Pratap Singh (1739-63) the Maratha ruler of Thanjavur, the Danes continued to buy slaves who were available and continued to transport them to South Africa.

The letter of the missionaries of Tranquebar to Francke at Halle in Germany dated 20 December 1741 complained that the people from Thanjavur and Ramanathapuram feared to come to Tranquebar and Poraiyar to meet the missionaries. The simple reason was that of the danger of being kidnapped at any time and shipped to Aceh or Cape Town where the slaves were in heavy demand.[50] Slaves brought to Aceh in Sumatra were often the children of indebted families.

THE REACTION TO THE DANISH SLAVE TRADE BY THE KING OF THANJAVUR, 1741-1744

Pratap Singh, the Maratha ruler of Thanjavur did his best since he disliked slave trade of the Europeans in the ports of his kingdom. He was totally against the natives who engaged themselves as slave dealers and brokers for the European companies. It has been mentioned in the missionary records that the slave traders were punished severely in the kingdom of Thanjavur. Muthu Nayakkan the Tamil catechist who travelled from Tranquebar to Puthakudi on 5 September 1741 found a hand hanging from a tree. He came to know on enquiry that it belonged to a convicted slave trader whose hand had been cut off as a punishment. He learnt that the slave trader had finally died of the injury.[51]

Again, it has been mentioned by Aaron, the Tamil pastor in his report that he saw two former slave dealers/traders on a stake near Kollimangudi on 5 September 1743. They were executed prior to being impaled for display.[52] Thus Pratap Singh the Maratha ruler of Thanjavur banned slave trade and exports and took stern measures. Slave traders were seen as malicious scoundrels, rogues and kidnappers and so they were hated, tortured cruelly and punished. Yet many men, women and slave children were traded secretly by the Europeans reaching the ports.

THE PROHIBITION ORDER ISSUED BY THE DANISH GOVERNOR FOR SLAVE TRADE IN TRANQUEBAR, 1745

The local Tamil elites in the surrounding villages of Tranquebar were very unhappy when their slaves ran away where the Danish Company gave shelter and refuge. The work of the missionaries also became controversial when Hindu slaves became Christians. Thus, serious conflicts arose between the kingdom of Thanjavur and the Danish administration in Tranquebar. At the same time, it contributed importantly to the formation of discourses of abolition. The Lutheran missionaries lobbied mainly for interventions to restrict the kidnapping and sale of involuntary slaves. The outcome of this necessity was the prohibition of the slave trade in Tranquebar, promulgated by an order by Carsten Carstensen the Danish Governor (1744-6) in 1745.

He issued a public proclamation on 20 July 1745 in Tranquebar prohibiting and abolishing the accustomed trade in slaves. However, it was still allowed to buy slaves for private use, those slaves, who of their own free will and intention sold themselves, or were put up for sale by their real parents.[53] The proclamation also made it clear the trade was prohibited in people, who were not already slaves. The purpose of the proclamation is framed in a discourse of evangelical enlightenment, making a reference to both natural law and the rights of people. This was done in order to prevent the trade and enterprise in innocent and freeborn human beings.[54] The missionaries made the demand to end the trade in slaves except for the quite legal one, in which natives let themselves be sold as slaves than die of hunger. This was considered an important victory by the missionaries, who continued to be supported and respected as critical observers of inhuman practices allowed in Tranquebar by the Danish Company.[55]

THE DEVELOPMENT OF ILLEGAL SLAVE TRADE AFTER THE PROHIBITION, 1745-1753

The proclamation of prohibiting the trading of slaves in Tranquebar was issued when the Danish Company was still a private enterprise. Illegal private trade in slaves had developed after 1745.[56] The Lutheran missionaries put pressure on owners of slaves in and around Tranquebar to send their slaves to school and let them be baptized. They argued subsequently that slaves who were Christians could not be sold, especially not to Muslims, which met with local opposition as Muslims offered and paid the best prices.

Europeans in Tranquebar continued to buy and sell slaves to the Dutch in Nagapattinam during 1746-7. It has been stated that the Dutch Company had no qualms about selling fellow Christians into slavery whether they were of Tamil or had mixed Tamil and European background. Lutheran missionaries noticed that many people were simply kidnapped by the slave dealers and brokers and though the Danish administration was officially opposed to such kidnappings, it did not take effective steps to stop the bad practice. The Danish Company trade in other commodities and goods had not been highly successful. It was estimated in 1750 that ten to twelve slaves per year were shipped from Tranquebar to Cape Town the central hub that connected the Indian Ocean and the Atlantic slave trade.[57]

THE ABOLITION OF SLAVE TRADE AND THE ORDER ISSUED BY THE DANISH GOVERNOR IN TRANQUEBAR, 1753

As the slave trade continued to thrive on secretly in Tranquebar, there was a need to proclaim the abolition of the slave trade in 1753. Controversy resulted in a proclamation of abolition at that time and the Danish Company directors in Copenhagen prohibited slave trade as Company trade.[58] There was much less missionary work amongst the people in the Portuguese congregation in Tranquebar because the congregation had dwindled and there were no new slaves in Tranquebar who could be baptized. Hans Ernst Bonsack (1746-53) the Danish Governor made every effort to stop the slave trade totally. The abolition also meant that missionaries could no longer be accused of being slave traders.

The Danish Company was taken over by the Danish Crown in 1777, after its monopoly on trade to the Cape and beyond, which had expired in 1772. Trade was liberalized and further proclamations were posted in the Danish colony of Tranquebar as a reminder that the slave trading had been prohibited. The letter by Johann Friedrich Köenig (1741-95) the Lutheran missionary in 1773 had reflected the circumstance under which slaves and slavery prevailed in Tranquebar. He said that it was far more bearable than in West Indies where slavery continued over generations where slaves had to do heavy work in the plantations.[59]

Slave trade stood condemned by 1780 on humanitarian grounds in the eyes of thoughtful and prominent members of the Danish government. A Lutheran missionary wrote in a letter dated 17 October 1780 that the Hindu slaves who received baptism had been urged to serve their masters even more faithfully.[60]

TRANQUEBAR BORN SLAVES IN SRI LANKA, CAPE TOWN, MAURITIUS AND DENMARK, 1775-1794

A record mentions Joana a manumitted slave who was born in Tranquebar. She was sold to the Dutch in Sri Lanka. She lived there according to records. She was the concubine of the slave Lakij who belonged to Van Hek, the under-surgeon in Galle.[61]

A woman slave in Tranquebar had become Christian. It is found that a daughter was born in Tranquebar to the slave

Aurora on 21 July 1774. She was baptized with the name Maria Magdalena in 1775 by the Moravian missionaries in Tranquebar. She was taken in by the Moravian missionary and went to Denmark with the closing down of the Garden of the Moravians at Tranquebar. She lived at Christianfeld in Denmark.[62]

Slaves purchased in Tranquebar also came to be exported to Mauritius where there was a demand. Naagan, a Tamil from Tranquebar boarded the ship *Beaute* in August 1784 and he had later testified that economic distress had forced him to come to Mauritius. He was told that he would be employed as a crew member in Mauritius. But on arrival he was sold at a slave auction in Mauritius to a freeman of Tamil origin who had already settled there.[63]

Slaves from Tranquebar who reached Cape Town were employed mainly in the households. The data of the privately owned slaves from the household inventories (preserved in the archives of the Master of the Orphan Chamber in Cape Town) shows that there were three male slaves from Tranquebar in 1749. Again it has been found that three male slaves and one female slave from Tranquebar were found between 1750 and 1794.[64] Slave trade continued because people tried to profit from the misery of others.

THE GOVERNMENT ORDERS ISSUED ENDING THE SLAVERY IN TRANQUEBAR, 1783-1790

The government order of forbidding export of slaves from the Danish territory of Tranquebar was issued on 20 June 1783 since many foreigners continued to purchase slaves and exported them. It ordered strictly that no slaves should be exported from the Danish colony.[65]

Again on 21 June 1783, the Danish Governor found it necessary to issue a decree, prohibiting slave trade and stating that punishment would be meted out to those who took slaves out by sea or by land.[66] Like the slave trade, abolition was clearly an ongoing business, it was thus directed more against kidnapping and abductions than against the trade in slaves as such and presupposes a colonial society in which the ownership of slaves as servants was commonplace and where the boundaries between slavery and contractual servitude were fuzzy and negotiable.

The government issued an order on 16 December 1790 in Tranquebar prohibiting slave owners to put their slaves in iron. It was stated that the government would punish unruly slaves according to the law.[67]

CONCLUSION

It has been observed the emergence of slave trade in Tranquebar under the Danes in the seventeenth century and its abolition at the end of the eighteenth century. Several discourses of abolition had been undertaken in the context of slaves of various types including the bonded labour. However all that had been related to this had been the types of slavery that existed in the region of Tranquebar prior and after the coming of the Danes. The development in slave forms had changed from time to time and it had moved from unfree labour from slavery to indenture linking slave trade from Tranquebar to ports of South East Asia, Sri Lanka, Africa and the Atlantic. One notices multinational dimensions of slavery that had chiefly led to prohibition in 1745 and to the next stage of abolition of slavery in 1753 and finally to the end of the slave trade. The Lutheran missionary enterprises based in the Danish colony of Tranquebar had contributed to the development of ideas of education, enlightenment and natural rights that fed into emerging discourses of abolition of slavery.

NOTES

1. S. Jeyaseela Stephen, *Tranquebar in Global History, 1620-1801: The Coromandel Coast and Europe in a World Network System*, Puducherry, 2020, pp. 13-14.

2. R.C. Temple and Lavinia Mary Anstey, eds., *The Life of the Icelander Jon Olafsson Traveller to India, 1622-5*, 2 vols., London, 1932, p. 151.
3. Martin Krieger, 'Danish Shipping and Trade between Tranquebar on the Coromandel Coast of India and South East Asia during the Seventeenth and Eighteenth Centuries', S. Jeyaseela Stephen, ed., *The Indian Trade at the Asian Frontier*, New Delhi, 2008, pp. 117- 42, see p. 124.
4. Ole Felbaek, 'No Ship for Tranquebar for Twenty–nine Years: Or the Art of Survival of a Mid–Seventeenth Century European Settlement in India', Roderich Ptak and D. Rothermund, eds., *Emporia, Commodities and Entrepreneurs in Asian Maritime Trade, c. 1400-1750*, Heidelberg, 1991, pp. 29-36.
5. Asta Bredsdorff, *Willem Leyels liv og farefulde rejse til Indien*, Copenhagen, Museum Tusculanus Forlag, 1999, p. 148.
6. Kay Larsen, *Dansk-Ostindiske koloniers historie*, Copenhagen, Centralførlaget, 1907.
7. William Foster, *English Factories in India: A Calendar of Documents in the India Office, British Museum and Public Relations Office*, XIII vols., 1906-27, vol. VI, p. 141.
8. Ibid.
9. Archivo General de Indias (hereafter AGI), Seville, Spain, Filipinas 193, n. 11 (1654-2-6).
10. Rigsarkivet (hereafter RA), København, *Danske Kancelli* (hereafter *DK*), B 246.
11. Ibid.
12. Asta Bredsdorff, *The Trials and Travels of Willem Leyel: An Account of the Danish East India Company in Tranquebar, 1639-48*, Copenhagen: Museum Tusculanum Press, 2009, pp. 148-9.
13. Asta Bredsdorff, *Willem Leyels liv og farefulde*, p. 149.
14. Mourids Christensen, *Skildringer fra et ophold I Ostindien (begyndte I Trankenbar 16.3. 1671) med nogle Portugisiske og Malebariske Gloser*, 1672. The text runs thus: *Mallebarerne naar dee lider trang for Føde, eller Dyre Aaringer er, Selger di bort till Huem som Köbe vill deris egne bøern, Piger och drenge, ia Manden sin egen Kone naar nøden er størst, och dersom hand endaa fattis selger manden sig selffuer och bageffter, och maa werre Slaffuer och arbeede som andre bæster deris Liffuis tid med Hug och slag, nøgen och suelt uden nogen modsigelße.*
15. Anthony Reid, 'Slavery and Bondage in Early Southeast Asian History', in *Charting the Shape of Early Modern Southeast Asia*, Singapore, 2000, pp. 181- 206.

16. *Der Königl. Dänischen Missionarien aus Ost–Indien eingesandter ausführlichen Berichten, Von dem Werck ihrs Ams unter den Heyden, angerichteten Schulen und Gemeinen, ereigneten Hindernissen und schweren Umstanden; Beschaffenheit des Malabarischen Heydenthums, gepflogenen brieflicher Correspondentz und mundlchen Unterredungen mit selbigen heyden*, Teil 1-9 (Continuationen 1-108), Waiserihaus, Halle, 1710-72 (hereafter HB=Hallesche Berichte), vol. 3, cont., 29, p. 470.
17. Gunnar Olsen, *Dansk Ostindien, 1616-1732*, in Vore gamle tropenkolonier, ed., Johannes Brøndsted, Copenhagen, Westermann, 1952, pp. 207-12.
18. Martin Krieger, *Danish Shipping and Trade*, p. 131.
19. Heike Liebau, *Cultural Encounters in India: The Local Co-workers of the Tranquebar Mission, 18th to 19th Centuries*, trs. Rekha V. Rajan, New York, Routledge, 2018, p. 152.
20. Ibid.
21. Ibid., pp. 148-9.
22. Ibid., pp. 148-54.
23. Archiv der Franckesche Stiftungen (hereafter AFSt), Halle, MSS MII A6: 5(3), 'Register of those persons, who through the proclamation of the Gospel by most gracious order of His Royal Majesty of Denmark and Norway, etc., owing to divine grace have been gathered to our pure Evangelical religion from blind heathenism and partly also from sinister papacy from Anno 1707, 12 May on until now 1708, 27 September and also since until the present day are being instructed in our Jerusalem Church in the Word of God on their salvation by Bartholomaus Ziegenbalg and Heinrich Plutschau, servants of the Divine Word among the heathens at the Jerusalem congregation.'
24. W. Germann, 'Bartholomaus Ziegenbalg als Bahnbrecher der lutherischen Mission', *Allgemeine Missions-Zeitschrift*, vol. X, Giltersloh, C. Bertelsmann, 1883, pp. 529-33. Daniel Jeyaraj, *Inkulturation in Tranquebar*, Erlangen, Verlag der Ev.-Luth. Mission, 1996, pp. 174, 319.
25. Jorge Simon Izquierdo Doaz, 'The Trade in Domestic Servants (Morianer) from Tranquebar for Upper Class Danish Homes in the First Half of the Seventeenth Century', Itinerario, vol. 43, special issue 2, *Colonial Entanglements: Cross Roads, Contact Zones and flows in Scandinavian Global History*, 2019, pp. 194-217.
26. W. Germann, 'Bartholomaus Ziegenbalg', p. 533.

27. Christiano Aletophilo, *Kurze und wahrhafte Relation von dem Ursprung und Fortgang der Danisch-Malabarischen Missionariorum, 1715*, in J. Ferd Fenger, *Geschichte der Trankebarschen Mission, Aus dem Danischen tbersetzt*, Grimma, J.M. Gebhardt, 1845, pp. 98, 277.
28. *Der Koniglich Danischen Missionariomm unter den Ost-Indischen Heiden abgendtigte Apologia Epistolis Bovingianis*, in Niels-Peter Moritzen, ed., *Bartholomaus Ziegenbalg, Johannes Ernst Grilndler, Von den Anfangen evangelischer Mission, Zwei unbekannte Missionsschriften von 1713 und 1717*, Bonn, Verlag fiir Kultur und Wissenschaft, 2002, pp. 91, 95.
29. E. Arno Lehmann, *It Began at Tranquebar: A History of the First Protestant Mission in India*, trs. Martin J. Lutz, second edition, Chennai, 2006, pp. 43-4.
30. Arno Lehmann, ed., *Alte Briefe aus Indien: Unverdffentlichte Briefe von Bartholomaus Ziegenbalg, 1706-19*, Berlin, Evangelische Verlagsanstalt, 1957, p. 83.
31. HB, Cont. 34, p. 1056.
32. Anders Nørgaard, *Mission und Obrigkeit: Die Dänisch-Hallische Mission in Tranquebar 1706-1845*, Gütersloh, Verlagshaus Gerd Mohn, 1988, pp. 33, 36-8.
33. AFSt, M2 B5: 7. 'Portugiesische Sklaven die Weitzen mahlen' and 'Eine Portugiesche Sklavin die zur Kirchen gehet'.
34. W. Germann, *Ziegenbalg und Plutschau. Die Grundungsjahre der Trankebarschen Mission*, Erlangen, Andreas Deichert, 1868, p. 15.
35. Gunnar Olsen, *Dansk Ostindien. 1616-1732*, pp. 231-9; Kamma Struwe, *Dansk Ostindien 1732-76: Tranquebar under Kompagnistyre*, second edition, Copenhagen, Fremad, 1967, pp. 113-16.
36. AFSt, M1 B3: 26, pp. 1-2.
37. Daniel Jeyaraj and Richard Fox Young (translated, introduced and annotated), *Hindu-Christian Epistolary Self-Discourses: 'Malabarian Correspondence' between German Pietist Missionaries and South Indian Hindus (1712-14)*, Harrassowitz Verlag, Wiesbaden, 2013, pp. 268-9.
38. Ibid., pp. 270-1.
39. Ibid.
40. AFSt, M1 F3: 5, p. 7, see, *Supplementum Des Verzeichnißes der glieder der Portugiesischen, Malabarischen Stadt-und Land-Gemeine vom 5 October 1728: bis d: 5ten October 1729. Nebst einem anhang von denen die in diesen Jahr abgegangen.*

41. HB, vol. 3, cont., 30, pp. 544-5.
42. HB, vol. 3, cont., 28, pp. 366-7. The text runs thus: *Einwohner wollen auch keine Sclaven mehr kaufen, ob man gleich einen für 2 bis 4 fanam . . . Denn sie bleiben nicht leben.*
43. HB, vol. 3, cont., 31, p. 701.
44. AFSt, M2 C15: 3, p. 5, *Supplementum des Verzeichnißes der Glieder der Portugiesischen und Malabarischen Stad-und Land-Gemeine vom 5 October 1740 bis 5 October 1741, Nebst einem Anhang von denen die in diesem Jahr abgegangen.*
45. AFSt, M2 C15: 9, p. 15, *IItes Supplementum Des Verzeichnisses der Glieder der Portugiesischen u: Tamulischen Stadt-und Land-Gemeine, vom 5ten Octobr 1746, bis 5ten Octobr 1747, Nebst einem Anhange von denen in diesem Jahr abgegangenen.*
46. AFSt, M1 B29: 29, p. 2.
47. AFSt, M2 C15: 3, pp. 3, 5.
48. HB, vol. 5, cont., 53, p. 786.
49. AFSt, M1 K5: 14, p. 3.
50. AFSt, M1 B29: 29, p. 2.
51. HB, vol. 5, cont., 54, p. 1003.
52. HB, vol. 5, cont., 60, pp. 1802-3.
53. Kay Larsen, 'Danmark og Slavehandelens Ophævelse', Historisk Tidsskrift, vol. X, no. 4, 1937, pp. 106-8; Martin Krieger, *Der dänische Sklavenhandel auf dem Indischen Ozean im 17. und 18. Jahrhundert, Jahrbuch für Europäische Überseegeschichte* vol. XII, 2012, pp. 9-30, see p. 21.
54. Kay Larsen, 'Danmark og Slavehandelens Ophævelse', p. 107.
55. Anders Nørgaard, *Mission und Obrigkeit*, pp. 159-61.
56. Martin Krieger, *Der dänische Sklavenhandel*, pp. 21-2.
57. Kamma Struwe, Dansk Ostindien 1732-76, pp. 59-64.
58. Søren Mentz, 'Handelsstationen Tranquebar, 1630-1750', in *Danmark og Kolonierne Indien: Tranquebar, Serampore og Nicobarerne*, ed. Niels Brimnes, Copenhagen, Gads Forlag, 2017, pp. 76-111, see p. 109.
59. Heike Liebau, *Cultural Encounters*, p. 154.
60. Ibid., pp. 154-5.
61. Sri Lanka National Archives (hereafter SLNA), Colombo, Dutch Central Government of Coastal Ceylon, 1640-1796, 1/4740, 1/4702, Criminal dossiers, fls.31r–v, Articles 1 and 2.
62. Unitats Archive (hereafter UA), Herrnhut, R.22.84.21. The Biography of Maria Magdalena Malabar. It is stated that she died on 10 May 1827.

63. Marina Carter, *Veils from Indenture: Experiences of Indian Migrants in the British Empire*, London, 1996, p. 92.
64. Nigel Worden, 'Indian Ocean Slaves in Cape Town, 1695-1805', *Journal of South African Studies*, 42(3), 2016, pp. 389-408, see p. 406.
65. *Calendar Containing Notifications (1779-1824) Issued by the Administration at Tranquebar 1779*, Danish Records, Serial No. 1, Government Press, Madras, 1908, p. 4.
66. Georg Christian Knapp et. al., *Neuere Geschichte der Evangelischen Missions-Anstalten zu Bekehrung der Heiden in Ostindien*, Waisenhaus, Halle 1770-8/95, 1848, 29. St, 531.
67. Calendar Containing Notification, p. 6.

CHAPTER 11

Slaves and Trading Voyages of the French from Pondicherry and Karaikal to Mauritius, Reunion Islands and France, 1687-1792

The French East India Company established a trading factory at Pondicherry in 1674. François Martin took care of the commercial activities of the French Company. He was approached by some local slave dealers in September 1687 who enquired whether he was in need of slaves for export since the Dutch East India Company had been conducting trade in slaves on large scale from the ports of Pulicat, Devanampattinam, Nagapattinam and Tuticorin on the Tamil Coast. Martin replied in the negative, and maintained that it was demeaning for the French to conduct slave trade.[1] However, according to records a slave boy of twelve years old had been purchased and exported from Pondicherry in 1687 to the Mascarenes Islands.[2]

SLAVE TRADE OF THE FRENCH FROM PONDICHERRY TO MAURITIUS, REUNION AND THE COMOROS ISLANDS, 1707-1760

After the death of François Martin, the officials of the French Company in Pondicherry decided to conduct slave trade. The company showed interest in the purchase and export of slaves to Isle de Bourbon (Le Reunion) which had been occupied by the French in 1670. The deliberations of the Superior Council of Pondicherry on 9 February 1707 reveal that there was a plan to buy Tamil slaves and export them to Isle de Bourbon.[3] For the first time, mention is made of the ship *St Louis* that sailed away with 25 slaves in September 1707 from Pondicherry.[4] Pierre Du Livier, the French Governor of Pondicherry, wrote, a letter to the Directors of the French East India Company in Paris in this regard on 1 October 1707. The next ship sailed from Pondicherry on 17 November 1707 with 4 males and 15 females who were mostly children. They were purchased at six *pagodas* (around 444 *livres*) each in Pondicherry the total amount invested was 26,444 *livres*. In Reunion Island the males were sold for 2,133 *livres* and the females were sold for 9,030 and the total was 11,163 *livres*.[5] Thus the profit margin was more than fourfold.

The French Governor in Pondicherry took keen interest in the slave trade and asked the Company servants to contact the native dealers for the supply of slaves to be exported on an annual basis. Meanwhile, *St Loui*s returned to Pondicherry in February 1708 and the investment for the purchase of slaves came in the form of silver to the tune of 11,000 *piastres* from Isle de Bourbon.[6] The French Company had paid *pagodas* (gold coins) to Pondicherry by that time and purchased 6 young girl slaves. Therefore, an order was passed by the French Governor to reimburse the amount in silver bullion. The slaves purchased were transported in ships to Isle de Bourbon under the careful supervision of the ship's captain. These slave girls reached Bourbon and were employed in the houses prepared for them. The ship *La Vierge* sailed from Pondicherry in April 1710 and it took 25 slaves. Two slaves died during the voyage. Three were reserved for the French Company and so 20 slaves were sold for 5,667 *livres* in Reunion.[7]

According to records, one finds Fr. Senet in Reunion had baptized 12 slaves in 1710. They had come in the ship St. Malo and St. Jean-Baptiste. He also baptized 22 slaves who came in the ship on 27 August 1710. Further he also baptized 3 slaves who came in the ship on 19 October 1710.[8]

Instructions were sent from Isle de Bourbon to the French Governor in Pondicherry who was requested to send adult slave boys in large numbers to be employed there. As French private merchants were banned from indulging in slave trade, the Directors of the French East India Company in Paris wrote to the Governor in Pondicherry to take all possible care in the export of slaves by the French Company.[9] The officials and servants of the French Company in Pondicherry were asked to contact the native slave dealers to ensure the supply of an adequate number of slaves for export to Isle de Bourbon. In the deliberations of the Superior Council of Pondicherry on 6 September 1718, one finds mention of the purchase of slaves in Arcot, the capital of the Nawab. Slaves purchased there were carefully transported to Pondicherry and finally, they were shipped to Isle de Bourbon in 1719.[10]

Mauritius, abandoned by the Dutch in 1710 and renamed Isle de France was first appropriated by the French in 1715. The island was occupied in 1721 by settlers from the neighbouring Isle de Bourbon. The French Governor in Pondicherry was asked to purchase more slaves for Reunion. He did so and the slaves were exported in ships. It is reported that most of the slaves were between the age of 18 and 25.[11]

According to records, 200 slaves were purchased and transported in 1737 from Pondicherry to Reunion island. The

TABLE 11.1: EXPORT OF SLAVES FROM PONDICHERRY TO REUNION BY THE FRENCH, 1729-1732

Date of Departure	*Number of Slaves*
14 February 1729	300
27 March 1729	173
April 1729	26
June 1730	45
15 February 1731	26
23 November 1731	14
24 December 1732	4
TOTAL	588

Source: ADR, C 596, C 599, C 601, C 603.

average length of slave voyages from Pondicherry including days of departure and arrival, was around 44 days.[12] There are references to slave mortality owing to disease in 1740. The slaves aboard vessels arriving from Pondicherry died at sea in large numbers and the death rate in 1740 was reported to be 92.5 per cent.[13] The French administrators of the Mascarenes Islands had sought agricultural labourers from Pondicherry actively since at least 1728.

THE NAWAB OF ARCOT AND HIS POLICY TOWARDS FRENCH SLAVE TRADE

Since the French East India Company in Pondicherry showed great interest in the purchase and export of slaves overseas, the French Governor wrote a letter to Dost Ali Khan the Nawab of Arcot, seeking permission to purchase and transport slaves. The Nawab replied through his letter dated 5 September 1738 and the text runs as follows:

> On what you have prayed to me by your letter asking to give a *parwana* (temporary permit issued by the provincial officials) that the passage of slaves purchased by you and arrested en route becomes effective. Although it is not our custom to permit any one to buy or take away any slave, I have passed beyond this consideration and have accorded you a *parwana*, which you have asked me on this subject. Ghulam Hussain Imam Khan made me understand your favourable dispositions by which you have maintained all the liaisons of sincere friendship of which you have frequently given me the mark. This gives me pleasure. You can count on me that I will always give you service whenever I can.[14]
>
> The Nawab added that 'we are given to understand that the Governor of Pondicherry was in need of slaves for his port or other places has given order to buy slaves, in some places of my dependency through which these slaves will pass. You would let them pass freely provided that they are not by religion Muslims because that is our wish. You take care that this is executed exactly'.[15]

The French Company was relieved of the burden of transporting slaves from the villages in the hinterland to the port of Pondicherry. Native slave dealers carried out such works and sold even Muslim slaves. It helped the French to buy, transport and export Tamil Muslim slaves officially in the ships of the Company violating the order of the Nawab of Arcot.

METHODS OF OBTAINING SLAVES FOR FRENCH OVERSEAS EXPORT

Entries found in the Tamil diaries maintained by the natives of Pondicherry mention slave dealers and the ways in which they managed to obtain slaves for supply to the French East India Company. Slaves were purchased at Bahoor, Ozhundiyapattu, Vriddachalam and Tiruvalanjuli and brought to Pondicherry for export. The price of a child was 10 *pagodas* while that of an adult was 15, and a female was 20 *pagodas*. These slave agents enticed many woodcutters through business conversations on the pretext of buying timber. Then they trapped them in the warehouses or lodged them in private buildings when needed, feeding them regularly and finally selling them off as slaves mercilessly to the French Company for export to Mauritius.[16] Even the French Company officials, on a number of occasions, intimidated, kidnapped and lured men, women and children immigrating for menial jobs with the help of native slave dealers. A man in Pondicherry revealed that he was inveigled into the building, on the promise of being employed as a *coolie* (wage labourer) to carry a bag and that when he entered, he was arrested, his head was shaved, fetters were placed round his legs and he was declared a slave. Another man announced that he was offered betel, lightly smeared with lime and when he chewed the betel leaf he felt giddy. Thereafter, he did not know what happened to him. On becoming conscious, he found that he was led away and found himself as a slave being sold to the French Company in Pondicherry.[17]

Slave dealers were skilled kidnappers who were in the regular habit of luring people who lived in villages. There was a separate house in a hamlet (name not mentioned) located west of Tranquebar town, where batches of 50 and 100 individuals were imprisoned and kept. They were transported silently at night in a boat to reach Ariyankuppam situated in the environs of Pondicherry. These slaves were confined again in a house belonging to Paramanandan, a great slave dealer. The heads of the slaves were shaved and they were given black clothes to wear. Each slave had a fetter placed around one of his legs. They were fed with *canjee* (boiled rice with water) and had to remain there until a sailing vessel came to take them away to the French islands near Africa.[18]

It had been reported that Paramanandan, the great slave dealer had kidnapped and arrested 4 *chetti* (trading caste) men and 1 *chetti* woman in 1743. He transported them by a boat to Ariyankuppam where the slaves spent a night in a house, and were then removed to another one which belonged to Louis Jude who divulged under Cornet, the keeper of the warehouse in the fort of Pondicherry. Some *chettis* who visited Louis Jude in connection with some textile business happened to see the slaves in his house, and questioned him. He said that he had purchased the slaves recently. When the *chettis* asked for further details, especially regarding the castes to which the slaves belonged, he became nervous and said that he would send them away if they were *chettis*. The news spread among the *chettis* and others and also reached the officials of the French Company, who sent some peons to the house of Louis Jude, who divulged the information. It was found that the slaves were *chettis*. The peons of the French Company searched for Paramanandan and pounced on him in the town. They arrested and produced him before the judge in the court. He ordered Paramanandan to be thrown into prison for he had trapped the *chettis*, the merchant caste, as slaves.[19] The native slave agents were greedy for money and, therefore, indulged in immoral traffic. They used unethical ways to supply slaves to the French Company as there was demand for slave exports from Pondicherry. Thus, slaves were trapped largely through deception, coercion and kidnapping by unscrupulous native agents. Arulanandan (Arlanden in French records) was another slave dealer who appeared in a case heard by the Superior Council of Pondicherry in 1743, where he was accused of illegal slave-trading and described as the valet/*dubashi* and broker of Louis Jude, the French merchant.[20]

SHIPPING SLAVES FROM TO MAURITIUS, REUNION AND THE COMOROS

Periodic slave exports by the French from Pondicherry in the eighteenth century show that children and young adults, many of whom had been kidnapped and sold into bondage, comprised the majority of slaves. Wars and famines forced desperate men and women to sell themselves or their children into slavery. When Chanda Sahib pillaged the region of Thanjavur in October 1738, the servants and officials of the French Company made captives and sent them as slaves to Mauritius. Due to continued droughts, slave trade thrived in the Cauvery Delta area. Slaves were purchased in the hinterland and came to be transported secretly to Pondicherry for export. In his diary entry on 25 June 1743, Ananda Ranga Pillai the chief *dubash* of the French Governor, mentioned that having developed direct overseas trade from Pondicherry to Port Louis, the French Company transported slaves in ships. The French also re–exported slaves who came from Pondicherry in ships to Mauritius to other places like the Comoros Islands located at the northern end of the Mozambique Channel. In 1743, the ship *St Pierre* directly sailed away from Pondicherry with plenty of slaves to the Comoros.[21] Another ship *St Benoit* had also directly sailed from Pondicherry to the Comoros in 1744 with slaves.[22]

In line with the metropolitan policy, the Superior Council of Pondicherry issued an order on 12 January 1742 instructing all Christian slave owners in Pondicherry to baptize their slaves within a year from that date. It was added that all slaves should be educated properly in the Catholic faith.[23] In 1746, the Superior Council of Pondicherry passed another order that no slave would be allowed to work on Sundays and Christian

TABLE 11.2: SAILINGS WITH SLAVES FROM PONDICHERRY TO MAURITIUS, 1729-1945

Year	*Number of Ship*
1729	Indien
1730	St. Pierre
1731	Dauphin
1731	St. Joseph
1732	St. Joseph
1734	St. Pierre
1744	St. Benoit
1744	Pondichéry
1745	Brilliant

Source: ADR, Alfred Martineau, ed., *Correspondance du Conseil Supérieur de Pondichéry et de la Compagnie, 1726-67*, 6 vols., Pondichéry, 1920-31; Edmond Gaudart, ed., *Procès–verbaux des délibèrations du Conseil Supérieur de Pondichéry du 1 er Fevrier 1701 au 31 Decembre 1739*, 3 vols., Pondichéry, 1913-15.

holidays without permission.[24] Ships with slaves sailed regularly from Pondicherry, and it was estimated that 20-5 per cent of them died en route to the Comoros islands.[25] There were 870 Tamil slaves in Mauritius (out of the total population of 12,196 slaves) in 1761. Thus, 7 per cent of the population of Mauritius comprised Tamil slaves.[26]

PONDICHERRY SLAVE IN FRANCE IN 1750 AND THE LEGAL BATTLE DURING 1759

Francisco (Francisque in French record) was born to parents of Indo-Portuguese origin and lived in Pondicherry. He was taken as a slave to France in a ship that sailed from Pondicherry in 1750 by a trader of the French East India Company who lived in the port of St. Malo. After serving for 7 years in the house of his master he ran away because of mistreatment. Later he sought another employer in 1757. His former master had him imprisoned and Francisco sued for his freedom, first in the Admiralty Court of France and then, upon appeal, before the Parliament of Paris.[27]

It is interesting to find that the lawyer of Francisco argued in 1759 for his freedom on the grounds of his Indian origins, the free soil principle and failure to comply with the Code Noir of 1685, the ordinance of 23 April 1615, the edict of 1716, edicts of July and September 1720, letters patents of 1723, the edict of 1724 and the declaration of 15 December 1738. The lawyer argued for the chief claim for an exclusive relationship between slavery and blackness. It was a more significant feature on the racialized nature of slavery then present in the French empire. Interestingly, the lawyer of Francisco had never quoted the 1739 order, despite the fact that it had been issued two decades earlier.[28] This was a crucial piece of legislation for claim to freedom and the order, issued by King Louis XV on 2 March 1739, prohibited the enslavement of Indians. It was also counter argued that French laws prohibiting the enslavement of Indians applied to American Indians, and not those of South Asia. The case did not drag on for years and the final judgement was delivered in favour of Francisco. This is the first metropolitan legal case which argued that slavery was justifiable only for Africans and their descendents, not to Indians or Indo-Portuguese/Indo-Europeans before the Parliament of Paris in 1759.

SLAVES FROM KARAIKAL TO PONDICHERRY AND THE GROWTH OF SLAVE TRADE OF THE FRENCH COMPANY, 1760-1778

After the seizure of Pondicherry on 16 January 1760 by the English East India Company, the French began to pay attention to Karaikal. They began to trade and purchased and exported slaves. A document of the French Company mentions that the price of a slave in Karaikal was around 3-4 Porto Novo *pagodas* in 1760.[29] Owing to the unavailability of adult slaves, the slave agents in Karaikal arranged for the sale of kids and children. A child, 2½ years old, was sold for 3 *pagodas* in January 1767. A girl, 9 years old, was purchased for 4 *pagodas* in March 1774. Girls, 8 years of age, were purchased for 3 *pagodas* and sometimes also for 3 *panams*. There was a mention of 2 boys aged 12 and 16, who were purchased for 6 and 16 *pagodas* respectively.[30] Another French record mentioned the sale of a male slave for 53 Arcot rupees in August 1769. The purchase price of slaves had been high, and was escalating at an alarming rate. The main reason was the heavy demand for slaves in Mauritius and Le Reunion by the French East India Company.

Names and castes are neatly mentioned in the sale deeds of slaves at Karaikal. Kumaran of the *vellala* caste remitted his son aged 12 to Appu. The father received 3½ *pagodas* for the transfer of his son on 8 November 1774.[31] Further, names like Veera, a boy of the *pariayar* caste and another called Pungaavanam, are mentioned. A slave, 10 years old was sold at Karaikal in 1774 for 50 rupees (20 *pagodas*). Naagaatha of the *vellala* caste sold her daughter Kamalayee.[32] It is interesting to find several buyers whose names often appear and they were French. It includes Ange Marie Nicolaz, the notary clerk of Karaikal (mentioned in 4 sale deeds), Alexandres de Rosaire (mentioned in 3 sale deeds) and Poly d'Aurbigny, the master-surveyor of Karaikal (mentioned in 3 sale deeds). Those slaves who were of *vellalar* caste exported to Mauritius, were employed in the plantations on arrival as they were professionally skilled in agricultural operations.

TABLE 11.3: SALE OF SLAVES FROM KARAIKAL FOR EXPORT TO MAURITIUS AND REUNION, 1766-1776

Year	*Male*	*Female*	*Total*
1766	–	1	1
1767	–	1	1
1771	1	–	1
1774	20	17	37
1775	3	2	5
1776	2	2	4

Source: Edmond Gaudart, *Catalogue des manuscrits des anciens archives de l'Inde Française, 1690-1789*, 8 vols., Pondichéry, 1926-42.

Pondicherry was restored to the French in 1765 and there were attempts in 1768 to purchase slaves for export. The French Company transported 329 slaves from Pondicherry to Mascarenes till 1775.[33] The *noirs* (adult males) and *caporl* (young males) were sent in large numbers as slaves. No young women were exported in this period. Pondicherry was again occupied by the English from August 1778 to February 1785.[34] Therefore, the slave trade of the French East India Company to Mauritius and Le Reunion came to a halt.

The customs duty on the export of slaves had been 4 per cent in Pondicherry since 1715. The French Company raised it from time to time with the aim of increasing the revenue. They also reduced the rate sometimes with a motive to attract traders. During January 1739, the Superior Council of Pondicherry ordered ½ per cent ad valorem duty to be levied on slaves brought into Pondicherry for export. A writer was appointed in Pondicherry, at the port, to maintain the accounts of customs duties on exports including slaves.[35]

HUMAN MERCHANDISE AT THE MARKET: INSIGHTS FROM THE SLAVE REGISTER OF PONDICHERRY

Though there is a lack of exact information regarding the conditions which determined the price of a slave in Pondicherry, there are some clues which are available. The price of a slave was determined by his/her age, skills and physical appearance. Slaves who were skilled cooks, carpenters and masons, were more valuable than unskilled slaves. Adult and good looking slaves were also more expensive than children or older slaves. Ananda Ranga Pillai, the chief *dubash*, mentioned in his private diary that the age of the native slaves primarily determined their value in the market. Those above 7 years and below 16 years of age had fetched a high price in the Indo-French town of Pondicherry. A Tamil document dated 25 November 1781, preserved in the southern zonal office of the National Archives of India, Pondicherry, describes some of the procedures followed in the sale of slaves in Pondicherry.[36] In the open slave market in Pondicherry, the slaves were present with their masters. Auction was conducted by public outcry and the slaves were sold. The sale transactions were confirmed through the registration of a deed. It was executed in the presence of the local officials along with the deposition mentioning that the absolute right over the slave vested with the buyer. The sale deed was written both in Tamil and French by the *ur kanakkar* (accountant of the place). The witnesses also signed the document. The money receipt was made by the *chavadi ur kanakkar* (court accountant of the place), and it was executed in the *chavadi* (court) of Pondicherry. On the sale of slaves, the French and other Europeans besides the natives in Pondicherry had to pay 5 per cent by way of tax and 1½ per cent for stamp paper.[37]

The French East India Company's sale register of the native slaves in Pondicherry contains the name of the slave, his or her probable age, place of origin along with the place from where the slave was brought, the name of the slave dealer, relationship if any, the name of the seller, the exact price for which the slave was sold, the date of sale, and the purchaser's name. It is learnt that children were sold in the auction only after consent was obtained from the mothers/grandmothers. The price varied between 3 rupees and 21 rupees. The percentage of sale of the male slaves was more than that of the female slaves.[38] The buyers included the Muslims (Mohammed Shah on 11 September 1783, Mohammed Thasty on 22 August 1783 and Khader Sahib on 4 September 1790), the Indo-Portuguese (Francisco Rodrigues on 12 September 1783) and the Hindus who had come from distant places (like Thondiayarpettai near Madras and Sriperumbudur) to participate in the auction in Pondicherry.[39]

According to the slave register, 149 slaves were sold in Pondicherry in 1783. The number decreased in the following years.[40] We find frequent mention of individuals like Muthu, Nalla Thamby, Thailamme and Muthammal, slave dealers who had been participating in the sale of slaves in Pondicherry.

TABLE 11.4: GEOGRAPHICAL ORIGIN OF SLAVES AND THE SELLING PRICE IN PONDICHERRY, 1783

Date	*Place*	*Price in Rupees*
13 July 1783	Kosapalayam	21
18 July 1783	Madras	4
24 July 1783	Muthirapalayam	10
28 July 1783	Arcot	4
28 July 1783	Villupuram	15
28 July 1783	Yembalam	7½
2 August 1783	Nellikuppam	10
2 August 1783	Villiyanallur	4
10 August 1783	Kalapet	5½
11 August 1783	Kanchipuram	15
12 August 1783	Sipouvanthittu	4
23 August 1783	Kumbakonam	5
25 August 1783	Panruti	3
26 August 1783	Thiruvennainallur	3
26 August 1783	Chingleput	64

Source: National Archives of India, Puducherry, *Eighteenth Century Documents*, folder no. 91.

Khader Sahib was found selling as well as buying slaves on different dates (3 December 1783 and 18 December 1783). The police chief in Pondicherry had issued regulations for the sale of slaves on 20 June 1778 since several complaints were lodged in the town. Additional rules were enforced on 18 December 1790 to avoid the problems encountered in slave purchases and sales. Large scale illegal slave sale transactions necessitated such measures in the town.[41] It was ordered that the sale deeds of slaves must be signed by the mothers or grandmothers, and not by the father. It is significant that mothers and grandmothers enjoyed the sole authority to relegate children to slave status. The local advisor also played his part.

The French East India Company in Pondicherry requested the weavers to produce *guineas* and *salempouris* that had been used as slave cloth. The same varieties were exported to Mauritius, Le Reunion, the Mascarenes and the Comoros islands for the use of slaves. Ananda Ranga Pillai supplied 1,500 pieces of slave shirts which were in great demand in the Mascarenes. Slave trade conducted by the French had facilitated the production of the coarse variety of cloth. There was a heavy demand for striped and checked *guinea* cloth required for clothes for the slaves. The slave cloth of *gurras* (coarse cloth), *futas* (strong and cheap calico) and *niqnarias* (stripped calico patterned in loom with 14¼ cubits long and 1⅛ cubits broad) produced in Pondicherry, were exported for the use of slaves.[42] Many Tamil slaves exported to Mauritius worked as cooks and household servants and helped the French population. Slaves also worked as palanquin bearers since 4-6 of them were needed for each vehicle.

Trade and traffic in slaves was abolished by the French National Assembly through a decree and it also came into force in Pondicherry from 1 November 1792 through the arrêtés (orders) of 11, 14 and 15 October 1792.[43] The Colonial Assembly of Pondicherry asked the natives in the town to dispose of the slaves acquired earlier. It also banned them from doing business in slaves. Thus, with the abolition of slavery in Pondicherry in 1792, the export of slaves to Mauritius and Le Reunion came to an end.

ESCAPE OF A TAMIL SLAVE FROM MAURITIUS TO PONDICHERRY IN A SHIP IN 1785

Slaves exported from Pondicherry to Mauritius were treated as private property. João (John) was a slave exported from Pondicherry to Mauritius and he served Lousteau his master for many years. A complaint was lodged by Lousteau at the police station in Port Louis, Mauritius, on 25 May 1785 wherein he stated that João his slave had been abducted. He also mentioned that his fugitive slave was of the *lascar* caste, a Tamil, dark in complexion, short in height, with a handsome, slightly thin face, a gentle appearance, long hair, abundantly endowed with clothes such as jackets and shorts, wearing small gold earrings and a pin with a gold heart on his shirt and having on the arm, a mark which read DM.[44]

On enquiry the police learnt that João the slave, was a skilled carpenter. He had managed to escape and sailed away in the ship *Le Brilliant* that left Port Louis on 20 May 1785 to Pondicherry. João had boarded the ship by mentioning himself as a freeman under the name of Joseph. On 16 December 1785, the police received information regarding João being in the service of M. Brousse, a lieutenant of the regiment of Isle de France, with whom he had disembarked in Pondicherry.[45] In spite of the fact that João was asked to be deported to Mauritius, nothing happened. He lived happily in Pondicherry and did not return. The French Company officials in Pondicherry could not take any effective steps in this case because there was no provision in the then prevailing legal system.

The Hindu slaves of Pondicherry in Mauritius who survive in records is because a significant proportion of slave owners were Hindus. In 1775, Muthu a free Tamil man owned a slave named Rama and he reported his death at 80 years.[46] Hindus were also kidnapped. In 1785 several Indians testified before the police in Port Louis calling for the liberation of Aadiya Paatham (Odia Padam) a Tamil who had been kidnapped by Jean de Silvas in 1775 and enslaved. It was reported to the police. Several Tamils testified before the police in Port Louis for liberation.[47] Hindu slave owners had ill-treated the slaves and committed acts of wanton cruelty. Chinna Thambi (Sinetamby), a free Indian in Mauritius had been described as a man of very bad character. In a local police report he described the suicide of one of his slaves, attributing to his harsh treatment. The police could not arrest him because there was no evidence and the needed proof. Chinna Thambi, on another occasion had been reported to ill-treat Arunachalan (Arnacelon) one of his Tamil slaves who was badly wounded with his arms bound. The slave was sent for medical treatment and the cost was charged to Chinna Thambi.[48] Jean Baptiste Pipon a French merchant in Mauritius mentioned a transaction involving three slaves, very handsome and aged between 12 and 18, who had been purchased in Pondicherry. He also mentioned the arrival of a female slave from Pondicherry in 1791 and advised the prospective buyer to do the needful immediately.[49] In 1792, three French vessels sailed from Pondicherry to the Mauritius with 1,200 slaves.[50] The French Company was able to obtain more slaves from the Cuddalore area and so two more French ships sailed away from Pondicherry with 300 Tamil slaves and the ship arrived at Mauritius on 3 February 1792.[51]

CONCLUSION

The French East India Company exported slaves from Pondicherry, Cuddalore and Karaikal areas to Mauritius, Reunion and Comoros Islands. The French Company attempted to enter into agreements with the port officials and rulers of the Tamil Coast requesting a legal stamp for the purchase and transport of slaves but it was of no use. However, religion had played an important role in slave trade. While the Nawab of Arcot desired that Muslims should not be exported as slaves and the European missionaries also wished not to export the slaves who became Christians.

In the beginning of the eighteenth century, the French Company preferred young slaves for overseas export so that they might lose memory of their parents and forget their own native place and knew nothing of what had happened when they were young. There would be a tendency also in that case not to run away from the masters and be very obedient and submissive. Natural calamities such as the failure of crops, drought and famine had been key factors for persons becoming slaves voluntarily. The relationship between lack of rainfall and food scarcity perhaps was the cause of rise for the slave market on the Tamil Coast. The slave supplies dried up when famine situation disappeared. The monetary value of slaves fluctuated over time and depended on age, gender, skills and market demands.

NOTES

1. Lotika Varadarajan, *India in the Seventeenth Century: Memoirs of François Martin* (hereafter *Memoirs*), 2 vols., Delhi, 1984, vol. II, pt. I, p. 1070.
2. Hubert Gerbeau, 'Des minorités mal connues: Esclaves indiens et malais des Mascareignes au XIXe siècle', in *Migrations, minorités et échanges en Océan Indien, XIXe-XXe siècle*, Aix-en-Provence: IHPOM, 1979, pp. 160-242.
3. Archives Nationales (hereafter AN), Paris, MSS Colonies Série C², no.12, fol. 219; See also MSS Colonies Série C², no. 68, fol. 214.
4. Bibliothèque Nationale de Paris (henceforth BNP), MSS *Nouvelles Acquisitions Françaises* (hereafter *NAFR*), no. 8929, fol. 275.
5. Archives Departmentales de la Reunion (hereafter ADR), Saint-Denis, C 2791, fls. 81r-82v.
6. BNP, MSS *Fond Français, Memoire sur la Compagnie des Indes Orientales*, no. 6231, fol. 39.
7. ADR, C 2792, fl. 9r.
8. ADR, GG 1, Saint-Paul nos. 748-756, 758-780, 782-783.
9. AN, MSS Colonies Série C², no. 72, fols. 141-2.
10. Edmond Gaudart, ed., *Procès-verbaux des délibèrations du Conseil Supérieur de Pondichéry du 1 er Fevrier 1701 au 31 Decembre 1739* (hereafter *Procès-verbaux*), 3 vols., Pondichéry, 1913-15, see 6 September 1718.
11. ADR, C 319.
12. Richard B. Allen, 'The Constant Demand of the French: The Mascarene Slave Trade and the Worlds of the Indian Ocean and Atlantic during the Eighteenth and Nineteenth Centuries', *Journal of African History*, no. 49, 2008, pp. 43-72, see p. 65.
13. J.M. Filliozat, *La Traite des Escalves vers le Mascareignes au XVIII e Siecle*, Paris, 1974, p. 226.
14. Alfred Martineau, *Lettres & Conventions des Gouverneurs de Pondichéry, avec differents princes hindous (1666 a 1793)*, Pondichéry, 1914, p. 58.
15. Ibid., p. 57.
16. Frederick Price, H. Dodwell and V. Rangachari, eds., *The Private Diary of Ananda Ranga Pillai, Dubash to Joseph François Dupleix, Knight of the Order of St. Michael, and Governor of Pondicherry: A Record of Matters Political, Historical, Social, and Personal, from 1736 to 1761* (hereafter *ARP Diary*), vol. I, 1904; vol. II, 1907; vol. III,

1914; vol. IV, 1916; vol. V, 1917; vol. VI, 1918; vol. VII, 1919; vol. VIII, 1922; vol. IX, 1924; vol. X, 1925; vol. XI, 1927; vol. XII, 1928, Madras; repr., Delhi, 1980, vol. I, pp. 227–30.

17. *ARP Diary*, vol. I, pp. 228–30.
18. Ibid. Ananda Ranga Pillai had mentioned that Paramananda Pillai of Karaikal was a rich merchant. He also said that Ramalinga Pillai of Karaikal was wealthy. *ARP Diary*, vol. IX, pp. 248-50.
19. Ibid., vol. I, pp. 227-30.
20. Centre des Archives d'Outre-Mer (hereafter CAOM), Aix-en-Provence, Inde, Série M/91.
21. S. Jeyaseela Stephen, 'Waves of Migration of Tamil Slaves and Skilled Artisans from Puducherry to Mauritius and Le Reunion under the French East India Company, 1707-93', *Journal of the Institute of Asian Studies*, vol. xxv, no. 2, March 2008, pp. 41-63, see p. 47.
22. Edmond Gaudart, *La criminalite dans les comptoirs français del'Inde au XVIIIe siecle*, Pondichéry, 1937, p. 17.
23. Edmond Gaudart, *Catalogue des manuscrits des ancienns archives de l'Inde Française, 1690-1789*, 8 vols., Pondichéry, 1926-42, vol. I, p. 9; Edmond Gaudart, *Procès-verbaux 1747*, document no. 29.
24. CAOM, Inde, B/28 and B/29. For more on the baptisms of French owned slaves, see CAOM, FM, F^3/238, fols. 525-6.
25. Marina Carter, 'Indian Slaves in Mauritius, 1729-1834', *The Indian Historical Review*, vol. XV, nos. 1-2, 1988-9, pp. 233-47.
26. CAOM, Aix-en-Provence, DFC, Memoire no. 132, *Extrait du recensement general de l 'Isle de France, 1761*.
27. *Mémoire signifié pour le nommé Francisque, Indien de nation, néophyte de l'Eglise Romaine, Intimé contre le Sieur Allain-François-Ignace Brignon, se disant Ecuyer, Appellan*, Chez P.G. Simon, Imprimeur du Parlement, Paris, 1759.
28. Ibid.
29. British Library (hereafter BL), London, *Oriental and India Office Collection* (hereafter *OIOC*), *The Verlee Collection, 1769-1836*, MSS EUR. F. 193, fol. 6, see the accounts of M. Bretel in August 1769.
30. CAOM, Aix-en-Provence, *Feuilles Volantes, Karaikal*, Serie Le-Indes, dossier nos. 3356, 3422, 3540, 3640, 3657, 3810 and 3871.
31. Edmond Gaudart, *Catalogue des manuscrits*, vol. IV, p. 144.
32. Ibid., vol. V, document no. 3648.
33. Richard B. Allen, 'The Constant Demand', p. 55, see Table 4.

34. S. Jeyaseela Stephen, 'Urbanism and the Chequered Existence of the Indo-French Town of Pondicherry, 1674-1793', *Revue Historique de* Pondichéry, vol. XIX, 1996, pp. 29-64.
35. W.H. Dalgliesch, *The Company of the Indies in the Days of Dupliex*, Easton, 1933, p. 68.
36. S. Jeyaseela Stephen, 'Puduvai Avana Kapagathil Ore Adimai Sasanam', *Avanam*, vol. 8, 1997, p. 96. The sale deed in Tamil was executed by Tayilaamma, the wife of Ponnanan of the *palli* caste in favour of Mariyamma.
37. National Archives of India, Puducherry (hereafter NAIP), *Eighteenth Century Documents*, folder no. 449, fol. 3.
38. *ARP Diary*, vol. XII, p. 18; vol. I, p. 269.
39. NAIP, *Eighteenth Century Documents*, folder no. 91, *Vente d' enfants et d' d'esclaves, 25 November 1781 to 22 December 1791.*
40. Ibid.
41. Plaidoyer de M. Ed. Thureau, *Indien, de l'esclavage et de la traite des Indiens*, Paris, 1844, pp. 17-18.
42. S. Jeyaseela Stephen, *Oceanscapes*, p. 490.
43. BNP, LK 19.18.
44. National Archives of Mauritius, Coromandel, Serie JB, 47, *Procedure Criminelle, 1785*, Evasion of João the slave of M. Lousteau.
45. Ibid.
46. CAOM, Aix-en-Provence, Registre Etat Civil, Isle de France.
47. Sadasivam Reddi, 'Aspects of Indian Culture in Ile de France between 1803 and 1810', in *History, Memory and Identity*, eds., Vijayalakshmi Teelock and Edward A. Alpers, Nelson Mandela Centre, Mauritius, 2001, p. 35.
48. M. Jumeer, *Les Affranchis et les Indiens Libres à l'Ile de France au xviiième siècle 1721-1803*, University of Poitiers Thesis, 1984, pp. 277-80.
49. Auguste Toussaint, *Le Mirage des Iles: Le negoce français aux Mascareignes au XVIIIe siècle*, Aix-en-Provence, 1977, p. 94.
50. British Library (hereafter BL), *Oriental and India Office Collection* (hereafter *OIOC*), P/241/31, fl.562, letter of Mathew Yeats to Sir Charles Oakley dated 22 December 1792.
51. BL, *OIOC*, P/241/36, fls. 6-19, the letter of Mathew Yeats to Major-General William Meadows, dated 3 February 1792.

CHAPTER 12

Conclusion
Closing the Curtains

Slavery was a recognized institution in the Tamil country since medieval times. The slaves came to be employed in the temples and with madams and were engaged in many kinds of labour. The institutions, being masters, had unlimited power over the slaves who had been placed at the bottom of the Tamil society. There had been no concrete evidences of manumission of slaves in medieval Tamil country. The causes for slavery show the influence of local practices of social mobility as well as debt bondage in determining the condition. Inequalities such as caste, indebtedness, slave lineage, birth rights and stigmas in addition to conflicts such as warfare and punishment had also been attributed.

The papal bull, 'Dum Diversas' issued in 1452 had authorized the Portuguese to conquer and enslave the Saracens, the pagans and other unbelievers inimical to Christ. The Portuguese missionaries in India faithfully applied the principle of religious conversion to slaves. It was believed that once a slave got converted to Christianity there was always the option of freedom. Portuguese traders began to transport slaves from various places to their own trading settlements. The African slaves brought to Goa were called coffrees. It must be said that the Portuguese considered Tamils a race superior to Africans and other Asians. Slaves converted in the Tamil Coast area were given Christian names with surnames which reveal the region or place of origin such as Coromandel, besides Negapatam (Nagapattinam) and Tuticorijin (Tuticorin). Missionary records mention that a large population of domestic slaves had lived in the Portuguese port settlements of the Tamil Coast.

I

The Jesuits on the Tamil Coast noticed the slave trade of the private traders who purchased men, women and children from natives. Since Tamil slavery was mainly domestic in nature, the missionaries reacted sharply when large scale exports from the Tamil Coast to Goa, Cochin and Melaka was carried on. One finds that at this time slavery and slave trade had developed as a theological problem for the missionaries. Time and again the provincial councils of Goa discussed the medieval notion of slavery. It challenged the local enslavement practices which could not be considered for they were unethical for the Christian recognition. The resulting decrees and the constitutions of the Archbishop of Goa became the general guidelines according to which disputes were to be resolved by ecclesiastical authorities. The priests debated the relation between slavery and the sacraments, the limits and rules governing master-slave relations, as well as the relations with non-Christians. The condition of the domestic slaves was reported to be very different from that of rising colonial slaves.

The Portuguese missionary letters and the Danish-Halle missionary reports provide information on the slave trade, slavery, social conditions and indigenous forms of bondage. These details had been found missing in the sources of the East India Company. These missionary descriptions provide information on the pattern of slavery and the system present in Portugal and Germany linking to Catholic and Protestant Christian religious view indicating the need and importance of making efforts to stop slave trading from the Tamil Coast extending throughout the world.

II

Portuguese private traders began slave trading within Goa, Cochin, Melaka and Manila. The Spaniards extended it by transporting Tamil slaves crossing the Pacific linking with colonial Mexico. The Spanish records show the nature, routes, and logistics of these voyages in detail and the importance of private slave traders in expanding the slave supply in the seventeenth century. Finally, both these circuits supplied slaves to meet the Portuguese and Spanish demands around the globe.

In early years of Dutch expansion on the Coromandel Coast between 1621 and 1651, in spite of commercial rivalry and competition with the Portuguese, the Dutch Company successfully purchased and transported plenty of slaves from the Coromandel Coast to Indonesia, Myanmar and Sri Lanka. It mostly happened when people were forced into slavery as a result of impoverishment and starvation after famines broke out. The Dutch transported slaves to Jakarta and also to increase the population in Sri Lanka after a series of conquests. On the other hand, there had been increase in slave trade and transport of enslaved people in groups with many voyages that were primarily fitted out for Dutch Company purposes. Such trade and transport of enslaved people subsequently became widespread in several ports on Coromandel. The flows gradually accumulated to bulk slave trade that grew to full cargo slave trade.

The quantifications found in Dutch records contribute to the growing insight that the slave trading by the Dutch Company was frequent and widespread between Coromandel and Indonesian archipelago. Carving out the patterns of slave trade through quantitative means, one finds local forms of bondage developed in response to global capitalist needs. The Dutch Company documents mention the names of the port, the number of slaves purchased in total for export along with the total amount paid. Since details of such expenditure incurred had been found, the price of each slave on an average could only be calculated though the price of men, women, boys, girls and infants would be varying.

It is gleaned that during the same year, in different months at the same port, the prices of slaves had varied. Further, prices also differed at various ports during the same year.

TABLE 12.1: SLAVE PRICE PAID BY THE DUTCH AT THE PORTS OF COROMANDEL COAST, 1631-1652

Year	*Place*	*Price per Slave in florins*
1631	Pazhaverkadu	42
1635	Devanampattinam	31:10
1636	Devanampattinam	26:16
1636	Pazhaverkadu	26
1636	Pazhaverkadu	35:04
1637	Pazhaverkadu	32
1640	Pazhaverkadu	27
1642	Pazhaverkadu	27
1643	Devanampattinam	50
1644	Tirumullaivasal	31:15
1644	Pazhaverkadu	30
1645	Pazhaverkadu	38
1645	Pazhaverkadu	37:16
1645	Pazhaverkadu	33:01:05
1646	Pazhaverkadu	15:11
1647	Pazhaverkadu	12:11
1648	Pazhaverkadu	21:15
1651	Devanampattinam	40
1651	Karaikal	38:05
1652	Karaikal	36:18

The escalation may be due to various factors such as availability and non-availability of slaves in the market. According to the master list of slaves, the Dutch had given the classification of slaves in Pulicat as Hindus and Muslims.

Long voyages were carefully planned by the Europeans while slave trading to take maximum advantage of the seasonal changes in wind direction, with special reference to the monsoons of the Indian Ocean. The southwest monsoon assisted outward voyages between April and October in the region. Europe bound ships via Cape Town made use of the northeast monsoon during the remainder of the year. The heaviest concentration of sailors was therefore to be found at the Cape of Good Hope between late December and early May. Improvements in ship construction in the interests of greater safety and efficiency took place. Indian teak began to replace oak and copper sheathing to protect it from the ravages of the worm in tropical waters. Crowded slaves and insanitary conditions caused the spread of disease and the medical attention was rough. Fever was common on the ships, respiratory complaints and dysentery was widespread and dietary deficiency led to scurvy. Meanwhile, slaves died unnecessarily and the death rate was often staggeringly high, even on voyages of moderate length. One finds 131 ships in total had sailed between June 1621 to November 1665 and 1,379 slaves had died during the voyage.

The cost of clothing a slave had been also mentioned. The slaves were commonly clothed in dungarees (*dongrys*), a simple coarse cotton cloth, much like a loincloth. Sometimes it was dyed red with a black stripe running through the middle. Dungarees were also used as sail cloth and for packing material, especially for wrapping textiles. The price of a piece of dungarees fluctuated from as little as florin 0:15:00 to as much as florin 1:10:00. Guinea cloth (*guinees lywaet or negros kleden*) for slaves has also been mentioned often. This was a coarse, cheap striped or chequered cotton cloth woven from yarn dyed in bright colours and cost around florin 0:11:00 per piece. It was often exported to the Gulf of Guinea, which gave it its name.

The cost of feeding a slave had been recorded. Each slave had a daily ration of 1.13 lbs of rice costing on an average about florin 0:00:07 per pound. The total daily cost of feeding a single slave including rice (*kanji*), dried fish (*karuvadu*) sesame oil was about florin 0:05:05. Dutch shipping lists regularly mention gingely or sesame seed oil which the slaves put on their bodies and its cost ranged from florin 0:09:00 to florin 0:16:00 per litre. The food and clothing from time of purchase till the slaves shipped at Devanampattinam in 1635 in total had been mentioned and the expenditure for each slave had been 33.08 florins. The documents also mention the cost of food: 17 parra of rice (714 lbs) incurred in total since slave arrival at Karaikal in 1651. The record also shows that a toll of 1 pagoda (4.04 florins) was paid for each slave in 1652.

III

Large scale export of slaves from various ports of Coromandel to Dutch settlements in Indonesia, Myanmar and Sri Lanka helped and facilitated the fortification works, paddy cultivation and agricultural works that incorporated slave labour. One finds that slaves exported at times found useless by the Dutch Company, were sent back from Syriam and Jaffna to the Coromandel Coast. It is to be noted that long-term slave based systems of agricultural production were perhaps absent in these places. The indigenous slavery in these regions must have merged earlier into a kind of serfdom or household membership. After the arrival of the Dutch in Jakarta slave holding practices were shaped profoundly particularly because the slaves were employed in pepper and nutmeg gardens, animal husbandry and fortification works. Slaves of Pazhaverkadu were employed in the Banda islands where nutmegs were produced in the estates. Chinna Thaai the female slave hailing from Nagapattinam was sold thrice by the Dutch and ended up with the Christian name Rosa and she was employed in 1763 at Groot Constantia's wine estate located outside the suburbs of Cape Town.

Slaves from Madras were sent by the English Company to St. Helena island for development of sugarcane plantations. Thus one finds that within the established accounts of slavery, there are not many geographic and historical variations which are to be usually acknowledged to European slave trade practices from Tamil Coast. One finds a distinct form of colonial slavery links in tune with the New World and Africa, where European systems were imported wholesale. However this system has been a form of exploitation of slave labour unheard of in medieval Tamil country.

There has been some kind universal method of application of slave labour by the Europeans. One finds European expansion leading to the growth of slave based production of key global commodities, such as pepper and nutmeg by the Dutch in Indonesia, sugar in St. Helena Island by the English, coconut palm cultivation plantations in Manila and Mexico by Spaniards and development of wine estates in South Africa through employment of Tamil slaves. This happened owing to the rising demand for labour that fuelled the long distance slave trade, which in turn stimulated enslavement through warfare, raiding, or the exploitation of local castes or bondage systems and debt.

IV

A striking aspect of the effect of political dynamics on slavery and slave trade happened when the rulers of the Coromandel Coast put up a strong resistance to European slave trading. Krishnappa Nayak the ruler of Gingee when approached by the Dutch for royal permission to undertake slave trade, he vehemently condemned it as a universal crime and shame. Shivaji the ruler banned the Dutch export of slaves totally from the ports of Devanampattinam and Porto Novo in his kingdom. The Nawab of Arcot did not encourage the French in Pondicherry but he was somewhat lenient and said that that no Muslim slaves should be transported from his territory and exported overseas by the French Company. Pratap Singh the Maratha ruler of Thanjavur expressed his grief over Danish slave trade and as a result the governor of Tranquebar prohibited it issuing an order in 1745. The European slave trade in turn, had a massive effect on local economies. Large-scale kidnapping, abductions and enslaving impacted the Tamil society deeply. Inhuman activities and slave trade by native agents and brokers were condemned. The king imposed severe punishments for those who indulged in the slave dealing and profited from the commercial transaction.

V

Christianity speaks of ethics where slaves have to be manumitted after a period of time as stipulated in the Old Testament (Exodus 21:2). The Tamil slaves transported to Sri Lanka and employed in the houses of the Europeans, came to be manumitted. A legal way of freeing a Tamil slave thus developed under the Dutch, but the transition to full freedom was generally very slow and the situation could be reverted if the ex-slave failed to show gratitude or to be helpful to the former master when required. In Dutch records one finds that according to the custom a master manumitted his or her slave in Sri Lanka, hailing from Tuticorin by declaring that he/she would be free only after his/her (the master) death. It was not a very welcome change of status for old slaves who could then hardly find a new buyer or master.

Manumission practice required almost always that the slave handed over a part of his value in cash to the former master. This was almost a kind of self-sale that permitted the master to buy a new slave. Manumissions without such value exchange were exceptional. These were motivated by pious intentions of the masters of gaining merits before God. Also such cases were often delayed till the slave was old and was of little use in terms of labour that could be exacted from him or her. In reality, manumission did not always correspond to the good intentions and legislation.

Manumission had been found conditional at times, requiring service during the life time of the owners and at times the condition of service could be required from the children of the manumitted slaves. But there had been cases in which the masters helped the manumitted slaves to be able to continue working to gain their livelihood. Though in rare cases, some masters gave a house and a piece of land. While emancipation deeds of slaves in Sri Lanka provide a wealth of information on name, regional origin of slave mentioning the name of the ports like Nagapattinam and Tuticorin, the gender, age and circumstances leading to emancipation, what happened once freedom was given to emancipated slaves and their families, is not recorded.

VI

The tendency of the slaves to run away was found common. The legislation took measures to block any assistance to such runaway slaves. There were even extradition laws to guarantee return of the slaves who crossed the borders of the country like that of Francisco the slave of Pondicherry found in France. Again the journey of Samuel Johannes the slave of Tuticorin to The Netherlands, his escape in Germany and finally travelling to Pennsylvania in British North America, point to the impact of the expanding long-distance slave trade and also on the local conditions and the strategies employed by slave owners.

The presence of Europeans on the Tamil Coast had led to an integration and intensification of slave trade systems throughout the continents of Asia, Africa, Europe and America. The chapters in the book had helped to increase one's understanding of the mechanisms of the systems of slavery, modes of enslavement and trade. In doing so, it accentuates the local contexts of bondage and how they were folded into transregional or transoceanic networks. The study of the specific routes of entry and exit into and from slavery, sheds additional light on the ways that different forms of slavery and bondage were interconnected and interacting.

VII

A slow end of European slave trading came about when the flow of supplies to the slave markets dried up with time. There was the emergence of a market for land and territorial conquest where the self-sufficiency of the labourers was a fact. The Anglo-French rivalry in the Carnatic region led to recruitment of African soldiers and brought to Fort St. David at Cuddalore besides maintaining native armies of sepoys. Artisans and skilled labour besides coolie (wage) labour became the need of the hour and so migration came to develop on these lines. Hence the French signed contracts and the labour migration spread from Pondicherry to Reunion Island between 1841 and 1883. Indenture labour migration developed from Pondicherry and Karaikal to French Guiana in South America between 1854 and 1872, to Martinique Islands in the Caribbean between 1854 and 1879, to Guadeloupe Island in the West Indies to be employed in sugar plantations between 1851 and 1890. Coolies were sent from Madras to Mauritius between 1842 and 1880. Wage labour migration from Tamil country to work in the coffee plantations developed under the British between 1828 and 1883. Here one finds return voyages of the coolies back to Tamil motherland in the nineteenth century. However, all these new developments happened by replacing the earlier slave mode of production introduced by the Europeans in the overseas. Enslavement and slave trade happened during the sixteenth to eighteenth centuries and it preceded migration of indentured labour on the Tamil Coast. Slave trade could not expand, spread and progress with the great movement of emancipation of slaves.

Bibliography

PRIMARY SOURCES

I. Manuscripts

DENMARK

Rigsarkivet, Kobenhavn

Danske Kancelli, B 246.

FRANCE

Archives Nationales, Paris

MSS Colonies, Série C^2, no. 12, Série C^2, no. 68, Série C^2, no. 72.

Bibliothèque Nationale de Paris, Paris

Fond Français, Memoire sur la Compagnie des Indes Orientales, no. 6231.

Nouvelles Acquisitions Françaises, no. 8929.

Centre des Archives d' Outre-Mer, Aix-en-Provence

Depot des fortifications des colonies, Memoire no. 132, Extrait du recensement general de l 'Isle de France, 1761.

Feuilles Volantes, Karaikal, Serie Le-Indes, dossier nos. 3356, 3422, 3540, 3640, 3657, 3810 and 3871.

Inde, Série B/28 and B/29; FM, F^3/238; M/91.

Registre Etat Civil, Isle de France.

GERMANY

Archiv der Franckesche Stiftungen, Halle

M1 B3: 26; M1 B29:29

M1 F3: 5, p. 7, see, Supplementum Des Verzeichnißes der glieder der Portugiesischen, Malabarischen Stadt–und Land–Gemeine vom

5 October 1728: bis d: 5ten Oct: 1729. Nebst einem anhang von denen die in diesen Jahr abgegangen.

M1 K5: 14, M 2 A 6: 5 (3); M 2 B 5: 7.

M2 C15: 3, Supplementum des Verzeichnißes der Glieder der Portugiesischen und Malabarischen Stad-und Land-Gemeine vom 5 October 1740 bis 5 October 1741, Nebst einem Anhang von denen die in diesem Jahr abgegangen.

M2 C15: 9, IItes Supplementum Des Verzeichnisses der Glieder der Portugiesischen u: Tamulischen Stadt-und Land-Gemeine, vom 5ten Octobr: 1746, bis 5ten Octobr 1747, Nebst einem Anhange von denen in diesem Jahr abgegangenen.

Unitats Archive, Herrnhut

R.4.B.V.b.3.8., Catalog Lindheim 1744.

R.6.a. A.74.4, Erdmuthe Dorothea von Zinzendorf to Chamberlain von Hund at Unwürde, 27 March 1754.

R.6.a. A.74, Order by Siegmund August von Gersdorf on behalf of Countess Zinzendorf, Herrnhut, 4 May 1754.

R.6.a. A.74, Pro nota regarding the extradition request, 11 May 1754.

R.6.a. A.74, Passport by the bailiff of Barby, 18 May 1754.

R.8.33.b.3, The Diary of Wetterau, 2 August 1742.

R.15.S.2, Diary of David Nitschmann and August Christian Friedrich Ellert's journey to Ceylon, vol. 2, 17 August 1740-24 November 1741.

R.21.A.28.47, Certificate of sale of the slave boy Maden to Christian Dober, 1 June 1739.

R.22.84.21, The Biography of Maria Magdalena Malabar.

R.27.291.13, The Register of Seminarians, Barby 1750.

INDIA

Historical Archives of Goa, Panaji

Moncoes do Reino, Livro 19C, 67-70/5-2.

National Archives of India, Puducherry

Eighteenth Century Documents, folder no. 91, Vente d' enfants et d' d'esclaves, 25 November 1781 to 22 December 1791.

——, folder no. 449.

Tamil Nadu State Archives, Chennai

Cochin Records, no. 352.
——, no 584, sale and transfer of slaves from 25 January 1755 to 5 August 1756.
——, no. 622, sale and transfer of slaves in 1758.
——, no. 632, sale and transfer of slaves in 1759.
——, no. 886, sale and transfer of slaves in 1770.
——, no. 896, sale and transfer of slaves in 1770-1.
——, no. 925, sale and transfer of slaves in 1772.
——, no. 957, sale and transfer of slaves, from 1 October to 31 December 1773.
——, no. 979, sale and transfer of slaves from 5 January 1774 to 5 June 1774.
——, no. 1003, sale and transfer of slaves from 1 April 1775 to 27 June 1775.
——, no. 1034, sale and transfer of slaves from 3 January 1776 to 29 April 1776.
——, no. 1062, deeds of sale and transfer of slaves from 19 July 1777 to 16 December 1777.
——, no. 1145, permits to export slaves from 18 February 1780 to 29 December 1787.
——, no. 1225, sale and transfer of slaves in 1784 and 1785.
——, no. 1266, sale and transfer of slaves in 1786.
——, no. 1288, sale and transfer of slaves from 12 February to 20 August 1787.
——, no. 1341, sale and transfer of slaves from 1 September 1789 to 27 November 1789.
——, no. 1369, deeds of sale and transfer of slaves in 1790-1.
Kantoor Bengalen te Chinsura en Rechtsopvolgers, Boxes 1677A, 1677B, 1679A, 1679B, 1694, 1696 and 1715.

INDONESIA

Arsip Nasional Republik Indonesia, Jakarta

Vendutiekantoor, 1, 1751-01-01, 1751-03-30, 1751-04-29.

MAURITIUS

National Archives of Mauritius, Coromandel

Serie JB, 47, Procedure Criminelle, 1785, Evasion of João the slave of M. Lousteau.

MEXICO

Archivo General de la Nación, Distrito Federal, México City

Seccion Civil, 680, N. 2 (1594).
Seccion Historia, 406, 407.
Seccion Indiferente Virreinal, caja 1355, exp. 34; caja 1355, exp. 36; caja 1355, exp. 37.
Seccion Inquisición, v. 355, exp. 44.
Seccion Jesuitas, IV-26.2, IV-50, IV-68.

Archivo Histórico del Municipio de Colima, Colima

Sección B, C. 23, exp. 4; Sección B, C. 23, exp. 5.

PHILIPPINES

National Archives of the Philippines, Manila

Protocolo de Manila, SDS 19763, Sale of slave Diego purchased by Miguel de Salazar, 1674.

REUNION

Archives Departmentales de la Reunion, Saint-Denis

C 319, C 596, C 599, C601, C 603, C 2791, C 2792, GG 1, Saint-Paul nos. 748-756, 758-780, 782-783.

SOUTH AFRICA

Western Cape Archives, Cape Town

Council of Justice 786, Sententiën, 1736-45.
Miscellaneous File, N 49, Serrurier Papers, Transfer deeds of slaves, 1763-6.

SPAIN

Archivo General de Indias, Seville

Seccion, Contaduria, 901-1601-02; Seccion, Contaduría, 1233, 2a pieza; Contaduría 1245, Tercera Pieza; Contaduría 1216.
Seccion, Escribanía de Cámara, 441B.

Seccion Filipinas, 10, R. 1, N. 25; Filipinas, 29-50, Filipinas, 29-63, Filipinas, 84, N. 46, Filipinas, 124, N. 10, Filipinas, 127, N. 17; Filipinas 193, n. 11.

SRI LANKA

Sri Lanka National Archives, Colombo

Dutch Central Government of Coastal Ceylon, 1640–1796, 1/4740, 1/4702, Criminal dossiers.

Protocols of Deeds of Emancipation of Slaves, 1/4145, (16 March 1739); 1/4145 (31 August 1750); 1/4145 (13 January 1751); 1/4146 (5 September 1779); 1/4146 (24 October 1781); 1/4146 (21 August 1784); 1/4146 (20 February 1786); 1/4146 (22 March 1786); 1/4146 (9 December 1786); 1/4146, (17 April 1787); 1/4146 (9 September 1787); 1/4146 (5 January 1791).

VOC 2712, Colombo Diary.

VOC Archives, Record group 1, Inventory number 9, Minutes of the Governor and Council in Colombo dated 16 November 1660; 1/20, Minutes of the Governor and Council in Colombo (29 October 1674), (3-26 November 1674); 1/24, Minutes of the Governor and Council in Colombo, Minutes of the Governor and Council in Colombo, 21 November 1678.

THE NETHERLANDS

Nationaal Archief, Den Haag

Bataviaasch Uitgaand Briefboek, VOC 876, VOC 884, VOC 890, VOC 891.

Overgekomen Brieven en Papieren, VOC 1073, VOC 1077, VOC 1079, VOC 1082, VOC 1083, VOC 1086, VOC 1087, VOC 1089, VOC 1090, VOC 1091, VOC 1092, VOC 1094, VOC 1095, VOC 1097, VOC 1100, VOC 1103, VOC 1109, VOC 1113, VOC 1117, VOC 1119, VOC 1122, VOC 1127, VOC 1133, VOC 1134, VOC 1135, VOC 1138, VOC 1143, VOC 1147, VOC 1151, VOC 1152, VOC 1156, VOC 1157, VOC 1158, VOC 1160, VOC 1161, VOC 1163, VOC 1164, VOC 1168, VOC 1184, VOC 1227, VOC 1231, VOC 1232, VOC 1233, VOC 1234, VOC 1236, VOC 1238, VOC 1240, VOC 1242, VOC 1245, VOC 1247, VOC 1248, VOC 1252, VOC 1274,

VOC 1315, VOC 1324, VOC 1332, VOC 1333, VOC 1348, VOC 1396, VOC 1351, VOC 1479, VOC 1506, VOC 1540, VOC 1628, VOC 1630, VOC 1641, VOC 1651, VOC 1653, VOC 2360, VOC 2419.

Resoluties, VOC 3324, VOC 3350, VOC 3402, VOC 3432, VOC 3433, VOC 3457, VOC 3483, VOC 3485, VOC 3516, VOC 3572, VOC 6035, VOC 7534 and VOC 7538.

Nederlandse bezittingen India: Digitale duplicaten Chennai, 1.11.06.11, 66, Scan 75, Case ID Database CR-66-11; 1.11.06.11, inv. no. 440, fls.1-39.

Verzameling Buitenlandse Kaarte, Leupe, no. 1083, 1087, 1089.

UNITED KINGDOM

British Library, London

India Office Records, B/37.

India Office Records: Series E: Correspondence to and from the London EIC.

E/3/87, Letter from London to Bantam dated 18 January 1670-1.

E/3/88, Letter from London to Fort St. George, 15 December 1676.

E/3/90, Letter from London to Fort St. George, 13 June 1683.

E/3/90, Letter from London to St. Helena, 1 August 1683.

E/3/90, Letter from London to St. Helena, 1 April 1684.

E/3/90, Letter from London to Bengal, 5 March 1683-4.

E/3/90, Letter from London to Fort St. George, 29 February 1684.

E/3/90, Letter from London to Bengal, 5 March 1684.

E/3/90, Letter from London to St. Helena, 5 April 1684.

E/3/91, Letter from London to Fort St. George, 16 March 1685.

E/3/91, Letter from London to Fort St. George, 28 September 1687.

E/3/98, Letter from London to Bencoolen, 20 March 1712/13.

India Office Records: Series G: Factory Records.

Factory Records of Fort St. George, no. 20.

G/19/1, 5 May 1655; G/19/4, Letter dated 21 June 1686; G/19/5.

G/35/2, Letter of Elihu Yale and Council at Fort St. George to Benjamin Bloome at Bencoulen, 8 November 1687.

G/35/3, 18 January 1696.

G/35/4, 20 October 1699.

Fort Marlborough Consultation, G/35/56, 19 November 1709; G/35/59, 20 August 1726; G/35/60, 3 May 1727; G/35/60,

24 October 1727; G/35/61, 29 September 1731; G/35/61, 21 April 1735, 28 April 1735.
St. Helena Consultation, 26 July 1709.
York Fort Consultation, G/35/57, 22 May 1712; G/35/57, 3 July 1711, 27 June 1715.
G/35/62, 1738 section and 1739 section; G/35/64; G/35/75.
Oriental and India Office Collection.
Collet MS D. 1153/2, Letter to Nathaniel Hodges dated 2 November 1712.
European Manuscripts, F. 193.
India Office Records: Series P: Public Records.
P/241/31, letter of Mathew Yeats to Sir Charles Oakley dated 22 December 1792.
P/241/36, letter of Mathew Yeats to Major-General William Meadows, dated 3 February 1792.
P/252/76, Letter of Charles Oakeley to Jacob Eilbracht dated 14 February 1792.

UNITED STATES OF AMERICA

Family History Library Genealogical Society of Utah, Salt Lake City

MF no. 1126936, Lubao, Bautismos.
MF no. 1126951, Lubao Matrimonios.
MF no. 35770, Asunción Sagrario Metropolitano, Defunciones de castas 1707-1733.

Moravian Archives, Bethlehem, Pennsylvania

Bethlehem Church Register, no. 11, 24 May 1763
Diary of the Bethlehem Congregation, vol. XVII, 20 April 1757; vol. XXVI, 1763-1764.

II. Printed Documents and Contemporary Chronicles

IN DANISH

Calendar Containing Notifications (1779-1824) Issued by the Administration at Tranquebar 1779, Danish Records, Serial No. 1, Government Press, Madras, 1908.
Christensen, Mourids, *Skildringer fra et ophold I Ostindien (begyndte I Trankenbar 16.3. 1671) med nogle Portugisiske og Malebariske Gloser*, 1672.

IN DUTCH

Bes, Lennart, *Plaatsingslijst van de Collectie van de familie prins–1656-Zost eeuw*, II vols., 2003.

Chavonnes, M.P. De, *The Reports of Chavonnes and his Council, and of Van Imhoff, on the Cape*, Cape Town: Van Riebeeck Society, 1918.

Chijs, J.A. Van der, *Nederlandsch-Indisch Plakaatboek*, 17 vols., Batavia/ S' Gravenhage, 1885-1900.

——, *Dagregister Gehouden int Casteel Batavia vant Passerende daer te Plaatse als Over Geheel Nederlandts-India, 1628-82*, 31 vols., The Hague- Batavia, 1887-1928.

Coen, Jan Pietersz, *Beschiden Omtrent Zijn Bedirjf in Indie*, 7 vols., ed. H.T. Colenbrander, The Hague, 1919-34.

Coolhas, W. Ph., ed., *Generale Missiven van de Gouverneurs-Generaal en Raden Aan Heren XVII der Verenigde Oostindische Compagnie*, 9 vols., 'S Gravenhage, 1960-84.

Hovy, L., *Ceylonees Plakkaatboek: Plakkaten en Andere Wetten Uitgevaardigd door het Nederlandse Bestuur op Ceylon*, 1638-1796, 2 vols., Verloren: Hilversum, 1991.

Pieters, Sophia, trs., *Memoir of Hendrick Zwaardecroon, Commandeur of Jaffnapatam, 1697*, Colombo, 1911.

Rakash, Om, *The Dutch Factories in India, A Collection of Dutch East India Company Documents Pertaining to India, 1617-23*, New Delhi: Munshiram, 1984.

Van Dam, Pieter, *Beschryvinge van de Oostindische Compagnie*, ed. F.W. Stapel and C.W. Th. Van Boetzelaer, 7 vols., 'S Gravenhage, 1927-54, repr., 1977.

Worden N., and G. Groenewald, *Trials of Slavery: Selected Documents Concerning Slaves from the Criminal Records of the Council of Justice at the Cape of Good Hope*, 1705-94, Cape Town: Van Riebeeck Society, 2005.

IN ENGLISH

Diary and Consultation Book, 1662-1746, 1749-57, ed. C.M. Schmidt, J.J. Cotton, A.V. Venkatarama Ayyar, B.S. Baliga et al., 90 vols., Madras, 1910-53.

Foster, William, ed., *The English Factories in India: A Calendar of Documents in the India Office, British Museum & Public Record Office*, vol. I (1618-21), vol. II (1622-3), vol. III (1624-9), vol. IV (1630-3), vol. V (1634-6), vol. VI (1637-41), vol. VII (1642-5), vol. VIII (1646-50), vol. IX (1651-4), vol. X (1655-60), vol. XI (1661-4), vol. XII (1665-7), vol. XIII (1668-9), Oxford, 1906-27.

Letters to Fort St. George, 45 vols., Madras, 1916-32.

Public Consultations, 1672-1750, 36 vols., Madras, 1910-38.

Yule, H., ed., *Diary of William Hedges*, London, 1887-9.

IN FRENCH

Gaudart, Edmond, ed., *Procès-verbaux des délibèrations du Conseil Supérieur de Pondichéry du 1 er Fevrier 1701 au 31 Decembre 1739*, 3 vols., Pondichéry, 1913-15.

——, *Catalogue des manuscrits des anciens archives de l'Inde Française, 1690-1789*, 8 vols., Pondichéry, 1926-42.

Martineau, Alfred, *Lettres & Conventions des Gouverneurs de Pondichéry, avec differents princes hindous (1666 a 1793)*, Pondichéry, 1914.

——, *Correspondance du Conseil Supérieur de Pondichéry et de la Compagnie, 1726-67*, 6 vols., Pondichéry, 1920-31.

Mémoire signifié pour le nommé Francisque, Indien de nation, néophyte de l'Eglise Romaine, Intimé contre le Sieur Allain-François-Ignace Brignon, se disant Ecuyer, Appellan, Chez P.G. Simon, Paris: Imprimeur du Parlement, 1759.

Thureau, Plaidoyer de M. Ed. *Indien, de l'esclavage et de la traite des Indiens*, Paris, 1844.

Varadarajan, Lotika, *India in the Seventeenth Century: Memoirs of François Martin*, 2 vols., Delhi, 1984.

IN GERMAN

Der Königl. Dänischen Missionarien aus Ost-Indien eingesandter ausführlichen Berichten, Von dem Werck ihrs Ams unter den Heyden, angerichteten Schulen und Gemeinen, ereigneten Hindernissen und schweren Umstanden; Beschaffenheit des Malabarischen Heydenthums, gepflogenen brieflicher Correspondentz und mundlchen Unterredungen mit selbigen heyden, Teil 1-9 (Continuationen 1-108), Waiserihaus, Halle, 1710-72.

Germann, W., *Ziegenbalg und Plutschau. Die Grundungsjahre der Trankebarschen Mission*, Erlangen: Andreas Deichert, 1868.

Jeyaraj Daniel and Richard Fox Young (translated, introduced and annotated), *Hindu-Christian Epistolary Self-Discourses: 'Malabarian Correspondence' between German Pietist Missionaries and South Indian Hindus (1712-14)*, Wiesbaden: Harrassowitz Verlag, 2013.

Knapp, Georg Christian et al., *Neuere Geschichte der Evangelischen Missions-Anstalten zu Bekehrung der Heiden in Ostindien*, Halle: Waisenhaus, 1770-8/95, 1848.

Lehmann, Arno, ed., *Alte Briefe aus Indien: Unverdffentlichte Briefe von Bartholomaus Ziegenbalg, 1706-19*, Berlin: Evangelische Verlagsanstalt, 1957.

Volck, Alexander, *Das entdeckte Geheimniss der Bosheit der Herrnhutischen Secte zu Errettung vieler unschuldigen Seelen, in sechs Gesprächen dargelegt*, Frankfurt: Heinrich Ludwig Brönner, 1750.

IN PORTUGUESE

Bulhão Pato, Raymundo Antonio de, ed., *Cartas de Afonso de Albuquerque*, Typographia da Academia Real das Sciencias de Lisboa, 1903.

Cunha Rivara, Joaquim Heliodoro da, *Archivo Portuguez Oriental*, 6 fasc in 10 vols., reprint, New Delhi, Asian Educational Services, 1992.

O Primeiro Concilio Prouinçial çelebrado em Goa, no anno de 1567, Goa, João de Endem, 1568.

Silva Rêgo, António da, *Documentação para a história das Missões do Padroado Português do Oriente*, X vols., Lisboa, Agência Geral das Colónias, 1947-58.

Wicki, Jose, ed., *O Livro do Pai dos Cristãos*, Lisboa: Centro de Estudos Históricos Ultramarinos, 1969.

——, *Documenta Indica*, 18 vols., Roma, 1949-88.

IN SPANISH

Icazbalceta, Joaquín García, *Fray Juan de Zumárraga: Primer o bispo y arzobispo de México*, Buenos Aires, Espasa-Calpe, 1952.

IN TAMIL

Maduraikanchi, ed. U.V. Swaminatha Aiyar, in *Pathupattu*, Madras, 1974.

Manimekhalai, ed. Venkatsamy Nattar, Tirunelveli: South India Saiva Siddhanta Pathippu Kazhagam, 1992.

Pathitrupaththu, ed. Avvai Duraisamy Pillai, second edn., Tirunelveli: South India Saiva Siddhanta Pathippu Kazhagam, 1955.

Pattinappaalai, ed. U.V. Swaminatha Aiyar, in *Pathupattu*, Madras, 1974.

Price, Frederick., H. Dodwell and V. Rangachari, eds., *The Private Diary of Ananda Ranga Pillai, Dubash to Joseph François Dupleix, Knight of the Order of St. Michael, and Governor of Pondicherry: A Record of Matters Political, Historical, Social, and Personal, from 1736 to 1761* (hereafter *ARP Diary*), vol. I, 1904; vol. II, 1907; vol. III, 1914; vol. IV, 1916; vol. V, 1917; vol. VI, 1918; vol. VII, 1919; vol. VIII, 1922; vol. IX, 1924; vol. X, 1925; vol. XI, 1927; vol. XII, 1928, Madras; repr., Delhi, 1980.

Puranaanuru, ed. U.V. Swaminatha Aiyar, Madras, 1971.

Thirukural, ed. M. Virasamy Pillai, Madras, 1849.

Tholkappiyam, Porul Athikaaram, ed. V.U. Chidambaram Pillai, Madras, 1941.

III. Travelogues

Bowrey, Thomas, *A Geographical Account of the Countries around the Bay of Bengal, 1669-79*, ed. Sir Richard Temple, Cambridge, 1905.

Bredsdorff, Asta, *The Trials and Travels of Willem Leyel: An Account of the Danish East India Company in Tranquebar, 1639-48*, Copenhagen: Museum Tusculanum Press, 2009.

Dames, M.L., ed., *The Book of Duarte Barbosa*, 2nd edition, London: Hakluyt Society, 1921.

Dampier, William, *A New Voyage Around the World*, London, 1695.

Lombard, Denys, *Memoires d'un Voyage aux Indes Orientales; Un Marchand Normand a Sumatra*, Paris, 1996.

Manucci, Nicolao, *Storio do Mogur or Mogul India*, 4 vols., ed. William Irvine, repr., New Delhi, 1981.

Mentzel, O., *A Complete and Authentic Geographical and Topographical Description of the Famous and (All Things Considered) Remarkable African Cape of Good Hope*, II vols., Cape Town, Van Riebeeck Society, 1925.

Navarrete, Martín Fernández de, *Viajes y descubrimientos españoles en el Pacífico: Magallanes, Elcano, Loaysa, Saavedra*, Madrid: Maxtor, 2011, originally published in 1919.

Polo, Marco, *Travels of Sir Marco Polo*, 2 vols., tr., Yule, London, 1903.

Temple, R.C., and Lavinia Mary Anstey, eds., *The Life of the Icelander Jon Olafsson Traveller to India, 1622-25*, 2 vols., London, 1932.

Valentijn, Francois, *Oud en Nieuw-Oost-Indien*, Dordrecht-Amsterdam, 5 vols., 1724-6.

Wright, Ione S., *Voyages of Álvaro de Saavedra Cerón, 1527-9*, Coral Gables, University of Miami Press, 1951.

IV. Epigraphical Sources

Annual Report on Epigraphy (including Indian and South Indian Epigraphy from 1881 to 1922, 1923-1945, 1950 to 2005), New Delhi/ Madras, 1887-2005.

South Indian Inscriptions, Publications of the Archaeological Survey of India, vols., I to XXXIV, New Delhi, 1890-1990.

SECONDARY SOURCES

ARTICLES

Allen, Richard B., 'The Constant Demand of the French: The Mascarene Slave Trade and the Worlds of the Indian Ocean and Atlantic during the Eighteenth and Nineteenth Centuries', *Journal of African History*, no. 49, 2008, pp. 43-72.

Arasaratnam, S., 'Slave Trade in the Indian Ocean in the Seventeenth Century', K.S. Mathew, ed., *Mariners, Merchants and Oceans: Studies in Maritime History*, New Delhi, Manohar, 1995, pp. 195-208.

Basu, Basanta Kumar, 'Notes on Slave Trade and Slavery in India during the Early Days of John Company', Calcutta, *Muslim Review*, vol. 4, 1930, pp. 20-2.

Carter, Marina, 'Indian Slaves in Mauritius, 1729-1834', *The Indian Historical Review*, vol. XV, nos. 1-2, 1988-9, pp. 233-47.

Chakravarti, Sudeshna, 'The Dutch East India Company and Slave Trade in Seventeenth-Century India: An Outline by Pieter van Dam, An Advocate of the Company', *Journal of the Asiatic Society of Calcutta*, vol. 39, no. 2, 1997, pp. 73-99.

Diaz, Jorge Simon Izquierdo, 'The Trade in Domestic Servants (Morianer) from Tranquebar for Upper Class Danish Homes in the First Half of the Seventeenth Century', *Itinerario*, vol. 43, special issue 2, *Colonial Entanglements: Cross Roads, Contact Zones and Flows in Scandinavian Global History*, 2019, pp. 194-217.

Felbaek, Ole, 'No Ship for Tranquebar for Twenty-Nine Years: Or the Art of Survival of a Mid–Seventeenth Century European Settlement in India', Roderich Ptak and D. Rothermund, eds., *Emporia*,

Commodities and Entrepreneurs in Asian Maritime Trade, c.1400–1750, Heidelberg, 1991, pp. 29-36.

Gerbeau, Hubert, 'Des minorités mal connues: Esclaves indiens et malais des Mascareignes au XIXe siècle', in *Migrations, minorités et échanges en Océan Indien, XIXe-XXe siècle*, Aix-en-Provence: IHPOM, 1979, pp. 160-242.

Germann, W., 'Bartholomaus Ziegenbalg als Bahnbrecher der lutherischen Mission', *Allgemeine Missions-Zeitschrift*, vol. X, Giltersloh, C. Bertelsmann, 1883, pp. 529-33.

Gerrit, Knaap, 'Europeans, Mestizos and Slaves: The Population of Colombo at the end of the Seventeenth Century', trans. Robert Ross, *Itinerario*, vol. V, 1981, pp. 84-101.

Krieger, Martin, 'Danish Shipping and Trade between Tranquebar on the Coromandel Coast of India and South-East Asia during the Seventeenth and Eighteenth Centuries', S. Jeyaseela Stephen, ed., *The Indian Trade at the Asian Frontier*, New Delhi, 2008, pp. 117-42.

——, 'Der dänische Sklavenhandel auf dem Indischen Ozean im 17. und 18. Jahrhundert', *Jahrbuch für Europäische Überseegeschichte* vol. XII, 2012, pp. 9-30.

Larsen, Kay, 'Danmark og Slavehandelens Ophævelse', *Historisk Tidsskrift*, vol. X, no. 4, 1937, pp. 106-8.

Leupe, P.A., Vertooch wegens den presenten staet van de generale Nederlantse Geoctroijeerde Oost-Indische Compe bij Rijckloff van Goens, extr ord raed van India ende commandeur over de retourvloot van Ao. 1655, *Bijdragen tot de Taal-Land-en Volkenkunde*, 1856, pp. 141-80.

Mentz, Søren, 'Handelsstationen Tranquebar, 1630-1750', in *Danmark og Kolonierne Indien: Tranquebar, Serampore og Nicobarerne*, ed. Niels Brimnes, Copenhagen, Gads Forlag, 2017, pp. 76-111.

Peucker, Paul, 'Aus allen Nationen: Nichteuropäer in den deutschen Brüdergemeinden des 18. Jahrhunderts', *Unitas Fratrum*, vols. 59/60, 2007, pp. 1-35.

Reddi, Sadasivam, 'Aspects of Indian Culture in Ile de France between 1803 and 1810', in *History, Memory and Identity*, eds., Vijayalakshmi Teelock and Edward A. Alpers, Mauritius: Nelson Mandela Centre, 2001, pp. 30-8.

Sastri, K.A. Nilakanta, 'Shivaji's Charters to the Dutch on the Coromandel Coast', *Proceedings of the Indian History Congress*, Calcutta: Third Session, 1936, pp. 1156-65.

Sousa, Lúcio de, 'Slave Networks and their Expansion through Macao to Europe and America', *Revista de Cultura*, no. 35, July 2010, pp. 84-94.

Stephen, S. Jeyaseela, 'Urbanism and the Chequered Existence of the Indo-French Town of Pondicherry, 1674-1793', *Revue Historique de* Pondichéry, vol. XIX, 1996, pp. 29-64.

——, 'Puduvai Avana Kapagathil Ore Adimai Sasanam', *Aavanam*, vol. 8, 1997, p. 96.

——, 'Slavery and Society: Experience of the Dutch and the French Trading Companies in Coastal Andhra, AD 1600-1800', in *Social Evils in Andhra Desa, 17th & 18th Centuries*, ed. R. Soma Reddy, M. Radhakishna Sarma and A. Satyanaryana, Hyderabad, 1999, pp. 75-96.

——, 'Waves of Migration of Tamil Slaves and Skilled Artisans from Puducherry to Mauritius and Le Reunion under the French East India Company, 1707-93', *Journal of the Institute of Asian Studies*, vol. xxv, no. 2, March 2008, pp. 41-63.

——, 'Economic Change, Institutional Development and Urbanization in Santhome, 1507-1676', in *Portuguese Presence in India During the Sixteenth and Seventeenth Centuries*, ed. Yogesh Sharma and Jose Leal Ferreira, Delhi, 2008, pp. 3-21.

Vink, Markus, 'The World's Oldest Trade: Dutch Slavery and Slave Trade in the Indian Ocean in the Seventeenth Century', *Journal of World History*, vol. 14, no. 2, 2003, pp. 131-77.

Worden, Nigel, 'Indian Ocean Slaves in Cape Town, 1695-1805', *Journal of South African Studies*, 42(3), 2016, pp. 389-408.

BOOKS

Balasubramanian, C., *The Status of Women in Tamilnadu during the Sangam Age*, Madras: University of Madras, 1976.

Bertrand, Joseph, *La Mission du Madure d' après de Documents in Edits*, 4 vols., Paris, 1847-54.

Blair, Emma Helen and James Alexander Robertson, eds., *The Philippine Islands, 1493-1898*, 55 vols., Cleveland, Ohio, Arthur H. Clark Company, 1903-7.

Bredsdorff, Asta, *Willem Leyels liv og farefulde rejse til Indien*, Copenhagen: Museum Tusculanus Forlag, 1999.

Brøndsted, Johannes, ed., *Vore Gamle Tropenkolonier*, Copenhagen: Westermann, 1952.

Carter, Marina, *Veils from Indenture: Experiences of Indian Migrants in the British Empire*, London, 1996.

Chirino, Pedro, *Relación De Las Islas Filipinas*, Manila: Historical Conservation Society, 1969.

Cushner, Nicholas, *Spain in the Philippines: From Conquest to Revolution*, Quezon City, 1971.

Dalgliesch, W.H., *The Company of the Indies in the Days of Dupliex*, Easton, 1933.

Fenger, J. Ferd, *Geschichte der Trankebarschen Mission, Aus dem Danischen tbersetzt*, Grimma: J.M. Gebhardt, 1845.

Filliozat, J.M., *La Traite des Escalves vers le Mascareignes au XVIII e Siecle*, Paris, 1974.

Gaudart, Edmond, *La criminalite dans les comptoirs français del'Inde au XVIIIe siecle*, Pondichéry, 1937.

Gil, Juan, *La India y el Lejano Oriente en la Sevilla del Siglo de Oro*, Seville: Biblioteca de Temas Sevillanos, 2011.

Heese, Hans F., *Cape Melting Pot: The Role and Status of the Mixed Population at the Cape, 1652-1795*, trs. Delia Robertson, Cape, 2015.

Jeyaraj, Daniel, *Inkulturation in Tranquebar*, Erlangen: Verlag der Ev.-Luth. Mission, 1996.

Larsen, Kay, *Dansk-Ostindiske koloniers historie*, Copenhagen: Centralførlaget, 1907.

Lehmann, E. Arno, *It Began at Tranquebar: A History of the First Protestant Mission in India*, trs. Martin J. Lutz, second edition, Chennai, 2006.

Liebau, Heike, *Cultural Encounters in India: The Local Co-workers of the Tranquebar Mission, 18th to 19th Centuries*, trs. Rekha V. Rajan, New York: Rutledgc, 2018.

Love, Henry Davison, *Vestiges of Old Madras, 1640-1800: Traced from the East India Company's Records Preserved at Fort St. George and the India Office, and from Other Sources*, 3 vols., London: John Murray, 1913.

Manickam, S., *Slavery in Tamil Country—A Historical Overview*, Madras: CLS, 1982.

Monumenta Ignatiana, Series Prima, Tomus Quartus, Madrid: Gabriel Lopez del Horno, 1906.

Mortizen, Niels-Peter, ed., *Bartholomaus Ziegenbalg, Johannes Ernst Grilndler, Von den Anfangen evangelischer Mission, Zwei unbekannte Missionsschriften von 1713 und 1717*, Bonn: Verlag fiir Kultur und Wissenschaft, 2002.

Nørgaard, Anders, *Mission und Obrigkeit: Die Dänisch-Hallische Mission in Tranquebar 1706-1845*, Gütersloh: Verlagshaus Gerd Mohn, 1988.

Pillai, Kanakasabhai, V., *The Tamils Eighteen Hundred Years Ago*, Madras, 1966.

Pillay, K.K., *A Social History of the Tamils*, Madras, 1969, rpt. 1975.

Raychaudhuri, Tapan, *Jan Company in Coromandel, 1605-1690: A Study in the Interrelations of European Commerce and Traditional Economies*, The Hague, 1962.

Royle, Stephen, *The Company's Island: St. Helena, Company Colonies and the Colonial Endeavour*, London: Bloomsbury, 2007.

Stephen, S. Jeyaseela, *Portuguese in the Tamil Coast: Historical Explorations in Commerce and Culture, 1507-1749*, Pondicherry, 1998.

——, *Expanding Portuguese Empire and the Tamil Economy: Sixteenth-Eighteenth Centuries*, New Delhi: Manohar, 2009.

——, *Oceanscapes: Tamil Textiles in the Early Modern World*, Primus, 2014.

——, *Subaltern Lives, Tamil History and Society from Medieval to Early Modern Age*, New Delhi: Kalpaz, 2019.

——, *Tranquebar in Global History, 1620-1801: The Coromandel Coast and Europe in a World Network System*, Puducherry, 2020.

——, *From European Dwelling Settlements to Global Cities: Ports of the Tamil Coast and the Colonial Modernity*, Primus, 2021.

——, *Tuticorin and its Trade with Asia, Africa and Europe, 1570-1880: Colonial Transformation, Human Migration and Interrelations*, Puducherry, 2022.

Struwe, Kamma, *Dansk Ostindien 1732-76: Tranquebar under Kompagnistyre*, second edition, Copenhagen: Fremad, 1967.

Subrahmanyam, Sanjay, *The Political Economy of Commerce: Southern India, 1500-1650*, Cambridge, 1990.

Toussaint, Auguste, *Le Mirage des Iles: Le negoce français aux Mascareignes au XVIIIe siècle*, Aix-en-Provence, 1977.

Wickramasinghe, Nira, *Slave in a Palanquin: Colonial Servitude and Resistance in Sri Lanka*, New York: Columbia University Press, 2020.

Worden, N., *Slavery in Dutch South Africa*, London: Cambridge University Press, 1985.

Index